Doing Research In and On the Digital

As a social space, the web provides researchers both with a tool and an environment to explore the intricacies of everyday life. As a site of mediated interactions and interrelationships, the 'digital' has evolved from being a space of information to a space of creation, thus providing new opportunities regarding how, where and, why to conduct social research.

Doing Research In and On the Digital aims to deliver on two fronts: first, by detailing how researchers are devising and applying innovative research methods for and within the digital sphere, and, second, by discussing the ethical challenges and issues implied and encountered in such approaches.

In two core Parts, this collection explores:

* content collection: methods for harvesting digital data
* engaging research informants: digital participatory methods and data stories.

With contributions from a diverse range of fields such as anthropology, sociology, education, healthcare and psychology, this volume will particularly appeal to post-graduate students and early career researchers who are navigating through new terrain in their digital-mediated research endeavours.

Cristina Costa is Associate Professor Digital Education and Society, University of the West of England, Bristol, UK.

Jenna Condie is a Lecturer in Digital Research and Online Social Analysis at Western Sydney University, Australia.

Routledge Advances in Research Methods

For more information about this series, please visit: www.routledge.com/
Routledge-Advances-in-Research-Methods/book-series/RARM

Doing Research In and On the Digital

Research Methods across Fields of Enquiry

Edited by Cristina Costa and Jenna Condie

Routledge
Taylor & Francis Group

LONDON AND NEW YORK

First published 2018
by Routledge
2 Park Square, Milton Park, Abingdon, Oxon OX14 4RN

and by Routledge
711 Third Avenue, New York, NY 10017

Routledge is an imprint of the Taylor & Francis Group, an informa business

British Library Cataloguing-in-Publication Data
A catalogue record for this book is available from the British Library

Library of Congress Cataloging-in-Publication Data
A catalog record has been requested for this book

ISBN: 978-1-138-67391-5 (hbk)
ISBN: 978-1-315-56162-2 (ebk)

Typeset in Times New Roman
by Wearset Ltd, Boldon, Tyne and Wear

Contents

Illustrations

Figures

Tables

Contributors

Naomi Barnes is social media researcher and casual academic in Brisbane, Australia. She used Facebook as a data collection tool for her PhD thesis to investigate the experiences of first year university students. Her research interests align with digital educational research, specifically how online communication can inform higher education pedagogy. She has worked as a curriculum coordinator, writer and educator at primary, secondary and tertiary levels. [email: n.barnes@griffith.edu.au]

Lily Bui is a PhD student in MIT's Department of Urban Studies and Planning and has an M.S. from MIT's Comparative Media Studies. Her work focuses on disaster and emergency management planning on island cities. In past lives, she worked on the STEM Story Project at the Public Radio Exchange (PRX) and was the Executive Editor at *SciStarter*, *PLOS CitizenSci*, and *Discover Magazine*'s Citizen Science Salon. Previously, she helped produce the radio show *Re:sound* for the Third Coast International Audio Festival out of WBEZ Chicago; worked on Capitol Hill in Washington, DC; served in AmeriCorps in Montgomery County, Maryland, at the Asian Pacific American Legal Resource Center; worked for a *New York Times* bestselling ghostwriter; and performed as a touring musician. At her alma mater, the University of California Irvine (ZOT!), she double-majored in Spanish and International Studies. [email: lilybui@mit.edu]

Jenna Condie is a Lecturer in Digital Research and Online Social Analysis in the School of Social Sciences and Psychology at Western Sydney University. Her research focuses on identity, place, belonging, and equality in a digitally mediated world. Jenna champions the use of social media and digital technologies to encourage participation, dialogue, and action within academic and community contexts. Her ambition is to be as networked, participatory and open in her scholarship as possible. She is a Chartered Psychologist with the British Psychological Society and an Honorary Fellow at the University of Salford, UK. [email: J.Condie@westernsydney.edu.au]

Cristina Costa is Associate Professor Digital Education and Society in the Department of Education and Childhood, University of the West of England,

Bristol, UK Her research focuses on the intersection of education and the participatory web through a sociological lens, especially Pierre Bourdieu's key concepts. She is also interested in broader issues regarding the participatory web in the context of a changing society. She is the co-editor of the Social Theory Applied blog/website www.socialtheoryapplied.com [email: cristina2. costa@uwe.ac.uk]

Glyn Davies is Service Development Director at Breaking Free Group in Manchester, UK. He played an instrumental role in the development of the Breaking Free Online interventions. He has an academic background in criminology and criminal justice, and previous experience of the commissioning and delivery of substance misuse and criminal justice services. [email: gdavies @breakingfreegroup.com]

Stephanie Dugdale is a Research Associate at Breaking Free Group in Manchester, UK, and is currently training for a professional doctorate in Health Psychology at Staffordshire University. Her role focuses on expanding the evidence base for Breaking Free Online (BFO), a computer-assisted treatment and recovery programme for substance misuse and comorbid mental health difficulties. Stephanie's current projects include designing and delivering smoking cessation interventions to offenders in prisons in the UK. [email: sdugdale@breakingfreegroup.com]

Sarah Elison-Davies is a Chartered Psychologist and Research Director at Breaking Free Group, a digital health company based in Manchester, UK. As part of her role as Research Director, she leads the ongoing programme of research into the implementation and efficacy of the Breaking Free Online computer-assisted therapy programme for substance abuse. Dr Elison-Davies has worked as an academic researcher at a number of UK universities and in the National Health Service, and has a background in behavioural science research and an interest in evaluating complex behavioural change interventions. [email: selison@breakingfreegroup.com]

David A. Ellis holds a 50th Anniversary Lectureship in Psychology at Lancaster University and an Honorary Research Fellowship at the University of Lincoln. He previously obtained an undergraduate degree in psychology from the University of Glasgow followed by an MSc and PhD (2013). Much of his work considers how recent methodological developments in technology and data collection (often referred to as digital traces) can reveal information about individuals and their behaviour. He has published on these topics in *PLoS Medicine*, the *International Journal of Neural Systems*, *The Lancet Public Health*, *Cyberpsychology, Behavior and Social Networking* and other journals. In addition to university-led research, David continues to work collaboratively with industry and government partners. This included an ESRC-funded placement at the Scottish Government in 2011. His research has also received funding from the Chief Scientist Office, DSTL, Unilever and the EPSRC. [email: d.a.ellis@lancaster.ac.uk]

Carol Haigh is Professor in Nursing at Manchester Metropolitan University in the UK, with over 30 years experience of working in healthcare settings in the United Kingdom. She was a committee member of the National Institute for Clinical Excellence in the UK, advising upon health resources and treatments, has acted as an expert advisor to the Royal College of Nursing and other health-related charities and maintains strong links with the wider clinical disciplines facilitating improvements in patient engagement and experience using social media. She has a special interest in ethics (she is chair of a Local Research Ethics Committee in the UK), and digital healthcare. [email: c.haigh@mmu.ac.uk or on Twitter @loracenna]

Iain Hamlin is a Research Associate at Strathclyde University, Scotland. His research focuses on group decision making, person perception and sources of accuracy in social judgments, especially judgments of veracity.

Pip Hardy has a degree in English Literature, an MSc in Lifelong Learning, and many years' experience developing and consulting on open and distance learning materials from conception to delivery. Pip's post-graduate work includes adult education, learning strategies, group work and counselling. She is the founder of the Patient Voices Programme (www.patientvoices.org.uk/) and a core member of the design team for the School for Health and Care Radicals, an initiative set up to support NHS Change Day and provide skills and knowledge for people wanting to bring about transformational change in health and care. [email: pip@pilgrimprojects.co.uk]

Donna James is a Masters of Research Student and Research Assistant with the School of Social Sciences and Psychology at Western Sydney University, Australia. In 2016, Donna completed a Bachelor of Arts, majoring in English and sub-majoring in social and cultural analysis, and education studies. Donna's research interests centre on the reproduction of gendered performances in technology, in particular, the hyper-masculine identity and its relationship with violence. Her work looks at women's experiences with navigating safety on location-aware social apps during travel.

Michaela Jones is a person in long-term addiction recovery and has engaged in a wide range of recovery-related activities across the UK. She has extensive experience of working with people at all stages in their recovery journey. This has included people in active addiction, people with multiple and complex needs, people seeking to leave treatment, reduce or cease medication, and people in sustained recovery. Michaela has worked with a large number of service user groups and recovery champions based in major treatment organisations and facilitated the development of community-based groups. Michaela would describe herself as a 'recoverist'.

Linda K. Kaye is a Senior Lecturer in the Department of Psychology at Edge Hill University, Lancashire, UK. Her research interests consider the positive psychological experiences associated with new and emerging technologies, with a particular focus on the psychosocial impacts of digital gaming. [email: Linda.kaye@edgehill.ac.uk]

Garth Lean is a Lecturer in Geography and Urban Studies in the School of Social Sciences and Psychology at Western Sydney University, Australia. His research and writing primarily investigate experiences of travel in a modern, mobile world. He is the lead researcher of the Transformative Travel Research Project (www.transformativetravel.com) and co-lead of the TinDA (Travel in the Digital Age) Project (www.tindaproject.com). He has published a variety of papers on travel, tourism and mobilities, along with the mono-graph, *Transformative Travel in a Mobile World* (CABI Books, 2016), and the edited volumes *Travel and Imagination* (Ashgate, 2014), *Travel and Transformation* (Ashgate, 2014) and *Travel and Representation* (Berghahn, 2017). He is Vice President of the Geographical Society of New South Wales and a member of the Geographies of Leisure and Tourism Research Group with the Royal Geographical Society.

Hannah L. Merdian is a Senior Lecturer in Clinical and Forensic Psychology at the University of Lincoln, UK. She started her university life at the University of Würzburg, Germany, and completed her PhD at the University of Waikato, New Zealand. Hannah is Co-Director of online PROTECT, a research and knowledge exchange programme addressing the safety of children and young people online and offline. She has published widely on offending behaviour concerning online child sexual exploitation material and provides consultation and training for offender management and child protection services. Her work is rooted in the Scientist-Practitioner Model, with a specific interest in the ana-lysis of 'real-life' data. [email: hmerdian@lincoln.ac.uk]

Rebecca L. Monk is a Lecturer in the Department of Psychology at Edge Hill University, Lancashire, UK. Her research focuses on the effect of context on substance use and associated cognitions, and on the development of new research methodologies. [email: monkre@edgehill.ac.uk]

Erinma Ochu is a Lecturer in Science Communication and Future Media at the University of Salford, UK. Trained originally as a neuroscientist at the University of Manchester, she went on to work as a writer and filmmaker in the creative industries. She is interested in the afterlives of creative practice and what remains from creating and experiencing intersectional work. She has benefited from career fellowships from: NESTA, the Wellcome Trust, Jerwood/Manchester International Festival and a Stuart Hall Library artists' residency. She collaborates with scientists, artists, designers, curators and activists via Squirrel Nation, a collective, that creates immersive experiences to stimulate debate, multi-modal inquiry and local action around global chal-lenges [email: e.e.ochu@salford.ac.uk | social media: @erinmaochu]

Cathy Ure is a doctoral candidate, and Project Research Manager in Public Health, at the University of Salford, UK. She has a Master's degree in Media

Psychology and is a member of the British Psychological Society (BPS). Cathy's particular focus of interest is on the use of social technologies to support patient health. Her PhD explores social media use by women living with and beyond breast cancer. [email: c.m.ure1@salford.ac.uk]

Tom Van Nuenen is Assistant Professor in Online Culture in the Department of Culture Studies of Tilburg University, the Netherlands. He has held visiting positions at Western Sydney University and Shanghai International Studies University. In his research, Tom asks how the digital age is influencing the way travel is experienced and reported. He investigates new media formats for travel writing, such as blogs, reviews and video games, and is especially interested in hermeneutic appliances of Digital Humanities strategies to analyse the interactions on these platforms. Tom's articles have been published in *Tourist Studies*, *The Journal of Popular Culture*, and *Games and Culture*. [email: tomvannuenen.nl]

Shireen Walton is an ERC Postdoctoral Researcher in the Department of Anthropology, University College London. She holds a BA in history from University College London and an MPhil and DPhil in Anthropology from the University of Oxford. Previously, Shireen has worked at the Centre of Migration, Policy, and Society (COMPAS) at the University of Oxford, and as a Teaching Fellow at UCL Anthropology. Shireen's research cuts across digital anthropology, visual culture, and migration, with regional interests in/between the Middle East and Europe. She has published with the Royal Anthropological Institute's Anthropology & Photography Series, and in the *Middle East Journal of Culture and Communication*. [email: shireen.walton @ucl.ac.uk]

Jonathan Ward is the Founder and Managing Director of Breaking Free Group in Manchester, UK. He led the team that developed the Breaking Free Online Interventions. Previously he practised as a clinical psychologist in the National Health Service, working primarily in adult mental health. [email: jward@breakingfreegroup.com]

1 Doing research in and on the digital

Cristina Costa and Jenna Condie

The web, as a social space, provides researchers both with a tool and an environment to explore the intricacies of everyday life. As a site of mediated interactions and interrelationships, the digital world has evolved from being a space of information to a space of creation, thus providing new opportunities regarding how and where to conduct research. This emergence of the digital web as a participatory platform provides citizens with a stage where they can play out aspects of their (social, professional, political, and even private) lives as a variant, complement and/or extension of their social existence. Online representations of daily life can in this way result in rich storylines; accounts of mediated experiences and events that are worth studying as a phenomenon of our contemporary society. In this vein, the digital world is ultimately transformed into an interactive memory container where participatory content becomes research data and digital users become research participants.

issue of consent?

It should then be no surprise that digital research methods are gaining prominence among researchers across different fields of inquiry. Researchers in the social and natural sciences, humanities and the professions alike are starting to employ digital tools for the collection of research data. Online surveys, for example, have become a mainstream practice in research while online interviews are increasingly more prominent given their affordances and affordability to reach research informants not only more easily and cheaply, but also in more dispersed locations. And although research on and within the digital world has become notoriously more abundant in the last few decades, given the opportunities enabled by the web, the majority of studies on digital phenomena still opt to employ more conventional research approaches, thus often creating a detachment from the tenets that compose the digital world as a space of knowledge creation and innovation.

Research on digital phenomena enables the development of digital research methods that go beyond the use of the web as a repository of data or a space where researchers tend to apply traditional forms of data collection. This is so because the emergence of the web as an alternative locus of participation and agency is blurring the boundaries of digital and physical spaces and, in so doing, it raises hard-to-answer ethical questions that steer less experienced researchers away from more advanced research approaches.

The objective of this book is to deliver on those two fronts by presenting examples of and reflection on how researchers across various fields are devising and applying innovative research methods when researching on and within the digital sphere and by discussing the ethical challenges and issues implied in such approaches.

Digital methods take on many different approaches, approaches which are not only related to the disciplinary tradition the researcher is associated with, but also intimately connected with the research phenomenon he/she is about to explore and the questions that are asked of it. As observed by Gubrium and Harper (2013), digital methods have more often than not become adaptations of traditional forms of inquiry than they have become participatory approaches. In this regard, the web is still predominantly regarded as a research tool rather than a research environment. This is an observation which we also have found through our own experience and observations as researchers, supervisors of post-graduate students and members of academic ethic committees. Just as in other areas of academic practice, there is an inclination to transfer to the digital world the practices that have marked one's activity before the emergence of the web. This is a natural way of exploring the 'new' with the knowledge one brings to the field and which ultimately characterise researchers' practices and experiences. However, with the expansion of the web to multiple communities and the widespread use of platforms that accommodate people's interactions and generate user-driven data, new possibilities for research are constantly emerging online as a space of unhampered social interaction.

Collecting research data is a core activity of empirical research, and the web has, in this regard, contributed immensely to the enhancement of data collection instruments through the technological solutions it offers, thus translating techniques used prior to the advent of the web into its digital form. Thus is the classic case of surveys and questionnaires that can now be sent to a multitude of participants via a link or even interviews that can be conducted online using Voice over Internet Protocol (VOIP) or video solutions that are time- and cost-effective (Costa, 2013). Although some may argue that conducting online interviews may present challenges when considering the lack of physical presence or the deficiency of human expression, the critique is less fierce when associated with research instruments that require the entry of participant data. Online solutions to the collection of questionnaire data are rarely questioned these days, thus showing a smooth transition from paper to online solutions of such approaches. Yet, other possibilities have been opened through the developments of web and mobile applications that may or may not be designed with a research purpose in mind. This multitude of prospects can both delight and alarm researchers, given that such opportunities call for an experimental mind as to how research can be conducted within the novelty brought by the web. However, it also requires a robust epistemological and ontological approach, one that is followed by an ethical approach which more often than not challenges both the role and activity of the researcher, given the novelty of the experience. Even though the literature is not always straightforward about the potential and advantages of conducting, in particular, qualitative research with the support of the digital tools and on digital environments, there is an increasing need to explore the alternatives presented by the web, given the social phenomena that are therein unveiled and the opportunities it presents for wider research opportunities in times of research budgetary cuts.

[handwritten margin notes: "a new phenomenon? once know how to study it?"]

Researchers have shown that since the advent of the web, especially since its read and write features have become mainstream, the digital world is ripe for research of a wide variety of phenomena and from a wide range of disciplinary perspectives. No less important is the realisation that both online devices and environments, such as Twitter, Facebook, Blogger, Tinder or Instagram, to name but a few, can be used both as tools of data collection and spaces of research participation. These are themes this book will explore. In other words, this book aims to provide examples and reflections of digital methods to work on and within the digital.

The structure of the book

One aim in editing this collection was to document the diversity of contexts in which digital methods are used and in which ways the digital serves as either a solution for data collection and/or engagement with research participants. The other key aim of the book was to contribute to ethical debates with critical perspectives anchored in practice, as a form of informing ethic committees and inspiring researchers to develop contemporary forms of doing research in light of a digital knowledge society. The book is organised into two distinctive Parts to accommodate the purpose mentioned above:

Part I Data collection: methods for harvesting digital data
Part II Engaging informants: digital participatory methods and data stories

The two Parts comprise chapters that explore digital research approaches from a range of methodological angles while also covering a wide variety of research areas, such as substance misuse, education, cancer research, or photoblogging practices, to name but a few. The research included in this collection has been selected with the purpose of providing the reader with as wide an understanding as possible of the application of digital methods in a wide range of contexts. Nonetheless, it should be noted that the list of topics by no means covers everything the ever-expanding digital field of inquiry includes, but rather should be regarded as an intellectual endeavour of conceptualising the 'digital' as both a tool and environment ripe for new research ventures. Furthermore, an objective of this book is to provide readers with examples that are useful across disciplines and which can be transferred and/or adapted to other fields of inquiry.

The chapters

From the discipline of Psychology, Kaye, Monk and Hamlin's contribution (Chapter 2) focuses on smartphone-enabled research as an alternative methodology in psychological research that offers researchers the ability to conduct contextually aware and ecologically valid research in 'real time'. The authors draw upon two research studies from quite different psychological fields: one study focuses on the assessment of alcohol consumption and related cognitions and behaviours, and the other focuses on digital gaming experiences. The two studies enable the authors to traverse a diverse range of issues, some of which are more pertinent to Psychology, such as acknowledging the importance of social context in human behaviour, but other issues can apply across fields. The authors consider how technology can be used effectively in the pursuit of knowledge across Psychology, including the potentials, pitfalls, practicalities and technicalities of conducting smartphone-enabled research.

In Chapter 3, Naomi Barnes takes us to the field of Education as she traces the methodological adaptions developed during a research project that takes Facebook status updates as research data. Using a phenomenography approach, the author sets out to explore first year students' experience at university. In so doing, the chapter provides an incisive discussion regarding a new approach to scholarship, one that relies on the digital. The chapter discusses the selection of phenomenography as an appropriate methodology and reflects how phenomenography is a valuable tool for digital research while elaborating on the ontological, epistemological and ethical questions the researcher faced as part of the research process. As well as showing how to do phenomenography, Barnes points out its conceptual underpinnings to consider what phenomenography can do for digital forms of scholarship.

From an applied and clinical psychological setting, in Chapter 4, Dugdale, Elison-Davies, Davies, Ward, and Jones reflect on how the digital world is reshaping the boundaries of traditional research methods by providing access to a wide range of data and affording a multitude of online data collection techniques. The authors go on to remind the reader that such technology-enhanced research methodologies, however, do not come without challenges, especially those regarding ethics. To illustrate their ethical considerations, the authors review a mixed-methods online study that investigated the use of online resources to support people in recovery from substance misuse as part of their psychosocial research. With digital research methods, the authors navigate the challenges of doing research with people in recovery from, or still using, substances, as admitting to substance-using behaviour can often incur legal implications.

Cathy Ure's research in Chapter 5 explores breast cancer bloggers' lived experiences of 'survivorship' and reflects on the ethical aspects of gaining access and analysing data available online. Breast cancer is a subject area that is generating significant online interest, but it is also an area of great sensitivity and subjectivity. The author explores this aspect through an inductive and reflexive approach to the research presented in the chapter, but not without addressing the ethical issues that emerged from such a research experience. Reflexive ethical approaches require researchers to consider and revise their role as part of the research process on a continuous basis. The author goes on to reflect on the challenges posed by the 'digital', including considerations of what 'informed consent' is and means in the digital era. She also ponders on the epistemological implications of undertaking a discursive analysis of blogs and how participants might feel about the research interpretations and findings. The chapter finishes with a reflection on the nature of online data regarding its open accessibility to a wider audience and how it should not necessarily be regarded as publicly available data for research purposes. Ure's decision to ask bloggers for their informed consent resulted in her data corpus consisting of content from one blogger who also requested 'proper credit' for the use of her blogged texts in research. From this chapter, we can see how ethical and responsible behaviour by the researcher can always be observed, even if that presents complications and challenges for the data sample.

Into the realm of Digital Humanities and continuing the epistemological and methodological considerations around discursive approaches but on a larger scale, Chapter 6 explores text mining research on online platforms. Using a case study focused on contemporary online forms of travel writing, Tom Van Nuenen discusses basic heuristic steps for explorative and unsupervised computational text research in current online environments, which he designates as a form of 'corpus-assisted discourse studies'. In so doing, he examines several methods of gathering, preparing, sorting and analysing online data and offers suggestions for the vacillation between so-called 'distant' and 'close' reading strategies. He concludes that digital methods allow researchers many avenues of insight, and that different data sortings and representations allow different epistemological approaches. The chapter concludes with some important reflections on the relationship between Digital Humanities and the broader Humanities and the contributions that Digital Humanities has to offer, that go beyond digital research tools to the scholarly questions these tools present to researchers.

Continuing the theme of travel, Chapter 7 explores how researchers can get closer to the phenomenon of location-aware technologies and move towards a conceptual position that understands humans and technology as inherently entangled with one another. Condie, Lean and James reflect and diffract upon their research on the use of location-aware social apps such as Tinder, by critically examining their research questions, how they have evolved and are evolving through their personal experiences of 'swiping right' into their research fields and through their engagement in new materialist scholarship. One contribution of this chapter is to highlight the challenges of resisting binary constructs such as human/non-human, subject/object, online/offline, and digital/material within research on digital phenomena. Their research focus on travel also brings to the fore how humans, technologies and place are inseparable and how knowledge and experience are always situated somewhere. Entering the research field has changed to using the phone in the researcher's hand, which can be included in the assemblages of research and knowledge production for responsible digital scholarship.

Chapter 8 offers a meaningful insight into the remote ethnography practices made possible by digital technologies. Shireen Walton provides us with a contribution from digital anthropology while using a technology-linked visual research approach. Engaging Iranian photobloggers as research participants, the author discusses how visual methods can be applied and developed to ask specific research questions, especially in cases where access to the site of inquiry is limited, as is the case of her study-example on Iran at a particular period of political and diplomatic unpredictability. Furthermore, Walton shows that a *digital* presence can be as effective in her research role of ethnographer. Finally, she suggests that digital and virtual ethnographic methods can raise a host of epistemological, ontological and ethical questions concerning how qualitative digital researchers 'be in', mediate and represent an increasingly interconnected world.

Part II of the book changes focus to consider more engaged and participatory research practices. We start with Ellis and Merdian's chapter (Chapter 9) on the visualisation of research data in the contexts of digital research dissemination. The authors also consider their approach to the collection, management and analysis of very large data sets as well as the observation of ethical research practices alongside secure data ownership. More concretely, the chapter constitutes a response to the increased digitalisation of research, especially within psychology and across the social sciences. It argues that digital research methods have the potential to revolutionise data management across disciplines, but that fact has so far failed to be recognised and/or implemented by the research community. The chapter also aims to highlight a way towards an improved research toolset for the psychological community and help improve access to future research for both their psychological peers and interested members of the public.

Bui's work (Chapter 10) provides reflections on a project involving a human-centred design research approach. It describes the redesign of a digital platform (iSeeChange) that combines two types (quantitative and qualitative) and scales (global and local) of climate data, data that is user-driven. The author takes the reader through the design process which reveals meaningful insights regarding how researchers situate both the digital tools and the design process itself within social research. The human-centred design approach bears resemblance to certain aspects of participatory action research approaches by placing emphasis on the generation and collection of collaborative data with the community being studied. Such approaches raise questions of transparency towards research participants. The chapter concludes that participatory approaches in the design of social research have the potential to lead to meaningful interactions between designers and researchers, and target audiences and communities on which the research is focused.

In Chapter 11, Erinma Ochu encourages researchers to think about who their research is for and reminds us about overlooked and unheard people or 'missing dreamers'. By centring personal histories, Ochu's autobiographical narrative of two digitally mediated citizen science projects highlights how who we are plays an important role in the research produced and its outcomes. Digital methods are only ~~*Dcoses*~~ part of Ochu's academic performance as her commitment to socially just research projects is enabled by the democratic, open, networked, digital and reciprocal practices she advocates. For marginalised scholars, this chapter provides encouragement to stick with research goals and embrace the time it might take to build the kinds of trusting relationships and partnerships required to leave your mark on the world. The author dreams of a digital commons and legacy for her digital research projects, and the methodological approaches that she employs enable the flexibility required for change, action and unforeseen ethical issues that arise during the research journey. Her autobiographical analysis provides us with insights into how digitally mediated citizen science projects emerge and their unexpected endings.

In Chapter 12, Carol Haigh and Pip Hardy discuss the use of digital stories in healthcare research while elaborating on the ethical and practical dilemmas they faced while conducting their research. In so doing, the authors reflect on issues of veracity and reliability, the concepts of power and consent, and how such ethical issues are dealt with within the digital storytelling format. The authors use case studies as examples of the reflections provided, making this a very practical reading which readers can apply and adapt to their own research contexts. According to Haigh and Hardy, digital stories can be regarded as units of raw data. They can, however, also be regarded as discrete auto-ethnographic and auto-analysed data that require ethical considerations, considerations that are an ongoing issue and they emphasise that the researcher need to be both aware of and constantly vigilant regarding this aspect.

The final chapter of this edited collection (Chapter 13) reveals some of the core issues we, the editors, found when reviewing the contributions of the chapters and respective authors. Nonetheless, these reflections are not exhaustive, nor do they aim to provide the last word on a topic as rich and varied as the one herein explored. We therefore recommend that readers engage in their own analysis of the different chapters and come up with their own interpretations and conclusions about the different research processes and inherent epistemological, ontological and ethical issues raised in this book.

The ultimate aim of the book is to develop the capacity of researchers, in particular of post-graduate students and early career researchers to successfully design appropriate and innovative methodologies for working on and within the digital realm. Importantly, the book will make a contribution to the ethical debates surrounding digital research in an attempt to provide ethical research committees with appropriate guidance in this area.

References

Costa, C. (2013). The participatory web in the context of academic research: landscapes of change and conflicts. University of Salford. Available at: http://usir.salford.ac.uk/28369/

Gubrium, A. and Harper, K. (2013). *Participatory Visual and Digital Methods*. New York: Routledge.

Part I
Collecting content
Methods for harvesting digital data

2 'Feeling appy?'

Using App-based methodology to explore contextual effects on real-time cognitions, affect and behaviours

Linda K. Kaye, Rebecca L. Monk and Iain Hamlin

A contextual issue

It is certainly not revolutionary to suggest that where we are and who we are with – one's environmental and social context – impact the way we think, feel and act. Indeed, Social Psychology has for years extolled the importance of social contexts on affect, cognitions and behaviour. Nonetheless, many traditional research methodologies fail to account for such contextual factors when examining human behaviour (Baker, 1968). That is, traditional psychological research findings are typically the product of retrospective self-reports or experimental manipulations, as opposed to reports of the experience in context, as lived (*in vivo*). Thus, there are a wide range of psychological research traditions which would benefit by employing alternative methodologies to provide further evidence of contextual influences on psychological concerns. In this chapter, it is argued that technology, specifically Smartphone technology, offers researchers the capability to conduct increasingly dynamic research and to collect vast amounts of contextually aware data. To aid in this overview, we talk generally about the value of Smartphones Applications (Apps) for research purposes, before drawing upon two example areas of research to further illustrate the utility of these alternative research methodologies: the assessment of alcohol consumption and related cognitions (for example, Monk and Heim, 2014a; Monk et al., 2015) and digital gaming experiences (cf. Kaye, 2016; Kaye and Bryce, 2012, 2014). In each instance, the important, yet largely hitherto unanswered research questions will be highlighted, as well as the potential utility of Smartphone Apps in such areas. The aim of this is not to suggest that these are the only areas of potential use. Rather, this chapter is intended to highlight, using specific examples, how technology may be used in the pursuit of knowledge across Psychology (Brown et al., 2014). The strengths, important considerations and potential pitfalls of such research are also outlined. We will argue that Smartphone-enabled research provides a more ecologically valid and contextually-aware perspective on psychological constructs.

The value of Smartphone App technology

The advent of increasingly advanced technology has begun to provide research-ers with the equipment to conduct real-time, contextually-aware research. Indeed, Smartphone methodologies have been identified as useful tools for gaining behavioural data (Miller, 2012) and Smartphone Apps have been readily applied as part of behaviour-change interventions (e.g. Stawarz, Cox and Bland-ford, 2015) and clinical/therapeutic strategies (Stoyanov et al., 2014). The use of electronic mobile devices in Psychology, however, is by no means a new phe-nomenon. Indeed, research adopting Experience Sampling Methodology (ESM) or Ecological Momentary Assessment (EMA), as it is also known) has typically used electronic 'beepers' to indicate the occasions (during participants' everyday lives) in which responses should be supplied (Csikszentmihalyi, Larson and Prescott, 1977; Diener and Emmons, 1985). Nonetheless, responses to such elec-tronic signals have not traditionally been obtained through electronic means, rather through more traditional methods such as paper-based questionnaires (e.g., Csikszentmihalyi et al., 1977). In other words, electronic devices have more traditionally been implemented to provide cue and reinforcement schedules rather than as data collection tools (Stawarz et al., 2015). In contrast, Smart-phone Apps enable functional responding, as well as data collection. They are therefore greatly beneficial in enhancing ESM methodologies. However, a recent review of free iPhone Apps, specifically those with a psychological basis, identi-fied that they have very limited scope and utility for research, and that there is a significant gap in the evidence base for such technologies (Harrison and Goozee, 2014, see also Wiederhold, 2015). Among these limitations are issues with installation costs and quality assurance, which is particularly important when such Apps are aligned for professional healthcare and therapy support (Harrison and Goozee, 2014). Clearly, empirical work is needed to ensure that such Apps are practically suitable for target users, as well as being effective and efficacious.

It is certainly the case that there has been a paucity of research using Smartphone-enabled ESM, and that research into their validity has been hitherto limited. Nonetheless, previous commentary has identified a number of key bene-fits of using Smartphones as research tools (Miller, 2012). Specifically, they have a positive scope for large, global-scale sampling. They also increase the convenience of conducting large-scale data collection and provide an unobtru-sive and simple way of responding (Miller, 2012). Specific technical capacities, such as participant response prompting, geo-location and photographic upload-ing, also offer further avenues for data-rich research. For instance, Golder (2008) proposes that photographs capture real-time events and social interactions/ dynamics. As such, they can be a powerful research tool (Plantié and Crampes, 2010). Indeed, recent research activity has moved towards the analysis of photo-graphs, particularly through social networking websites (Plantié and Crampes, 2010). This makes sense when one considers the popularity of Smartphone-based Apps, which are designed to allow and encourage the taking and sharing of photographs. The social networking site, Facebook, records that three hundred million photos are uploaded every day (Poltash, 2013) and Snapchat and Instagram have increased the trend whereby people document their lives by taking and sharing photographs via the Internet. Similarly, there has been a noticeable recent trend towards capturing the data supplied in Twitter, for research purposes (for example, Aphinyanaphongs, Ray, Statnikov, and Krebs, 2014). Geo-location also offers researchers a key opportunity to assess participants' current location in relation to any other variables of interest. For instance, Smartphone Apps for clinical samples of alcohol users have been used to assess the effect of current geo-location on subjective craving and relapse (Gustafson et al., 2011, 2014).

Another key strength of Smartphone technology is to facilitate real-time research, beyond the laboratory. Indeed, the ecological validity of Smartphone-based research is one of the main strengths highlighted by Miller (2012). The ability to collect data in real time can have particular importance for exploring issues which may be particularly susceptible to contextual influences. This chapter will now highlight the utility of Smartphone Apps to assess the effect of context, using two research exemplars: alcohol consumption (and related cognitions) and digital gaming experiences.

Alcohol cognitions and behaviours

It has long been suggested that substance use is the product of physiological, cognitive and environmental factors – the 'drug, set and setting' (Zinberg, 1984). A detailed overview of the research supporting this assertion is beyond the scope of this chapter. Nonetheless, it is well established that drug use (e.g. Robins, 1993) and alcohol use (e.g. Martin, 2006) are driven by one's current situational context. For example, the 'wetness'[1] of the situation has been shown to be an important determinant of consumption, drinking being heavier at parties and in bars than in restaurants (Martin, 2006).

In order to understand such changes in alcohol consumption, researchers have spent decades examining people's alcohol-related beliefs, and how they link with consumption. This indicates that alcohol-related beliefs reliably predict alcohol consumption (Jones, Corbin and Fromme, 2001). For example, those who expect alcohol consumption to result in positive outcomes (termed high positive outcome expectancies) subsequently consume greater quantities of alcohol (e.g. Leigh and Stacy, 1993, 2004; Stacy, Widaman and Marlatt, 1990). Similarly, believing one's alcohol intake to be lower than the norm (norm misperception) is claimed to create an increase in consumption (e.g. Carey, Borsari, Carey and Maisto, 2006).

It has been noted for some time that such alcohol-related beliefs may vary across different contexts (Wall, McKee, and Hinson, 2000) and there has been growing research to this effect (for example, Monk and Heim, 2013a, 2013b). Nonetheless, there remains a reliance on the use of retrospective reports in this area of research (Monk and Heim 2013c, 2014b, for reviews). This is problematic for a number of reasons. First, the task of making retrospective reports about one's alcohol-related beliefs in by-gone drinking scenarios is cognitively demanding and dependent on memory. However, given the fallibility and limitations of memory, such research may have questionable validity. This problem may also be further exacerbated if alcohol consumption occurred during the target period, as alcohol may further impair memory (Walker and Hunter, 1978). Second, the difficulty of retrospectively recalling multiple occasions may be heightened when it is considered that assessment in a non-alcohol-related environment necessitates recall in the absence of any associated environmental stimuli, to aid memory (Godden and Baddeley, 1975).

In light of such concerns, research has begun to assess alcohol-related cognitions using more ecologically-aware testing environments such as simulated bars (e.g. Larsen, Engels, Wiers, Granic and Spijkerman, 2012) or wine-tasting events (e.g. Kuendig and Kuntsche, 2012). In this vein, social contexts and alcohol-related environments have been shown to be associated with increases in positive expectancies (e.g. Monk and Heim, 2013a, 2013b). While pointing to the importance of social and environmental contexts in shaping alcohol-related beliefs, these studies have tended to test participants in environments which, to a greater or lesser extent, are removed from realistic drinking contexts.

As such, the question as to how such cognitions change across real-time contexts may be better assessed using Smartphone technology, which allows researchers to analyse cognitions in the real world. In other words, Smartphone technology offers researchers the chance to assess important cognitions when participants are actually in alcohol-related environments and in the presence of social groups. This also facilitates comparisons with cognitions that were provided in alcohol-neutral environments and in solitary contexts. Accordingly, research has begun to use participants' mobile phones to collect EMA data via phone calls (Courvoisier, Eid, Lischetzke and Schreiber, 2010) or text messages (Kuntsche and Robert, 2009), which has proved highly popular among participants (Kuntsche and Labhart 2014). The advent of highly sophisticated Smartphone Apps, nonetheless, presents a 'next step' in the use of such technology for research purposes (Kuntsche and Labhart, 2014). Accordingly, Monk and Heim (2014a) used a web-hosted Smartphone technology to conduct experiential sampling (EMA). This administered a bespoke App to assess participants' current cognitions and to simultaneously track their present situational and social context, to provide a contextually-dynamic perspective on alcohol-related cognitions. Here, it was revealed that *in-vivo* social and environmental contexts accounted for a significant proportion of variance in outcome expectancies. Prompts which occurred while participants were among friends or in a pub/bar or club were associated with heightened outcome expectancies in comparison with other settings (Monk and Heim, 2014a). Further research in this vein is therefore strongly recommended in order to further elucidate the nature of the cognitions which drive consumption. In so doing, it is hoped that researchers will be able to better inform clinicians who attempt to treat problem consumption via targeting alcohol-related beliefs. Specifically, by providing clients with the tools to be able respond to and address their contextually varying cognitions.

In addition to understanding alcohol-related cognitions, questions about the nature of alcohol consumption itself may also be better addressed using Smartphone technology. Indeed, it has long been questioned whether reports regarding consumption are accurate, particularly when one considers the afore-mentioned limitations of memory, and the potential for exacerbated memory deficits resulting from intoxication. Accordingly, research suggests that self-reported alcohol consumption is up to 40% lower than the amount of alcohol actually sold (Boniface and Shelton, 2013). Real-time assessments of consumption may thus allay fears about the accuracy of alcohol consumption reports. Further, the environments in which alcohol consumption assessments take place are often far removed from the setting in which the drinking occurs, by nature of their post hoc design (Verster, Tiplady and McKinney, 2012). As previously noted, there are difficulties associated with attempts to recall information processed in a different context from that in which the information was originally encoded (Godden and Baddeley, 1975). As Smartphone technology is contextually-aware, questions about the role of context in the recall of alcohol consumption may also be assessed.

The use of EMA to assess real-time substance use has been previously pioneered in the study of varying substance use, providing episode-based reports of real-time smoking and drinking (Alessi and Petry, 2013; Collins, Kashdan and Gollnisch, 2003; Collins, Morsheimer, Shiffman, Paty, Gnys and Papandonatos, 1998; Kuntsche and Labhart, 2014, 2015; Piasecki et al., 2011; Shiffman et al., 1997, 2002; Toll, Cooney McKee and O'Malley, 2005) To this end, recent research has used a native App to track alcohol consumption over the course of a week. Such real-time reports were then compared with both daily and weekly retrospective accounts of consumption. Furthermore, variability in reports across drinking contexts was also assessed (Monk et al., 2015). Here, retrospective accounts appeared to underestimate the amount of actual, real-time alcohol consumed, and increased consumption appeared to exacerbate differences between real-time and retrospective accounts. Environmental and social contexts also appeared to interact with the type of alcohol consumed and the time frame given for reporting (weekly vs. daily retrospective) to further impact such discrepancies. For example, real-time consumption in a bar/pub was associated with increases in the discrepancy observed between real-time and weekly retrospective accounts of consumption (ibid.). Similarly, Smartphone-based assessments of student drinking have indicated that drinking as part of larger friendship groups is associated with increases in hourly drinking frequency (Thrul and Kuntsche, 2015). Continued research in this area, using Smartphone technology, may therefore offer researchers key insights into the dynamic and contextually varying nature of consumption and associated beliefs. This approach is strongly advocated in order to provide policy-makers with a better insight into tackling excessive consumption and the associated economic and health demands.

Digital gaming

Another psychological area of enquiry that would further benefit from this form of methodology is digital gaming, particularly when there is still much to be understood about the role of social contexts in the experience of this activity, and the differential effects this may hold on gaming outcomes.

There is an increasing acceptance that digital gaming is not a solitary and socially-isolating activity. Rather, it often serves two main interpersonal functions. First, it facilitates players' sense of connectedness to others. Second, it promotes enjoyable social gaming experiences (Cole and Griffiths, 2007; Gajadhar, de Kort and Ijsselsteijn, 2008; Poels, de Kort and IJsselsteijn, 2007). However, there has been minimal attention to exploring real-time gaming within social contexts of play. Conversely, the majority of research in this area is undertaken in laboratory-based contexts. For example, manipulations of social presence within a laboratory have been undertaken in order to assess its role on participants' psychological, emotional and physiological outcomes (e.g. Bracken, Lange and Denny, 2005). The paucity of real-world research means that the literature regarding social gaming experiences may not necessarily translate to real-world gaming (Kaye, 2016; Kaye and Bryce, 2014), particularly given that gaming experiences are understood to be largely diverse and varied (Bryce and Kaye, 2011). In an attempt to be more contextually-aware, researchers have attempted to replicate social gameplay by allocating participants to engage in collaborative or competitive gaming tasks (Eastin, 2007). However, one could question the extent to which this is reflective of typical, real-world gaming experiences and play patterns, which typically occur with friends. Indeed, evidence shows that gameplay experiences are enhanced with friends compared to strangers (Ravaja, Saari, Turpeinen, Laari, Salminen and Kavikangas, 2006). Thus, experimentally-derived social groups may not be reflective of those patterns typically experienced in the real world.

Questionnaire-based methodologies may provide some solution to this issue, by permitting participants to provide retrospective accounts of real-world gaming experiences (Kaye, 2016; Kaye and Bryce, 2014). In this way, researchers may gain more accurate insights into the dynamic and varied nature of gaming experiences in respect of their occurrence in real-world contexts, rather than in artificially-designed social settings (Kaye and Bryce, 2014). For example, previous studies have been able to account for contextual variations in experiences of flow and post-gameplay mood, through obtaining gamers' self-reported accounts between solo and socially-based gaming experiences (Kaye, 2016; Kaye and Bryce, 2014). Nonetheless, such reports are clearly restricted by their retrospective nature, and reliance on participants' memory capabilities, as noted in the preceding section. Given these shortcomings, methodologies that are able to capture real-life gameplay experiences, as-and-when they occur (*in vivo*), appear highly advantageous. Specifically, such research allows the exploration of the dynamic nature of the social aspects of gaming. Assessing constructs such as flow (a psychological sense of feeling 'in the zone' when undertaking an activity) (Csikszentmihalyi 1975), may benefit particularly via this approach. Indeed, it has been noted that experimental conditions may not represent typical gaming contexts which optimise experience of flow. However, although traditionally subjected to ESM research (Csikszentmihalyi, Larson and Prescott, 1977), flow has not been explored within digital gaming in this way. There is therefore an apparent need to increase the understanding of flow in real-world gaming, and App-based research may provide the tools for such explorations. In this fashion, a heightened understanding of other contextually variable aspects of the gaming experience, such as emotional indicators, may also benefit from such methodologies (Ravaja, Salminen, Holopainen, Saari, Laarni and Järvinen, 2004).

The authors' ongoing research to this end has therefore sought to explore the contextual influences on emotional and psychological experiences of real-world digital gaming. Here, gamers were asked to complete real-time assessments of their mood, flow and expectancies relating to gameplay in different contexts (online, offline, solo). These assessments took place over the period of up to two weeks and were recorded by way of a bespoke Smartphone App. Specifically, this was intended to provide data to explore the extent to which gaming-related affect and cognitions varied as a function of social context. These were completed in reference to shooting games only, to avoid the type of game confounding the responses. Analyses of this data have therefore begun to shed insights into the extent to which experiences of gaming vary as a product of social context. This research substantiates the current literature and highlights the need for a fuller account of contextual factors that may be influential on gaming outcomes. To encourage wider acceptance of this form of research paradigm, the authors highlight the key practical and ethical considerations of App-based research in the following sections. This is important, given there is an apparent need for more App-based research if psychology is going to effectively respond to the criticism that it has failed to assess dynamic behaviours and cognitions in the real world (Baker, 1968). In an attempt to aid such future endeavours, the following section now examines the key considerations of conducting such research, using an example from the authors' digital gaming and alcohol-related research as illustrative examples. Emphasis will be placed on highlighting the potential benefits and issues associated with such research. Practical and ethical considerations of this form of research will be presented.

Ethical considerations

Adherence to the usual ethical principles outlined by the British Psychological Society is a standard requirement when doing research with human participants in the UK (BPS, 2009, 2010). Nonetheless, further considerations are necessary when conducting Smartphone-based research. Another important ethical consideration relates to the anonymity of data gained through this type of research strategy. That is, there are additional assurances to be made when tracking participants (and their data) over a longer period of time through the use of Apps, particularly when data is stored on an external server rather than on an individual user's device (which is not typical owing to potential issues with data loss). Namely, participants' data needs to be identifiable for analysis purpose in order that individual, cross-contextual variations can be assessed (as well as group-level variance). Concurrently, anonymity of participants' data must be assured. This can be done via typical means of obtaining unique participant codes or number strings which allow the data to be individually identified without removing participant anonymity. Previous research has used these sorts of strategies, specifically unique number-strings within web-hosted Apps (Monk et al., 2015) so that each participant accesses a URL with a unique number stream (allowing individual tracking) and random participant number generation from a native App (i.e. one that is downloaded to their Smartphone) (Monk et al., 2015). Each participant is thus tagged and can then be tracked using a random number generated at the start of study participation. Ethical panels will therefore require a well-considered strategy in this regard and so advanced consideration of this point is strongly advised early in the design process, to avoid unforeseen delays.

It is also important to consider the possible financial costs incurred by the participant as a result of taking part in such research. Specifically, costs can result from the use of mobile phone data (which incur charges) when using a web-hosted App to provide responses (if extended internet access is required by the App) or when downloading the Apps for subsequent use. It is therefore necessary to inform participants at the Briefing Stage that they should ensure that they have sufficient data to enable them to take part, and that they should consider the impact of accessing the App in instances where they may be using mobile data (as opposed to free WiFi). When the research App is web-based, participants do not have to download it. Instead, the App is hosted through a web-based platform, thus eradicating any associated download charges. However, participants will have to use the internet to transmit their responses. In most cases, the use of the internet in this way may not be clear, and it is therefore important to highlight this to participants in order to avoid unforeseen costs. For this reason, it is also advisable to limit the amount of time an individual responds during ESM sessions. When a native App is being used, any files should be compressed, in order to limit the download size and, again, limit potential data costs. A consideration of the type of research, and the sample population, will help researchers in such data use considerations. Specifically, if participants are likely to be at home when using the App, and thus have access to free Wi-Fi (e.g. in gaming research), data use issues may be less of a concern. However, if it is likely that participants may be moving around or engaging in the target behaviour in multiple contexts (e.g. alcohol consumption research), free Wi-Fi may not be available and hence the potential for incurring data use charges is higher. Researchers therefore have a duty to consider this, and to warn their participants accordingly, making sure all possible avenues have been pursued in order to minimise potential costs.

A final issue relates to the research placing undue demands on participants. EMA research, such as that facilitated by Smartphone Apps, requires numerous assessments over the course of an extended time period. It is therefore necessary to be mindful of the implications of participants feeling constrained by the demands of the research. One way to address this concern is by allowing participants to actively initiate the App themselves, to commence participation (and to desist) at a time which suits them. This can be facilitated using a 'Go' button on the home page of the App, which in the illustrative research, was used to indicate that a gaming session was commencing. This method contrasts other ESM research formats where prompts are sent at pre-defined intervals (or randomised) every day, over the course of the participation period. In this way, the demands placed on participants are limited and this promotes a greater sense of autonomy for participants in their data provision (as reported in qualitative assessments in pilot research for alcohol-related research, in Monk and Heim, 2014b). Furthermore, this approach removes the potential of asking questions which are presently irrelevant. For example, if one's research is interested in specific aspects of gaming or alcohol consumption behaviour, asking questions about alcohol or gaming when respondents are not currently engaged in that activity will capture no useful information, and may lead participants to question the veracity of the research. Hence, this type of response capture system is most suitable for capturing events that are temporal or periodic, occurring at only selective periods of times. If one's research is interested in ubiquitous factors, such as cognition, a more traditional ESM approach, as described above, is more appropriate. Here, while the researchers may suspect that cognitions change from time to time, that human beings are continually involved in cognitive thought processing is well established, hence a participation prompt at any interval gives the participant the opportunity to provide relevant and potentially important information. For example, assessing alcohol-related cognitions across varying contexts (both alcohol and non-alcohol-related) has given researchers insights into the dynamic and changing nature of such beliefs (cf. Monk and Heim, 2014b).

Practical considerations

Matching the data collection method to the research

The above highlights an important, related, consideration: Whether one's proposed question is suited to an App which only records data when the participant activates it. For the monitoring of periodic events such as gaming, or indeed alcohol consumption, this approach is suitable. However, for the assessment of processes that are continuous and constantly evolving, a more traditional Smartphone-enabled EMA approach (using regular, daily prompts) would be necessary. For example, emotions or thoughts are ongoing and evolving. However, it is not feasible to assess participants' thoughts continuously, nor is it possible to ask participants to activate the App when they have specific thoughts. Indeed, here it is perhaps necessary to note a greater theoretical question. By asking questions, are researchers changing the very nature of the thing they wish to study, by asking questions that bring otherwise largely unconscious processes into conscious awareness (Dewey, 1910)? Clearly such a discussion is beyond the scope of this chapter. Nonetheless, the wider point is an important one in that the type and spacing/timing of the questions asked by an App must suit the area that one is wishing to examine. As research capabilities currently stand, perhaps the best a researcher can therefore hope for is to take key 'snapshots in time' of certain psychological phenomena, using an App. This will provide information about given moments over time and allow the statistical modelling of the effect of varying contextual factors on the dependent variable of interest.

Technical requirements

Smartphones represent a diverse assemblage of different types of hardware and software. Consequently, one of the key issues in mobile App design is the potential lack of compatibility between the programming code, the different mobile devices and their operating systems and browsers. If a researcher chooses to use a native App, then individual applications must be made for each operating system (e.g. iPhone and Android). Alternatively, researchers must purposefully recruit participants who have a compatible mobile device. For example, Monk et al. (2015) designed an Android-only application. Here, the application and interface were built using HTML and JavaScript and JavaScript's jQuery mobile library. Phone Gap was used to convert the web-based application into a native application that could be downloaded onto the users' own device by scanning a QR code. Local Storage within the application was used to temporarily store all of the users' answers, before data were remotely transferred to Google Analytics. However, this sort of App must then be adapted for use on non-Android platforms, such as Apple, as one version of a native App will not be fully compatible with all operating systems. While native Apps may allow researchers to collect more data, and access more of the phone's features (e.g. the camera), the need to design multiple versions of an App (for different platforms) can considerably increase costs associated with programming services, unless a member of the research team is familiar with a number of programming languages and has access to the necessary software.

Perhaps the simplest way to produce a mobile App which works across most devices is to create it using HTML and JavaScript and embed it in a web page. These two widely used languages have been integral to the creation of most websites for more than 20 years, so most mobile phone browsers are able to run HTML and JavaScript code without serious issues. This means that only one App needs to be designed. A consideration of the type of App required for research – and the associated costs of the different approaches – is therefore strongly recommended prior to research commencement.

Two additional benefits of using mobile Apps as a series of JavaScript applets embedded in a webpage are also worthy of consideration. First, the resultant software is completely web-based and so may be less likely to deter potential participants, who may not feel comfortable with (or understand) the process of installing additional software on their phones. Second, the complexity of developing a native mobile App means that the vast majority of psychology researchers lack the skills required to produce an App in this fashion. Outsourcing the development of a mobile App to a software developer can be beneficial although financially prohibitive. However, some systems which use HTML and JavaScript webpages are not too complex, so this method may therefore be much easier for psychologists to master and be practical without financial support. Furthermore, JavaScript syntax resembles some of the languages that many psychologists regularly use when developing lab-based experimental software and data analysis algorithms, such as C++ and Python.

Although HTML and JavaScript run on most mobile phone web browsers and operating systems, careful programming is required to ensure that the resulting App is compatible with many different types of phone hardware and software. In respect of hardware, perhaps the main challenge for the programmer is to produce an App that displays similarly across a wide variety of different screen sizes. Nowadays, this can be easily achieved using a line of CSS code which automatically detects the screen size of the device it is running on and fits the page content to the screen accordingly. Web Apps can also be programmed so that participants' response mechanisms are interactive, determined by the users' Smartphone. Methods of responding to questions derived through Smartphone Apps will vary as a function of the specific software and device, but will largely be touchscreen responding. For example, iPhone or Android users indicated their responses by pressing or 'dragging' the onscreen response items while those without touch screen technology responded in a fashion compatible with their phone (Monk et al., 2014a).

It is much more challenging, however, to ensure that an App runs identically across the plethora of operating systems and browsers installed on participants' Smartphones. For example, in Apple's OIS operating system, JavaScript can only play a sound if it is directly triggered by a user action. On the other hand, on Android operating systems, the JavaScript code itself can play a sound element without the need for direct user initiation. Where such discrepancies exist and need to be mitigated, imaginative programming solutions are often required. Thankfully, the JavaScript and HTML lexicons are flexible enough that workarounds can usually be created to circumvent the differential compatibility of browsers with JavaScript syntax. For example, although OIS will not allow JavaScript to implement a time delay between a user action and a resultant sound event, the desired time delay can be achieved by playing an audio clip composed of the required sound event preceded by a period of silence equivalent to the required time delay. If the sound clip is preloaded using HTML to allow immediate presentation, then the expression of the time delay will exactly mirror the way the time delay would be expressed if controlled by programming code.

Although HTML and JavaScript provide most of the functionality required to produce a fully-functional mobile App, some server-side code is then required to send the data held by the JavaScript App to the researchers. For example, a few lines of PHP code can be used, which corresponds to the website on which the

App is embedded. This sends each participant's data to a dedicated email account that can be created specifically for the project in question. Before being passed to the PHP code for mailing, the outputted data is then organised into a suitable format by the JavaScript code. For convenience, the App should also organise the data into a space-delimited string, such that each data point is separated by a tab, space or comma, allowing it to be read by spreadsheet software. This data string then forms the content of each participant's data email, which can be automatically sent on completion of an experimental session. The data string can then be cut and pasted into a text file so as to be subsequently read and formatted by Excel. This process was used for the authors' gaming research.

The choice of where to host the completed website has important consequences for the functionality of the embedded code and perhaps even the likelihood of participants choosing to take part in the research. Several companies offer free web-hosting. Although an intuitively attractive option, there are often several problems associated with such offers. Free websites often expire after a set period of inactivity. For example, if the webpage on which the App is embedded is inactive for a number of weeks, the page may automatically be deleted. It is therefore essential to check for such rules prior to hosting. Free webhosting companies also often make their money from online advertising revenue, so the websites they host regularly feature banner and pop-up adverts that can compromise the display of page content. Furthermore, free websites often do not support the types of server-side code required to send participants' data from the webpage to a researcher's email account. A final problem with free hosting is that the generic web addresses (e.g. www.freewebhostingservice.psychology experiment.com/app.html) may seem unprofessional to potential participants, and perhaps even suspicious. Such factors may deter potential users and thus this too should be carefully considered. Hosting experimental software on a domain owned by one of the researchers or the host research institution may therefore be beneficial. The process of acquiring such a domain is cheap and simple and mitigates the issues highlighted above.

Obtaining the right amount of data

One factor which needs to be considered from the outset of such research is the amount of data points (or number of sessions completed) that will be required to provide sufficient data. For Apps which enable ESM research, researchers should consider the number of prompts needed per day (and for how many days should participation take place). For a native App, researchers must decide the time intervals for the participation prompts, once the App is activated. Researchers should then stipulate the participation requirements during recruitment (i.e. the number and regularity of prompts). For example, for the illustrative gaming research, it was explicitly started that consent should only be given if participants were able to commit to completing responses within at least five gameplay sessions (preferably in different contexts), over a maximum period of two weeks. The regularity of prompts should be determined based on the research area and a consideration of the practicalities of responding. For instance, it would not be pertinent to set overly regular prompts which may lead to quick participant fatigue and thus increase participation drop-out rates. Also, excessively demanding response times may not be practical for people whose work commitments would not allow them regular access to their mobile devices, particularly when using this web-hosted App. An ESM-based App, which requests a set number of responses per day, avoids some of these issues, although the researchers must still decide upon the regularity of the prompts once the App is activated. However, this alternative mechanism is by no means foolproof either, as participants may not be willing or able to respond at the prompted time. Data for that time period will therefore be blank. The amount of data gained within such Apps will therefore vary greatly, regardless of the design. Questions as to how to maximise data potential are therefore vital at the start of the research design. Nonetheless, researchers may be comforted by the knowledge that the multi-level analyses (which are required to analyse the inherently related nature of data from such App-based research) is well equipped to handle a degree of missing data, without compromising data validity. There are hitherto no accepted standards for the amount of data points required to conduct such analyses. However, most App-based research yields very large data sets, even when samples are relatively small, meaning that the resulting data should be sufficient to allow at least a basic level of analyses. One rule of thumb is that 200 assessment points are considered sufficient for most linear structural equation applications (Kline, 2005). Thus, for example (Monk and Heim, 2014a), if researchers obtain a number of pieces of data per response, and five responses over seven days are taken, even a relatively small sample size ($n=69$) will yield a very high amount of data (e.g. 10,560).

Recruitment of participants and management of data

Participant recruitment is necessary across all psychological research and is a perennial concern. Recruitment through a web-based advertisement can, however, lessen this demand. For App-based research, online adverts can easily direct participants to a web-link where more information can be supplied and where the App itself can be hosted. As the requirements of such research are more complex than typical psychology studies, a video tutorial can also be developed and hosted online which outlines the App to participants prior to their decision to take part.

Proceeding from this, once participants have viewed all the information and instructions relating to a given study, this may be a useful opportunity to issue them with a randomly generated participant number, which they are required to provide every time they complete a responding session. This allows matching of data across the whole period of the research, as well as ensuring participant anonymity. Using a stringent system of participant numbers is key within this form of research to ensure the large quantities of data across sessions can be matched accordingly to undertake within-participant analyses.

To manage the way data is transferred from an App to a given response database, one strategy is to use a system whereby responses are sent to a designated email address associated with the App. This enables a separate email to be received for each completed response. In the illustrative example of the researchers' gaming research, an email including the participant's unique number, followed by their item responses was sent after each participant response. These were transmitted in the form of a 25-item data string (representing the 25 responses to the items completed within each response set). For example, a typical format of psychometric scales (e.g. 1 = not at all, 2 = a little) represented the extent of participants' mood, flow and expectancies in gameplay. For categorical variables, such as identification of the gameplay context of the respective gaming session, these codes were determined by the research team (e.g. 1 = playing solo, 2 = offline with friends). This data can then be easily copied into an Excel file with the corresponding question item as a column header for analysis. An alternative mechanism (cf. Monk and Heim, 2014b; Monk et al., 2015), is to use Google Analytics to capture the data provided. This also has the added benefit of allowing researchers to analyse a wide range of additional data that is automatically captured. That is, this data is not actively supplied by the user, but rather it is passively stored by Google. This includes geographic location, the mobile device used, start and end times for the response session, and time taken to complete each question. Such information can be particularly useful for in-depth analysis of question veracity. For example, pilot research can highlight problematic questions if response times to particular questions are repeatedly longer than average. The recording of response time is also highly useful for experiential sampling research. Here, researchers can be sure that the responses obtained are real-time, as opposed to retrospective accounts which are, as noted previously, subject to the limitations associated with autobiographical memory. Specifically, researchers can compare the time of response with that of participation prompt. Any response supplied in excess of 15 minutes from prompt time can thus be excluded as such data can no longer be reliably held as an indication of the participant's thoughts or behaviours at the time of interest (cf. Monk and Heim, 2014b). Rather, such responses are retrospective accounts of what was happening at the time of interest, which is of less value to those researchers wishing to conduct real-time, experiential research.

Conclusion

Psychological research has been critiqued for its perceived failure to assess dynamic behaviours and cognitions in the real world, although it is contended that this is feasible (Baker, 1968). Indeed, using practical examples from our own work, this chapter has identified that not only is it important to consider the effect of context, but that it is feasible to do so within a viable research paradigm. From this perspective, the benefits of Smartphone Apps within research are plentiful. Not only does this constitute a novel approach in the discipline of Psychology, but it has the capacity to advance conceptual insight regarding the effect of context as a fundamental determinant of attitudes and behaviours.

This chapter has sought to advocate the utility of Smartphone technology across the discipline of Psychology, using examples from our own experiences. Smartphone technology offers researchers the capacity to conduct increasingly dynamic research and to collect vast amounts of contextually-aware data. Specifically, the mobile nature of Apps designed for research purposes mean that they enable researchers to easily capture a whole host of behaviours and beliefs as they occur, and change, in real time. Apps for use as research tools also marry more effectively with the evolving nature of everyday interactional behaviours (between individuals, as well as between user and system). Indeed, to understand issues which take place in online or virtual contexts (e.g. gaming, online social networking, email), it makes sense to use methodologies which take place in the equivalent context, particularly given that some online behaviours can vary from real-world ones (McKenna and Bargh, 2000). These methodologies may therefore provide researchers with access to more natural forms of interactions and behaviours than more traditional methodologies. In the context of digital gaming, real-life cues such as the presentation of the games themselves and the proximity of other players (physical or virtual) may change the nature of a gamer's experiences. Resultantly, beliefs and behaviour may vary. Smartphone-enabled research provides a more ecologically valid and contextually-aware perspective on such constructs. Not only do Apps allow researchers to measure these changes, but they provide a level of insights that may not be possible with laboratory-based research, where cognitive and behavioural processes may operate differently owing to the inherent differences between said contexts.

A practical summary

As a practical summary, we provide a list of critical questions we urge readers to consider before embarking on this form of research methodology.

* Are contexts fundamental to understanding your research enquiry? That is, is this methodology useful for developing understanding in your area?
* Will different contexts of responding present different demands for participants, which may result in varied response patterns?
* Are the contexts of interest appropriate for participant responding? Are there any confounding factors which may be relevant to consider?
* Is a Smartphone an appropriate medium through which to administer your *in-vivo* questions?
* Are the questions short and snappy and easily submitted by participants?
* What is the overall duration of the research? How long will participants be operating within the requirements of the study?
* How many contexts are relevant to examine and how many responses will you require per context?
* Do you hold adequate technical expertise to develop a bespoke App or to understand the requirements of how an off-the-shelf App may be adapted for your own research?

Note

1   In respect of alcohol consumption, 'wet' refers to a culture or context where alcohol consumption is commonplace, while 'dry' refers to a culture or environment where there is little or no alcohol consumption.

References

Alessi, S.M., and Petry, N.M. (2013). A randomized study of cell phone technology to reinforce alcohol abstinence in the natural environment. *Addiction, 108*, 900–909.

Aphinyanaphongs, Y., Ray, B., Statnikov, A., and Krebs, P. (2014). Text classification for automatic detection of alcohol use-related tweets: A feasibility study. In *IEEE 15th International Conference on Information Reuse and Integration (IRI), 2014* (pp. 93–97). IEEE.

Baker, R.G. (1968). *Ecological Psychology: Concepts and Methods for Studying the Environment of Human Behavior*. Stanford, CA: Stanford University Press.

Boniface, S., and Shelton, N. (2013). How is alcohol consumption affected if we account for under-reporting? A hypothetical scenario. *The European Journal of Public Health, 23*(6), 1076–1081. doi:10.1093/eurpub/ckt016.

Bracken, C.C., Lange, R.L., and Denny, J. (2005, October). Online video games and gamers' sensations of spatial, social, and co-presence. Paper presented at the Future-Play Conference, Lansing, Michigan.

British Psychological Society (2009). *Code of Ethics and Conduct: Guidance published by the Ethics Committee of the British Psychological Society*. Available at: www.bps. org.uk/system/files/documents/code_of_ethics_and_conduct.pdf.

British Psychological Society (2010). *Code of Human Research Ethics*. Available at: www.bps.org.uk/sites/default/files/documents/code_of_human_research_ethics.pdf.

Brown, H.R., Zeidman, P., Smittenaar, P., Adams, R.A., McNab, F., Rutledge, R.B., and Dolan, R.J. (2014). Crowdsourcing for cognitive science: the utility of smartphones. *PLoS ONE, 9*(7), e100662 doi:10.1371/journal.pone.0100662.

Bryce, J., and Kaye, L.K. (2011). Computer and videogames. In G. Brewer (ed.), *Media psychology* (pp. 101–114). London: Palgrave Macmillan.

Carey, K.B., Borsari, B., Carey, M.P., and Maisto, S.A. (2006). Patterns and importance of self-other differences in college drinking norms. *Psychology of Addictive Behaviors, 20*, 385–393.

Cole, H., and Griffiths, M.D. (2007). Social interactions in Massively Multiplayer Online Role-playing gamers. *CyberPsychology and Behavior, 10*(4), 575–583. doi:10.1089/cpb.2007.9988.

Collins, L.R., Kashdan, T.B., and Gollnisch, G. (2003). The feasibility of using cellular phones to collect ecological momentary assessment data: Application to alcohol consumption. *Experimental and Clinical Psychopharmacology, 11*, 73–78.

Collins, R.L., Morsheimer, E.T., Shiffman, S., Paty, J.A., Gnys, M., and Papandonatos, G.D. (1998). Ecological momentary assessment in a behavioral drinking moderation training program. *Experimental and Clinical Psychopharmacology, 6*, 306–315.

Courvoisier, D.S., Eid, M., Lischetzke, T., and Schreiber, W.H. (2010). Psychometric properties of a computerized mobile phone method for assessing mood in daily life. *Emotion, 10*, 115–124.

Csikszentmihalyi, M. (1975). *Beyond boredom and anxiety: Experiencing flow in work and play*. San Francisco: Jossey-Bass Publishers.

Csikszentmihalyi, M., Larson, R., and Prescott, S. (1977). The ecology of adolescent activity and experience. *Journal of Youth and Adolescence, 6*, 281–294.

Dewey, J. (1910). *The Influence of Darwin on Philosophy*. New York: Henry Holt and Co.

Diener, E., and Emmons, R.A. (1985). The independence of positive and negative affect. *Journal of Personality and Social Psychology, 47*, 1108–1117.

Eastin, M.S. (2007). The influence of competitive and cooperative group game play on state hostility. *Human Communication Research, 33*, 450–466.

Gajadhar, B.J., de Kort, Y.A.W., and Ijsselsteijn, W.A. (2008, April). Influence of social setting on player experience of digital games. Paper presented at CHI 2008 Conference, Florence, Italy.

Ghonsooly, B., and Hamedi, S.M. (2014). An investigation of the most flow inducing genres. *International Journal of Research Studies in Education, 3*(4), 99–108.

Godden, D.R., and Baddeley, A.D. (1975). Context-dependent memory in two natural environments: on land and underwater. *British Journal of Psychology, 66*, 325–231.

Golder, S. (2008). Measuring social networks with digital photograph collections. In *Proceedings of the Nineteenth ACM Conference on Hypertext and Hypermedia, 1*.

Gustafson, D.H., Boyle, M.G., Shaw, B.R., et al. (2011). An e-health solution for people with alcohol problems. *Alcohol Research and Health, 33*(4), 327–337. PMID: 23293549.

Gustafson, D.H., McTavish, F.M., Chih, M.-Y., et al. (2014). A smartphone application to support recovery from alcoholism: A randomized clinical trial. *JAMA Psychiatry, 71*(5), 566–572.

Harrison, A.M., and Goozee, R. (2014). Psych-related iPhone apps. *Journal of Mental Health, 23*(1), 48–50.

Jones, B.T., Corbin, W., and Fromme, K. (2001). A review of expectancy theory and alcohol consumption. *Addiction, 96*, 57–72.

Kaye, L.K. (2016). Exploring flow experiences in cooperative digital gaming contexts. *Computers in Human Behavior, 55*, 286–291. doi:10.1016/j.chb.2015.09.023.

Kaye, L.K., and Bryce, J. (2012). Putting the "fun factor" into gaming: The influence of social contexts on experiences of playing videogames. *International Journal of Internet Science, 7*(1), 23–37.

Kaye, L.K., and Bryce, J. (2014). Go with the flow: The experience and affective outcomes of solo versus social gameplay. *Journal of Gaming and Virtual Worlds, 6*(1), 49–60. doi:10.1386/jgvw.6.1.49_1.

Kline, R.B. (ed.). (2005). *Principles and practice of structural equation modeling* (2nd edn). New York: The Guilford Press.

Kuendig, H., and Kuntsche, E. (2012). Solitary versus social drinking: An experimental study on effects of social exposures on in-situ alcohol consumption. *Alcoholism: Clinical and Experimental Research, 36*, 732–738.

Kuntsche, E., and Labhart, F. (2014). The future is now: using personal cellphones to gather data on substance use and related factors. *Addiction, 109*, 1052–1053.

Kuntsche, E., and Labhart, F. (2015). ICAT: development of an Internet-based data collection method for ecological momentary assessment using personal cell phones. *European Journal of Psychological Assessment, 29*, 140–148.

Kuntsche, E., and Robert, B. (2009). Short message service (SMS) technology in alcohol research: a feasibility study. *Alcohol, 44*, 423–428.

Larsen. H., Engels, R.C., Wiers, R.W., Granic, I., and Spijkerman, R. (2012). Implicit and explicit alcohol cognitions and observed alcohol consumption: Three studies in (semi) naturalistic drinking settings. *Addiction, 107*, 1420–142.

Leigh, B.C., and Stacy, A.W. (1993). Alcohol outcome expectancies: Scale construction and predictive utility in higher order confirmatory models. *Psychological Assessment, 5*, 216–229.

Leigh, B.C., and Stacy, A.W. (2004). Alcohol expectancies and drinking in different age groups. *Addiction, 99*, 215–227.

Martin, A.L. (2006). Drinking and alehouses in the diary of an English apprentice, 1663–1674. In: M.P. Holt (Ed.), *Alcohol: A social and cultural history* (pp. 93–106). New York: Berg.

McKenna, K.Y.A., and Bargh, J.A. (2000). Plan 9 from Cyberspace: The implications for the Internet for personality and social psychology. *Personality and Social Psychology Review, 4*(1), 57–75.

Miller, G. (2012). The Smartphone Psychology Manifesto. *Perspectives on Psychological Science, 7*(3), 221–237.

Monk, R.L., and Heim, D. (2013a). Environmental context effects on alcohol-related outcome expectancies, efficacy and norms: A field study. *Psychology of Addictive Behaviors, 27*, 814–818.

Monk, R.L., and Heim, D. (2013b). Panoramic projection: Affording a wider view on contextual influences on alcohol-related cognitions. *Experimental and Clinical Psychopharmacology, 21*, 1–7.

Monk, R.L., and Heim, D. (2013c). A critical systematic review of alcohol-related outcome expectancies. *Substance Use and Misuse, 48*, 539–557.

Monk, R.L., and Heim, D. (2014a). A real-time examination of context effects on alcohol cognitions. *Alcoholism: Clinical and Experimental Research, 38*, 2452–2459.

Monk, R.L., and Heim, D. (2014b). A systematic review of the Alcohol Norms literature: A focus on context. *Drugs: Education, Prevention and Policy, 21*, 263–282.

Monk, R.L., Heim, D., Qureshi, A., and Price, A. (2015). 'I have no clue what I drank last night': Using Smartphone technology to compare in-vivo and retrospective self-reports of alcohol consumption. *PLoS ONE,* e0126209.

Piasecki, T.M., Jahng, S., Wood, P.K., et al. (2011). The subjective effects of alcohol–tobacco co-use: An ecological momentary assessment investigation. *Journal of Abnormal Psychology, 120*, 557–571.

Plantié, M., and Crampes, M. (2010). From photo networks to social networks: Creation and use of a social network derived with photos. In *Proceedings of the International Conference on Multimedia, 1*, 1047–1050.

Poels, K., de Kort, Y.A.W., and IJsselsteijn, W.A. (2007, November). 'It is always a lot of fun!' Exploring dimensions of digital game experience using focus group methodology. Paper presented at the Futureplay 2007, Toronto, Canada.

Poltash, N.A. (2013). Snapchat and sexting: A snapshot of baring your bare essentials. *Richmond Journal of Law and Technology, 19*, 14–14.

Ravaja, N., Saari, T., Turpeinen, M., Laari, J., Salminen, M., and Kavikangas, M. (2006). Spatial presence and emotions during video game playing: Does it matter with whom you play? *Presence, 15*(4), 381–392.

Ravaja, N., Salminen, M., Holopainen, J., Saari, T., Laarni, J., and Järvinen, A. (2004). Emotional response patterns and sense of presence during video games: Potential criterion variables for game design. In *Proceedings of the Third Nordic Conference on Human-Computer Interaction.* New York: ACM.

Robins, L.N. (1993). Vietnam veterans' rapid recovery from heroin addiction: A fluke or normal expectation? *Addiction, 88*, 1041–1054.

Shiffman, S., Gwaltney, C.J., Balabanis, M.H., Liu, K.S., Paty, J.A., Kassel, J., et al. (2002). Immediate antecedents of cigarette smoking: An analysis from ecological momentary assessment. *Journal of Abnormal Psychology, 111*, 531–545.

Shiffman, S., Hufford, M., Hickcox, M., Paty, J.A., Gnys, M., and Kassel, J.D. (1997). Remember that? A comparison of real-time versus retrospective recall of smoking lapses. *Journal of Consulting and Clinical Psychology, 65*, 292–300.

Stacy, A.W, Widaman, K.F., and Marlatt, G.A. (1990). Expectancy models of alcohol use. *Journal of Personality and Social Psychology, 55*, 918–928.

Stawarz, K., Cox, A.L., and Blandford, A. (2015, April). Beyond self-tracking and reminders: Designing Smartphone apps that support habit formation. Paper presented at CHI 2015, Seoul, Republic of Korea.

Stoyanov, S., Hides, L., Dingle, G.A., Tjondronegoro, D., Zelenko, O., Papinczak, Z., Koh, D., Edge, S., and Kavanagh, D. (2014, July). Mood enhancement using Smartphone apps. Paper presented at the 7th European Conference on Positive Psychology, Amsterdam.

Thrul, J., and Kuntsche, E. (2015). The impact of friends on young adults' drinking over the course of the evening: An event-level analysis. *Addiction, 110*(4), 619–626.

Toll, B.A., Cooney, N.L., McKee, S.A., and O'Malley, S.S. (2005). Do daily interactive voice response reports of smoking behavior correspond with retrospective reports? *Psychology of Addictive Behavior, 19*, 291–295.

Verster, J.C., Tiplady, B., and McKinney, A. (2012). Mobile technology and naturalistic study designs in addiction research (Editorial). *Current Drug Abuse Reviews, 5*, 169–171.

Walker, D.W., and Hunter, B.E. (1978). Short-term memory impairment following chronic alcohol consumption in rats. *Neuropsychologia, 16*, 545–553.

Wall, A.M., McKee, S.A. and Hinson, R.E. (2000). Assessing variation in alcohol outcome expectancies across environmental context: An examination of the situational-specificity hypothesis. *Psychology of Addictive Behaviors, 14*, 367–375.

Wiederhold, B.K. (2015). Behavioral health apps abundant, but evidence-based research nearly non-existent. *Cyberpsychology, Behavior and Social Networking, 18*(6), 309–210.

Zinberg, N.E. (1984). *Drug, Set, and Setting.* New Haven, CT: Yale University Press.

3 Adapting a method to use Facebook in education research

Taking phenomenography online

Naomi Barnes

Introduction

This chapter explains how methodological adaptions developed during a research project that used Facebook status updates as data. The research approach was phenomenography and the phenomenon studied was the first year experience at university. The traditional outcome of phenomenography is to determine a finite number of ways a group of people experience a phenomenon by finding the similarities between individual experiences captured at a moment in time (Marton, 1981; Bowden and Green, 2005). The variation between understandings of a phenomenon is generally used to design learning activities that progress expansion of knowledge from basic to complex. I initially chose phenomenography as a method for understanding transitions to university because I saw no difference between learning physics or mathematics (the disciplines out of which the research approach was developed) and learning a new social environment.

The aim of this chapter is not to report my findings. While the development of the methodology is grounded in empirical research, there is not the space to explain them here. If you are interested in the findings, please see Barnes (2014). Rather, in this chapter, I discuss an approach new to digital scholarship. First, how I went about selecting phenomenography as the most appropriate methodology. Second, because phenomenography's *reason for being* aligned with the type of online research I wanted to conduct, I needed to adapt the methodology for the new environment. Phenomenography is a boutique research approach that is usually situated in education research in order to inform classroom practice. Its practitioners are conscious of ensuring that phenomenographic research remains faithful to design, leading to debates about what constitutes phenomenography. Through this chapter, I weigh into this debate by arguing that with a few adaptions, phenomenography could be both sociological and become a valuable tool for digital research.

Researchers interested in extending phenomenographic methodology are presently investigating ways to extend and reach out beyond their *tribal borders* (Hallett, 2014) to engage more robustly with the wider research community (Gibbings, Lidstone, and Bruce, 2015). While engaging with a methodology from a theoretical point of view may be mundane in the wider qualitative research tradition, it is a way of thinking that is emerging from within phenomenography, which has sometimes been critiqued for its lack of theoretical muscle (Hallett, 2014; Hasselgren and Beach, 1997; Richardson, J., 1999). When a research approach reaches a crossroads: 'it is necessary, at a certain moment, to turn against Method, or at least to regard it without any founding privilege' (Barthes, 1986, p. 319). In other words, method is malleable and we need to interrogate its limits and possibilities for the ultimate goal of knowledge production, representation or performativity. If the rules do not fit perfectly but the conceptual framework does, adjust the rules. Methodologies should be developed that celebrate the findings and possibilities of research. Method is simply the journey. How we get to our destination should be as organized and creative as the researcher is themselves. I propose that phenomenography has a conceptual underpinning rarely pointed out in methodological literature that is usually focused on how to do phenomenography rather than what phenomenography can do for scholarship.

The aim of this chapter is to describe how I came to choose phenomenography and highlight the elements of the research approach that I found attractive for digital research. Phenomenography is a relatively new research approach, in that it was conceptualized in the late 1970s, and it has become a regular contributor to higher education research. As with all qualitative research, phenomenography has its sceptics and has worked to find ways to address its criticisms. Unfortunately, it has developed an arguably tribal mentality (Hallett, 2014) that has limited its options in engaging with the wider research field. In recent years, key phenomenographic researchers have been looking for ways to breach these self-imposed tribal borders and to extend the research approach, leading to debates about how much a methodology can be changed before it is no longer that methodology (Collier-Reed and Ingerman, 2013; Gibbings et al., 2015). This places phenomenographic researchers at a very exciting point in time where they can either remain in their tribal lands and continue to plug gaps in the methodological walls, or they can move steadfastly forward and explore lands new to phenomenography, such as those online, which, it can be argued, it is greatly suited to doing with only a few minor adjustments.

I begin by briefly describing my research and the ontological and epistemological foundations that attracted me to phenomenography. I will also explain how the (debatable) idea of phenomenography being non-dualist and participant-oriented begins to address the ethical problems of authenticity and reliability sorely needed in digital research. I argue that going online provides an alternative way to approach problems inherent in the highly criticized phenomenographic interview. I also outline how I employed phenomenographic techniques to analyse online artefacts. Through this chapter I propose that by looking at ways to adapt phenomenography to work better for what a researcher is looking to discover, a way that phenomenographers can breach their tribal borders can be found.

The core of the research: what I wanted to find out

I was interested in finding out how high school students transformed into university students. Throughout the rest of this chapter, I will use the generic term 'school leavers'. This term refers to students who have completed Year 12 or 6th form and are attending university within two years of graduating. The students who informed my research were 17–19 years of age, and I was concerned with their transition experiences, not just in the classroom, but in the life of the students. What did their transition look like? How can universities use that understanding to better develop programs for transition?

The majority of the literature about the first year of university positions the transition process as 'universally experienced and normalised' (Gale and Parker, 2012, p. 11) but the world is becoming increasingly individualized and 'liquid' (Bauman, 2000). Students are arriving in higher education along numerous pathways, bringing with them a vast range of experiences, and with a variety of reasons for valuing (or not) higher education. In this vein, an emerging school of thought about the first year of university suggests that students' experiences of transition are not linear but continuous and chaotic (Palmer, O'Kane, and Owens, 2009; Penn-Edwards and Donnison, 2011). The world of the first year student has changed dramatically during the last decade and current first year of higher education research has noticed this change, but I believe it has not sufficiently tried to understand the change.

I wondered if it was possible to arrive at a generalist qualitative understanding of the difficulties students face when they are transitioning that could be used to propose a future direction in research and complement established research in the field of transitions. In reviewing the literature, I noticed that in the expansive and rich library of research into the first year of university that the studies used either broad quantitative methods to conduct longitudinal national and institutional censuses of first year students (for the latest Australian version, see Baik et al., 2015), or small targeted qualitative studies of similar students either from the same class or course cohort. This limitation has been commented upon almost since its inception in the early 1980s. In 1984, Astin suggested that it might be nice for students to keep a diary 'showing the time spent in various activities such as studying, sleeping, socializing, daydreaming, working, and commuting' (1984, pp. 526–527). In 2001, McInnis suggested finding a way to follow students from high school to the end of their first degree might reveal some more detailed insights. In 2005, now ubiquitous technology was invented that could make those suggestions a reality. In 2005, Facebook was launched to the world and millions of people (especially school leavers) began to keep detailed diaries of their lives over long periods of time. In 2007, iPhone was launched and with it the ability for people to update their social networks *on the go*. In 2010, I became aware that the information people were putting on Facebook could add a missing piece of the puzzle of understanding the first year experience.

The online world is a networked entanglement of experiences that is a far cry from the ordered findings of offline research where the researcher conducts and organizes the participants. I wanted to use the raw online postings of first year university students and I did not wish to adulterate what was being posted through asking guiding questions. I found, however, that some form of map was needed that could signpost a way through research online in the field of transitions. I decided to see if I could write a generalized curriculum of the first year of university to act as a working document for future research into the phenomenon.

There were several problems to solve before I could begin the collection of data. Social media research in 2010 was under-theorized, or the theory that was widely used was technological determinism which looked to control and manipulate social media rather than use it to gather live unadulterated data (Selwyn, 2012). I needed a research approach that did the following:

1   Accepted the research participants' experiences at face value because in 2010 social media research was viewed with suspicion, particularly with respect to authenticity and reliability (Kaplan and Haenlein, 2010).
2   Privileged the participants' experiences over the researcher's theoretical background; quite oppositional to the majority of first year university research which was researcher- or institution-oriented.
3   Complemented pedagogy and curriculum development in order to make a contribution to the education research community.

The research method: selecting phenomenography

After deliberations, phenomenography appeared as a methodology that could help me develop a map for further exploration of the details of transition experiences. Most empirical and methodological literature that defines phenomenography will quote Ference Marton along these lines, saying that it is: 'the empirical study of the limited number of qualitatively different ways in which various phenomena in, and aspects of, the world around us are experienced, conceptualised, understood, perceived and apprehended' (Marton, 1994, p. 4425). Much current critique and debate about the research approach have centred on the meaning of the words *experience* and *conception, understanding, perception* and *apprehended* (Collier-Reed and Ingerman, 2013; Hallett, 2014). While it is important to interrogate meaning, when choosing a research approach, it is important that the approach works for the research question first and foremost. Phenomenographic researchers have justified the interchangeable use of these words by leaving it up to the individual researcher to choose the best word in accordance with their qualitative data (Collier-Reed and Ingerman, 2013). Others have criticized the phenomenographic method for being too generalist because it seeks to find a limited number of differences within a phenomenon rather than exposing the infinite variability of experiences but by its very name, phenomenoGRAPHY is about a generalized overview or a *map* of a phenomenon that can be used to explore it further (Bowden and Green, 2005). Maps are not hyper-detailed but that does not mean that there is a denial of the details. The generalizability of the research approach and the adaptability of the language are what made it useful.

Phenomenography is designed to capture multiple ways of seeing and understanding a phenomenon, and social media is a virtual bank of diverse points of view on events, ideas, ways of learning and knowing. By using phenomenography, an understanding of a phenomenon is built through capturing the diverse experiences and mapping them to form a clearer picture. As NASA overlaps multiple photographs of the Earth to produce a cloudless view of the planet, so phenomenography seeks to construct a clear view of a phenomenon. The more personal snapshots that the phenomenographic researcher collects, the more there is a likelihood of a clear, multidimensional view of the phenomena being studied. A phenomenographic researcher not only explores the descriptions of the phenomena but also how aspects within the phenomenon are seen to relate to each other and the participants' overall reality (Bowden, 2000). In other words, phenomenographers are also aware of where the experiences are taken from and the perspective used. Just as NASA would not be able to form an accurate image of Earth if the photographs were taken from different distances away from Earth, so phenomenographers endeavour to create their picture of a phenomenon from one place.

Phenomenography was born out of observations of science and mathematics educators that students could arrive at the solution for a problem along more than one pathway, and that each pathway could be ranked from conceptually basic to complex. Some phenomenographic researchers (including myself) have seen that the method offers potential for the development of a learner-centred curriculum where how the students learn is used to design activities that embrace different levels and styles of learning (Åkerlind et al., 2010; Barnes, 2014). A curriculum is a map of a learning experience and a map is a guide for exploration.

First year university research in the last five years has been interested in developing transition pedagogies and curricula for guiding first year university students into higher education (Kift, 2009; Kift, Nelson, and Clarke, 2010). Phenomenography seems to provide an appropriate method for developing a transition curriculum based on student focus at certain points during their first year of university.

In selecting phenomenography, I asked myself three questions: (1) does an online first year of university experience exist as a phenomenon?; (2) can phenomenography be used to create a theory/map/curriculum of the online first year experience as a guide for future investigation?; and (3) can phenomenography help us to understand online student experiences? In answering from a phenomenographic theoretical and methodological perspective, the answer was *Yes* to all three. Once I believed phenomenography was suitable, I then explored phenomenography to see if it would align with my need for a research approach that centralized student experiences.

Phenomenography should take online experiences at face value because, according to Marton and Booth (1997), it is non-dualist. Phenomenography holds that what is known cannot be separated from how it is known; that each person's experience of learning is inseparable from how he/she learns it. There is also no distinction between the individual, the group, the inner (personal life) and the outer (public life) as one of these realities cannot exist without the other realities. Phenomenography does not distinguish between the inner and outer world, therefore, there should be no distinction between the online and offline world. The research approach should therefore acknowledge that the information a person broadcasts on social media is a true description of their experience (as far as one can express an experience in text) at the time it was posted online without judgement of the accuracy or the truth.

It is debatable whether phenomenography is non-dualist because the primary form of data collection is the interview and when participants are asked to recall their experiences, and researchers in turn interpret those recollections, then subjectivism begins to creep in, whether intentional or not (Hallett, 2014). The interview has been criticized in all qualitative research as an academic construction, familiar to the researcher but not necessarily to the participant (Ashworth and Lucas, 1998). The interview is also political. A person's power is written on their body through the embodiment of gender, sexuality, race, class and age (Nairn, Munro, and Smith, 2005; Probyn, 1991). No matter how many pilot studies an interviewer conducts to limit influence, the interviewer will always remain in a position of power, and the setting will never be completely comfortable for the participant. The interviewer and the participant are from different cultural contexts, and past research suggests that interviews are affected by cultural norms (Hong, Morris, Chiu, and Benet-Martinez, 2000). In response to this criticism, phenomenographic researchers report intensive training in interview techniques that extends to recommendations that learning the research approach needs an apprenticeship with an experienced phenomenographic researcher (Bowden and Green, 2005). It recommends that several pilot studies are implemented to refine techniques for non-dualist interviews intent on capturing a snapshot of what the participant is recalling about his or her experience at the moment the interview is conducted, without changing the conception through subjective questioning or body language.

The decision to use Facebook was seen to address the conundrum of the interview in phenomenography. While underused, diary entries and historical artefacts are considered appropriate as phenomenographic data (Marton, 1994; Prinsloo, Slade, and Galpin, 2011). With this in mind, I chose to use Facebook status updates as data. Status updates are an instantaneously captured representation of the users' experience (such as updates which are transmitted live from a lecture or tutorial). Status updates are raw and immediate, providing unique insight into a phenomenon that is usually reported through recollection. When experiences are archived via social network sites, the researcher is bodily separate from the participant. As a researcher, in my project I only interacted with the participants for recruitment purposes. For the majority of the data collection period, I simply observed and archived status updates and associated commentary. The likelihood of me influencing their status updates was minimized.

While subjectivism is still an issue in interpreting the data, phenomenography presents a set of guidelines for researchers to remove (or bracket) themselves from the data analysis to preference the face value records of the participants. Bracketing is the process by which researchers make conscious their relationship with the data, participants and phenomenon in order to ensure that external influences and understandings do not impose 'preconceived ideas' (Marton, 1994, p. 4428). The phenomenographic researcher endeavours to maintain interpretive awareness (Sandbergh, 1997) because the reliability of phenomenographic research lies in the researcher's ability to 'acknowledge and explicitly deal with' her subjectivity (p. 209). The phenomenographic researcher works hard to be consistent with her approach across the development of the findings. In designing, conducting and evaluating the study, she uses phenomenographic bracketing as outlined by Bowden and Green (2005), to ensure rigour in analysis. The phenomenographic researcher explicates the various relationships between herself, the data and the participants so that the reader might understand her 'unique signature' (Eisner, 1998, p. 34) that influences the interpretation of the data.

While the attempt to avoid prejudging data is a conundrum for all researchers, phenomenography has it written into the epistemology that the participants' experiences should be privileged over the researcher's understandings (Marton and Booth, 1997). This approach is useful when dealing with social media data where questions of authenticity and reliability are seemingly more important than in other equally constructed, though maybe more traditionally collected, data. Phenomenographic research values the experiences of the participants by taking the descriptions of the experiences at *face value* (Marton and Booth, 1997). It is a valuable tool for understanding participants' experiences because it makes no judgement about why choices are made. Rather, phenomenography notes that a choice has been made and explores the participants' experiences of the ramifications of that choice. Phenomenography approaches research from what Marton (1981) termed a second-order perspective. Researchers who use the second-order perspective explore the experiences of participants in their study through participant voices. First-order perspective studies describe how the researcher understands the learners and their background, is frequently related to the researcher's own experiences, and is usually within an explanatory framework (Marton and Svensson, 1979). A first-order perspective research question within the field of first year university transitions would be 'What can Facebook status updates tell us about how the first year student becomes a university student?' Instead, I asked a complementary second-order perspective question, 'How do school leavers describe, on Facebook, their transitioning experiences of first year university?' Second-order research should complement first-order research, together revealing the multidimensionality of learning about a phenomenon.

The process of the research: using phenomenography

Data for the study was collected through manual data crawling (Wilson, Gosling, and Graham, 2012). The 31 participants made their status updates (status data) and any further comments they made on those status updates (commentary data) available for collection, provided the content related to university. A study-specific Facebook profile allowed me to collect conversations about university experiences 24 hours, seven days per week. I collected both their status updates and any further commentary the participants made within the thread initiated by the status update. While I did not collect the commentary from the participants' Facebook network, I extracted enough information to enhance/explicate the participants' meaning. The transcription of data is the status and commentary data of the participants.

Data collection only occurred during specific phases during the university year. The times were based on those nominated by the first year student particip-ants in Penn-Edwards' and Donnison's (2011) study as being critical points of engagement: in the first weeks of orientation, after the first assignment is returned, end of the first semester and end of the first year. These latter two phases fell around the time of submission of final assignments and examinations. The four critical times also defined the four phenomena to be compared:

1   Orientation week
2   First assessment
3   End of semester 1
4   End of the year.

There were three reasons for monitoring the participants' Facebook status updates during these four times. The first reason was the logistical ease of recruiting participants for the study while they were in attendance at university. Second, it removed the need to monitor the students constantly for ten months; thereby creating the four distinct snapshots in time for analysis. The third advantage was that these phases during the university year were when first year students were expected to be emotive about their university experience (Penn-Edwards and Donnison, 2011).

Ethical clearance for the project was gained by following the procedures out-lined by my university's Ethics Committee. The key concern for the Ethics Committee was the protection of the universities, so they stressed the need to ensure the anonymity of the universities, lecturers and course names. The age of the majority of participants (17) was initially of concern, but the Ethics Com-mittee ruled that if they were able to attend university, they would be able to consent.

One hurdle I faced was that associated with Facebook's terms and conditions. As part of Facebook's terms and conditions, online researchers are required to obtain consent from participants, make it clear that it was not Facebook who was collecting data, and post a privacy policy (Facebook, 2014 Term 5.7). I complied with these requirements by posting the informed consent materials on the Face-book profile and direct messaged each of the participants to ensure they were mindfully consenting. Despite all protocols being in place, Facebook determined the recruitment process was a threat because the people being recruited were not personally known by me offline. I was prevented from recruiting via the befriending tool on Facebook and informed I would have to recruit offline. In the end, approximately two-thirds of the participants were recruited via email where they were asked to add my Facebook profile to their network and informed consent details were attached to the email.

Analysis of the research: formulating a method

While traditional phenomenography looks to find hierarchies in how people understand a phenomenon, the data collection and analysis were framed by the accepting that there is no hierarchy of complexity of how people come to understand a social experience. Each person's journey is specific to them. It is not something that can be ranked.

In order to avoid hierarchies, focus became the key idea for how to map social understandings. Focus was chosen because those who write transition programs would be better served by information about what the people transitioning are focusing on at the different stages of their transition. For example, if school leavers are intently focused on making friends in the first few weeks of university, they may not be ready to hear a depth of information about academic ethics and study skills. Spotlighting that information may be more useful later on in the transition, when the students are focusing on assessment.

When analysing the status updates, I made note of those updates which were both frequent and impassioned. For example, I determined that cursing and frequent broadcasting were indicators of anxiety, and therefore focus, and took them into consideration when ranking the focus of the participants' transition experiences. This was a major modification made to phenomenography data collection: the addition of a basic quantitative technique that simply counted the number of times a certain category was referenced in the data. Though not unheard of in phenomenography, it is definitely contentious and the subject of debate as to whether using it still qualifies the methodology as phenomenography (Gibbings et al., 2015). I contend that it does remain phenomenography because it is simply another technique used for mapping a phenomenon. The qualitative part of the definition of phenomenography is malleable. I used the quantitative (frequency) and qualitative (impassioned) nature of the data to determine focus and design the map (or outcome space) of the findings.

Inspired by descriptions of Husserl's an illuminated theatre in phenomenology (Brough and Husserl, 2012), a research approach that allegedly inspired phenomenography (Richardson, 1999), I used a one-point drawing perspective, applied to a proscenium theatre stage, to illustrate the mapping of findings, known in phenomenography as an outcome space (Figure 3.1).

Simply explained, if the participants are the audience in the arena, the major focus is the happenings on stage, the minor focus is the scenery, and the peripherals are the detailing of the theatre and the box seats. The actors on stage may be the smallest element, but they are still the focus because they are where the action is located. The phenomenographic maps I developed show the focus as being where the action is located. The major and minor foci are the active

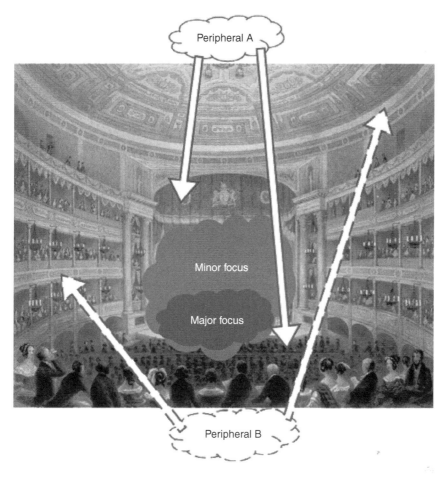

Figure 3.1 The proscenium stage and the phenomenographic map. This figure illustrates the thinking behind the outcome space representations.

Source: 'Drury Lane Theatre: *As You Like It*, Antique Engraving,' 2013/1842.

descriptions (frequent and/or emotive) and the peripherals drift in and out of focus. The frequency and level of emotion, interpreted from the participants' descriptions, determined the difference between the major and minor foci and peripherals.

I compiled one map for each phenomenon studied (the four points in time) using Figure 3.2 as a generalized guide. The shapes represent the concentration or intensity of the experiences. The darker and smaller the shape, the stronger the participants are focusing on the experience or conception (like a laser). The block colour shapes represent those experiences that are persistently in focus. The peripherals, represented by block and dashed lines, are the experiences that float around the focus and occasionally drift into focus. The amorphous shapes

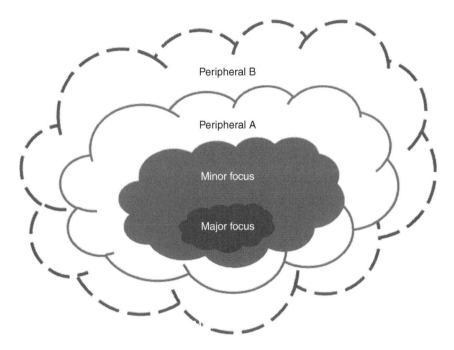

Figure 3.2 The control map. This figure shows how the outcome space is graphically represented in this method.

were chosen to acknowledge the qualitative nature of the analysis and to avoid misleading assumptions of precise outcomes that circles or squares could represent.

Each focus was determined by an iterative process of determining key similarities between the status updates. Decisions were made easier by using the participants' language. The majority of the status updates remained but some were discarded as they were deemed unrelated to the research question.

A challenge that arose from using social media was the massive amount of data available for analysis. Phenomenographic studies must sample enough participants to show enough variation in conceptions to form useful categories of description. Between 20 and 30 subjects, closely related to the phenomenon, is recommended (Bowden and Green, 2005). Over the four phases in time, there were useful contributions for the purposes of this study from 26 of the 31 student recruits. While the number of participants fell within phenomenographic recommendations, the transcribed size of potential data collected from the 26 students over a ten-month period needed to be contained. Analysing the data from ten months of archived status updates would have been a considerable task; too big for a lone researcher. At this stage in my digital scholarship, I still prefer manual analysis rather than software, although computational analysis for phenomenography, such as Leximancer, has been proposed (Penn-Edwards, 2010).

The selection of status updates was limited to content about university. I selected the useful status updates direct from the study's Facebook Newsfeed. The status data that was not clearly about the participants' experiences of university was not collected. The traditional phenomenographic researcher would transcribe all their interview data and then select the utterances that pertain to their research question. However, the participants of this study were recruited with the understanding that I would only archive status updates that were related to university experiences. This was an important ethical consideration due to the possibility of participants sharing sensitive material on their Facebook profiles.

Reflecting on the research: using phenomenography for researching using social media

One of the most-cited hurdles to conducting ethical digital social research is the authenticity and credibility of what is broadcast and who is broadcasting it. This is fast becoming an outdated assumption. In every environment in which data is collected, questions of the credibility and authenticity of the data are raised (James, Krause, and Jennings, 2010). A concern particular to using social media is verifying the identity of the participants, but the authenticity of nominal data is of concern for all methodologies and should not be considered any more critical online. Furthermore, commentators, for over a decade, have shown that many Facebook users believe that they are broadcasting a credible representation of their offline personae (see, for example, Lampe, Ellison, and Steinfield, 2006). Weisbuch, Ivcevic, and Ambady (2009) found that people are presenting themselves online as they want to be perceived offline in the day-to-day world. Additionally, Back et al. (2010) found that people are often networked through Facebook with others associated with several of their different 'identities', such as child, peer, or student. They suggest that this multi-identity connection is the reason Facebook identity is credible because people are held accountable by their network of *friends* for inauthentic behaviour. However, there is still much to learn about how people juggle and formulate their public online identities in continuously changing environments, such as social network sites (Baym and boyd, 2012). Regardless, people will exhibit a constructed identity according to the context; online identity is simply another context in a person's reality.

Phenomenography addressed problems of authenticity decades before people went online *en masse* because its core assumption is to take what people say at face value. As phenomenographic researchers take what their participants say at face value, moving the research approach into the online world seemed like a natural extension. In a space where authenticity and credibility are usually questioned, it is useful to have a research approach that embeds answers in the conceptual framework. By working in a phenomenographic framework, issues surrounding accuracy of representation were addressed because the research method was designed to centralize the participant, therefore it values the participants and the knowledge they have about a phenomenon without judgement.

In other words, the online Facebook status data were automatically assumed to be authentic.

Phenomenographic research can also aid with maintaining the anonymity of the research participants as direct quotations of raw data are not necessary to the phenomenographic map (Åkerlind, 2012). Phenomenography has been criticized by quantitative researchers for being too qualitative and by qualitative researchers as being too generalised (Richardson, 1999). This is because a phenomenographic outcome is essentially a map of the phenomenon: it contains enough detail to understand that a diversity of experiences make up a phenomenon, but it is more interested in what connects those experiences than what separates them (Marton, 1986). This generalized research approach means that the individual participants are not targeted in the analysis, rather the generalized experiences of all the participants are the focus (for a more detailed discussion, see Barnes, Penn-Edwards, and Sim, 2015).

Reflecting on the research: social media in general

While the ethics of using social media in research continues to be problematic, I believe the more interesting conversation is in how people are intentionally putting themselves 'out there'. Twitter users are hashtagging their conversations so that it can be saved for future consideration, researchers are putting their data online, daring others to become a part of a grand collaboration where data is free, not to mention the movement to and debate around open access publication. The problem with this freely offered data is that research may decide to settle for what is easy, rather than taking risks and pushing boundaries to try and use social media to find data that is hidden and nuanced. I regularly have PhD students contact me to find out ways they could use Facebook to find out about delinquency and criminal activities. I do not have the answers for them. In fact, I do not think we are there yet and I am not sure we should be. These are the kinds of ethical conversations we need to be having.

Social research online is a moveable space. Researchers need to make decisions in the moment and be worthy of what is presented to us, even before we know what we will find out (Richardson and St. Pierre, 2005). No matter how hard I tried to show the similarities between the transition experiences of the students in the findings of my research, the diversity of their experience kept trying to force its way out. While phenomenography only requires a map of the phenomena, the participants were not objects that can be known. They were provocateurs that took me on a 'line of flight to elsewhere' (Richardson and St. Pierre, 2005, p. 972). I had duty of care to my participants not to back their experiences into an empirical dead end. I also have a responsibility to my audience not to assume the authority of representation, rather, my results are malleable and open to interpretation with further analysis and research. This is the conceptual intention of phenomenography that intends to be complementary to other research approaches. The map of each phenomenon can provide a starting point for further exploration. With such rich data I could not contain myself within the traditional phenomenographical method. I needed to become a traveller across the universe of research; to move 'across our thresholds, toward a destination which is unknown, not foreseeable, not pre-existent' (Deleuze and Parnet, 1987, p. 25, cited by Richardson and St. Pierre, 2005, p. 972).

As an online researcher I want to hold in my mind's eye Derrida's (1994) vision of a future democracy; Richardson and St. Pierre's (2005) sociological imagining of different and fertile relationships where people thrive; and a conceptualization of Rancière's radical intellectual equality (Otoide and Alsop, 2015). A paradoxical utopia that is not reachable but, if I want to continue to theorize and methodologize the use of social media in educational sociology, I must continuously work towards such practice. Phenomenography can contribute to the methodologizing and theorizing of the online space. As a democratizing research approach that privileges the participants' experiences and takes them at face value, the research approach is well positioned to enter the world of online research. The catch is that phenomenographic researchers need to be willing to take their well-ordered maps, look outside their tribal boundaries, and realise that they have the potential for charting new territories.

References

Åkerlind, G. S. (2012). Variation and commonality in phenomenographic research methods. *Higher Education Research and Development, 31*(1), 115–127. doi:10.1080/07294360.2011.642845.

Åkerlind, G. S., Carr-Gregg, S., Field, R., Houston, L., Jones, J., Lupton, M., et al. (2010). A threshold concepts focus to first year law curriculum design: Supporting student learning using variation theory. Paper presented at the 13th Pacific Rim First Year in Higher Education Conference, Adelaide, Australia.

Ashworth, P., and Lucas, U. (1998). What is the "world" of phenomenography? *Scandinavian Journal of Educational Research, 42*(4), 415–431. doi:10.1080/0031383980 420407.

Astin, A. W. (1984). Student involvement: A developmental theory for higher education. *Journal of College Student Development, 40*(5), 518–529.

Back, M. D., Stopfer, J. M., Vazire, S., Gaddis, S., Schmukle, S. C., Egloff, B., and Gosling, S. D. (2010). Facebook profiles reflect actual personality, not self-idealization. *Psychological Science, 21*(3), 372–374. doi:10.1177/0956797609360756.

Baik, C., Naylor, R., and Arkoudis, S. (2015). *The first year experience in Australian Universities: Findings from two decades, 1994–2014.* Available at: Melbourne: www.cshe.unimelb.edu.au/research/rec_publications/FYE%202014%20FULL%20report%20-%20FINAL%20-%20web.pdf.

Barnes, N. (2014). Facebook status updates about the first year at university: how student experience informs a learner-centred transition curriculum. Unpublished PhD thesis. Griffith University, Brisbane.

Barnes, N., Penn-Edwards, S., and Sim, C. (2015). A dialogic about using Facebook status updates for education research: A PhD student's journey. *Educational Research and Evaluation, 21*(2), 109–121. doi:10.1080/13803611.2015.1024429.

Barthes, R. (1986). *The rustle of language.* Oxford: Basil Blackwell.

Bauman, Z. (2000). *Liquid modernity.* Cambridge: Polity Press.

Baym, N. K., and boyd, d. (2012). Socially mediated mublicness: An introduction. *Journal of Broadcasting and Electronic Media, 56*(3), 320–329. doi:10.1080/08838151.2012.705200.

Bowden, J. A. (2000). The nature of phenomenographic research. In J. A. Bowden and E. Walsh (Eds.), *Phenomenography* (pp. 1–18). Melbourne: RMIT University Press.

Bowden, J. A., and Green, P. (2005). *Doing developmental phenomenography.* Melbourne: RMIT University Press.

Brough, J. B., and Husserl, E. (2012). *On the phenomenology of the consciousness of internal time (1893–1917).* Amsterdam: Springer Netherlands.

Collier-Reed, B., and Ingerman, Å. (2013). Phenomenography: From critical aspects to knowledge claim. In M. Tight (Ed.), *Theory and method in higher education research* (pp. 243–260). Bingley: Emerald Group.

Derrida, J. (1994). *Spectres of Marx: The state of the debt, the work of mourning, and the new international* (P. Kamuf, Trans.). New York: Routledge.

Drury Lane Theatre: *As You Like It*, Antique Engraving. (2013/1842, 16/10/2013). CollectorsPrints.com: Antique prints and vintage art. Retrieved from www.collectorsprints.com/1153/antiqueprint/drurylanetheatre.

Eisner, E. W. (1998). *The enlightened eye: Qualitative inquiry and the enhancement of educational practice.* Upper Saddle River, NJ: Bobbs Merrill.

Gale, T., and Parker, S. (2012). Navigating change: A typology of student transition in higher education. *Studies in Higher Education, 39*(5), 734–753. doi:10.1080/03075079.2012.721351.

Gibbings, P., Lidstone, J., and Bruce, C. S. (2015). Engineering phenomenography. In J. Huisman and M. Tight (Eds.), *Theory and method in higher education research* (pp. 295–310). Bingley: Emerald Group Publishing Limited. (Reprinted from: In Press).

Hallett, F. (2014). The dilemma of methodological idolatry in higher education research: The case of phenomenography. In J. Huisman and M. Tight (Eds.), *Theory and method in higher education research II* (pp. 203–225). Bingley: Emerald Group Publishing Limited.

Hasselgren, B., and Beach, D. (1997). Phenomenography – a "good-for-nothing brother" of phenomenology? Outline of an analysis. *Higher Education Research and Development, 16*(2), 191–202. doi:10.1080/0729436970160206.

Hong, Y.-Y., Morris, M. W., Chiu, C.-Y., and Benet-Martinez, V. (2000). Multicultural minds: A dynamic constructivist approach to culture and cognition. *American Psychologist, 55*(7), 709–720. doi:10.1037/0003-066X.55.7.709.

James, R., Krause, K.-L., and Jennings, C. (2010). The first year experience in Australian universities: Findings from 1994 to 2009. Retrieved from http://citeseerx.ist.psu.edu/viewdoc/download?doi=10.1.1.723.8190&rep=rep1&type=pdf.

Kaplan, A. M., and Haenlein, M. (2010). Users of the world, unite! The challenges and opportunities of social media. *Business Horizons, 53*(1), 59–68. doi:http://dx.doi.org/10.1016/j.bushor.2009.09.003.

Kift, S. M. (2009). *Articulating a transition pedagogy to scaffold and to enhance the first year student learning experience in Australian higher education: Final report for ALTC senior fellowship program.* Retrieved from Strawberry Hills, Australia. Retrieved from http://fyhe.com.au/wp-content/uploads/2012/10/Kift-Sally-ALTC-Senior-Fellowship-Report-Sep-092.pdf.

Kift, S. M., Nelson, K. J., and Clarke, J. A. (2010). Transition pedagogy: a third generation approach to FYE: A case study of policy and practice for the higher education sector. *The International Journal of the First Year in Higher Education, 1*(1), 1–20. doi:10.5204/intjfyhe.v1i1.13.

Lampe, C., Ellison, N., and Steinfield, C. (2006). A Face (book) in the crowd: Social searching vs. social browsing. Paper presented at the 20th Anniversary Conference on Computer Supported Cooperative Work, Alberta, Canada.

Marton, F. (1981). Phenomenography: Describing conceptions of the world around us. *Instructional Science, 10*(2), 177–200. doi:10.1007/BF00132516.

Marton, F. (1986). Phenomenography: A research approach to investigating different understandings of reality. *Journal of Thought, 21*(3), 28–49.

Marton, F. (1994). Phenomenography. In T. Husen and T. N. Postlethwaite (Eds.), *International encyclopedia of education* (2nd edn, Vol. 8, pp. 4424–4429). London: Pergamon.

Marton, F., and Booth, S. (1997). *Learning and awareness.* Hillsdale, NJ: Lawrence Erlbaum.

Marton, F., and Svensson, L. (1979). Conceptions of research in student learning. *Higher Education, 8*(4), 471–486. doi:10.1007/bf01680537.

McInnis, C. (2001). Researching the first year experience: Where to from here? *Higher Education Research and Development, 20*(2), 105–114. doi:http://dx.doi.org/10.1080/07294360125188.

Nairn, K., Munro, J., and Smith, A. B. (2005). A counter-narrative of a 'failed' interview. *Qualitative Research, 5*(2), 221–244. doi:10.1177/1468794105050836.

Otoide, L., and Alsop, S. (2015). Moments with Jacques Rancière: Sketches from a lived pedagogical experiment in an elementary science classroom. *Canadian Journal of Science, Mathematics and Technology Education, 15*(3), 234–247. doi:10.1080/14926156.2015.1062939.

Palmer, M., O'Kane, P., and Owens, M. (2009). Betwixt spaces: Student accounts of turning point experiences in the first-year transition. *Studies in Higher Education, 34*(1), 37–54. doi:10.1080/03075070802601929.

Penn-Edwards, S. (2010). Computer aided phenomenography: The role of Leximancer computer software in phenomenographic investigation. *The Qualitative Report, 15*(2), 252–267.

Penn-Edwards, S., and Donnison, S. (2011). Engaging with higher education academic support: A first year student teacher transition model. *European Journal of Education, 46*(4), 566–580. doi:10.1111/j.1465-3435.2011.01501.x.

Prinsloo, P., Slade, S., and Galpin, F. (2011). A phenomenographic analysis of student reflections in online learning diaries. *Open Learning: The Journal of Open, Distance and e-Learning, 26*(1), 27–38. doi:10.1080/02680513.2011.538562.

Probyn, E. (1991). This body which is not one: Speaking an embodied self. *Hypatia, 6*(3), 111–124. doi:10.1111/j.1527-2001.1991.tb00258.x.

Richardson, J. (1999). The Concepts and Methods of Phenomenographic Research. *Review of Educational Research, 69*(1), 53–82. doi:10.3102/00346543069001053.

Richardson, L., and St. Pierre, E. A. (2005). Writing: A method of inquiry. In N. K. Denzin and Y. S. Lincoln (Eds.), *The Sage handbook of qualitative research* (3rd edn). Thousand Oaks, CA: Sage Publications.

Sandbergh, J. (1997). Are phenomenographic results reliable? *Higher Education Research and Development, 16*(2), 203–212. doi:10.1080/0729436970160207.

Selwyn, N. (2012). Making sense of young people, education and digital technology: The role of sociological theory. *Oxford Review of Education, 38*(1), 81–96. doi:10.1080/03054985.2011.577949.

Weisbuch, M., Ivcevic, Z., and Ambady, N. (2009). On being liked on the web and in the "real world": Consistency in first impressions across personal webpages and spontaneous behavior. *Journal of Experimental Social Psychology, 45*(3), 573–576. doi:http://dx.doi.org/10.1016/j.jesp. 2008.12.009.

Wilson, R. E., Gosling, S. D., and Graham, L. T. (2012). A review of Facebook research in the social sciences. *Perspectives on Psychological Science, 7*(3), 203–220. doi:10.1177/1745691612442904.

4 An exploration of lived experience in a digital world

How technology is revolutionising substance misuse recovery

Stephanie Dugdale, Sarah Elison-Davies,
Glyn Davies, Jonathan Ward and Michaela Jones

Introduction

Advances in digital technologies are re-shaping the boundaries of traditional research methods. With access to a wide range of available online data, and a multitude of online data collection techniques, research can be conducted with large populations of people from across the world, at any one time. However, these new technology-enhanced research methodologies are also stimulating debates around research ethics. Increasingly, it is becoming apparent that existing ethical guidelines may not be appropriate for new and emerging online approaches to research. To illustrate such ethical considerations when conducting social research using online data collection methods, this chapter overviews a recently completed mixed-methods online study which investigated the use of online resources to support people in recovery from substance misuse. Of interest to the scope of this book are the online data collection methodologies that were used in this study, which included an online quantitative survey and online, real-time, live qualitative interviews. This chapter describes this study in detail, and the practical and ethical issues faced during the research process are discussed, alongside reflections on the use of online methodologies in psychosocial research.

Background

Alongside the growing problem of online marketplaces widening opportunities to purchase illicit substances (EMCDDA, 2016), there has been an increasing prominence of online and technology-enhanced treatment and recovery resources for substance misuse. There is a wealth of online resources aimed at people embarking on the process of recovery from substance misuse (please note that as this research was conducted in the UK, examples provided were typically UK-based resources, and therefore this discussion is also situated in the UK context). For example, there are general online information resources, such as NHS Choices (www.nhs.uk), which may be accessed by individuals seeking information about certain substances (e.g. their effects and legal status), and treatment services that are available to support people in recovery. There are also thera-peutic resources, including online psychosocial interventions such as Breaking Free Online (Elison et al., 2013, 2014), online mutual aid groups such as those facilitated by SMART recovery (Hester et al., 2013) and 12-step organisations such as Alcoholics and Narcotics Anonymous (Yarosh, 2013). Additionally, there are a number of online recovery forums such as 'in2recovery' (www.in2 recovery.org.uk) and 'Soberistas' (www.soberistas.com) that are created and moderated by people within the recovery community, and Facebook and Twitter groups which can also be used for peer support and developing an online recovery community.

These online resources can support individuals who are trying to reduce or stop using substances through teaching therapeutic coping techniques, and by creating opportunities for peer support and self-help. Thus, the benefits of accessing these online resources may extend beyond directly supporting people to reduce their substance use by providing opportunities to create supportive social networks and empower those in recovery to take ownership of their recovery process. Central to this is the building of 'recovery capital' (Best and Laudet, 2010), which provides a basis on which recovery from substance misuse can be sustained. Recovery capital refers to the sum of internal or external resources that an individual has at their disposal which helps them to progress in their recovery and develop the skills needed to make wider positive changes to their life.

Building recovery capital via online social networks and support link to ele-ments of 'social' and 'human' capital (Cloud and Granfield, 2008). Social capital relates to the resources acquired through social support and relationships, developed through online forum-based interactions, for example. In contrast, human capital relates to personal resources such as skills, health and aspirations (Cloud and Granfield, 2008). Online recovery communities may enhance social capital by extending the range of accessible social support from traditional face-to-face methods, and also human capital in terms of strengthening digital skills developed while accessing these online resources. Other forms of recovery capital, in addition to social and human capital, are implicated in the recovery process, including physical resources and cultural values, although these sources of recovery capital are not explored in this chapter, which focuses on social and human capital specifically.

In addition to online technologies widening access to treatment and recovery support for substance misuse, technologies are also playing an increasingly significant role in conducting research into substance misuse and how people in recovery from substance misuse might best be supported. Substance misuse researchers are beginning to use online technologies to allow mass collection of data, such as those demonstrating quantitative treatment outcomes (Morley et al., 2015). This has led to an increase in 'big data' quantitative studies, one example being the Global Drug Survey (Winstock, 2015), which has influenced the devel-opment of best-practice guidelines on substance misuse treatment and harm reduction approaches (PHE, 2014). To date, digital methodologies, conducted within the field of substance misuse, have mainly focused on the collection of this kind of quantitative data. Although there are some examples of qualitative research using digital technologies for data collection within the wider research literature (e.g. Ison, 2009; James, 2007; Seymour, 2001), there are very few instances of the use of digital technologies in qualitative research into substance misuse research specifically.

Of the qualitative online data collection methods that have been reported in the literature, email as a methodological tool has been used since the 1990s, this being not long after the introduction of the 'World Wide Web' in 1991. For example, Foster (1994) used email interviews to investigate how university lecturers conducted their lesson planning. Additionally, a review of the online qualitative research literature indicates that most studies using email interviews as a means of data collection, were intended to explore the online activity of participants, or investigate the use of email as a suitable method of data collection (Meho, 2006). A review by Meho (2006) also indicates a change in the demographics of participants recruited to such studies over the past few decades, from a majority of 'professionals' in the 1990s (e.g. Murray, 1995; Young et al., 1998) to groups of consumers and service users in the 2000s (e.g. Curasi, 2001; Murray and Harrison, 2004), potentially reflecting changes in the use of email technology as it has become more widely used throughout society as a means of communication.

Qualitative data collection via email can be considered 'asynchronous', as it is not conducted in 'real time' and is not live. The relative cost effectiveness, lack of a need to travel to attend interviews, and large participation rates compared to face-to-face interview techniques, make this methodology viable for many researchers (Meho, 2006), potentially contributing to the relative longevity of this method of data collection. In contrast to asynchronous qualitative data collection methods, 'synchronous', or real-time, qualitative data collection methods have also been employed in research, using online communication resources such as chatrooms and instant messenger services. For example, Chou (2001) used a designated chatroom to conduct individual and group-based interviews about participants' experience of internet addiction. Additionally, Gruber et al. (2008) were able to recruit participants to a synchronous online qualitative study using a quantitative online survey, which acted as a springboard to identify potential participants for interviews about use of digital music players.

The examples of online interview studies cited above demonstrate that, although these methods are limited throughout the research literature generally, and certainly within substance misuse more specifically, they can be effectively employed within a wide range of areas of research, particularly to study participants' online behaviours, such as use of websites and online resources. Therefore, given the lack of online qualitative research in substance misuse, and scarcity of formal research around the utilisation of online recovery resources for substance misuse, this chapter reports on a recently conducted mixed-methods study exploring the use of online recovery resources within the substance misuse recovery community. This study was conducted with the UK Recovery

Foundation (UKRF), which was established in 2010, to support and build a community around recovery from substance misuse. This use of online methodologies was appropriate to explore the different types of online recovery resources accessed by participants and gain a wider understanding of how these different types of online resources are used. The use of both online quantitative and qualitative data collection approaches in this study also enabled triangulation of findings (Creswell, 2013). To clarify, this utilisation of both data collection methods allows for a convergence of findings, augmenting a comprehensive understanding of the overall outcomes with consideration of both objective and subjective views. This further increases the validity of the results by reducing the bias caused by using either one of the methods alone (Campbell and Fiske, 1959).

Exploring online recovery resources for substance misuse using online research methodologies

To conduct this investigation into the use of online substance misuse recovery resources, the research team was comprised of individuals with a wide variety of knowledge and experience in the field of substance misuse. Of this group, two were researchers trained in Psychology and specialising in behaviour change methods (SD and SE). GD has previous experience of the commissioning and delivery of substance misuse and criminal justice services, and co-developed the online treatment and recovery programme, Breaking Free Online. JW is a clinical psychologist and led the development of Breaking Free Online. MJ is in long-term recovery and is engaged in a variety of roles, with a focus on building sustainable recovery communities.

The use of digital online methods to collect data in this study seemed particularly appropriate, given the aim was to explore the use of online resources to support treatment and recovery from substance misuse. Therefore, people using these methods of online support for substance misuse (the population of interest) would be assumed to already have both the digital skills and access to online technologies required for participation in the study. Furthermore, online methodologies potentially facilitate access to 'hidden' populations of substance users, given the often nefarious behaviours individuals might engage in when obtaining and using substances (Neale et al., 2005). Online research, such as the Global Drug Survey, for example, has already been conducted to gain access to a wide range of substance users, including those using alcohol, cannabis, opioids and novel psychoactive substances (Winstock, 2015). The Global Drug Survey has also demonstrated that digital online methods can be very successful in recruiting large numbers of participants from across the substance-using population (McCabe et al., 2002; McCabe, 2004), such as the recent survey of 22,889 respondents (Lawn et al., 2014).

Research has also suggested that online methods can enhance the anonymity of research participants and may result in a more balanced power relationship between the participant and the researcher (Hewson, 2007), evidenced by indications that digital methods demonstrate higher rates of self-disclosure from participants compared to face-to-face methods (Joinson, 2001). This anonymity could be particularly important for self-disclosure in the substance-using population, as substance use is often linked to criminal behaviour (Budd et al., 2005; Butler et al., 2011; Fazel et al., 2006; Mumola and Karberg, 2006) and other multiple and complex difficulties, such as mental health issues (Buckley, 2005; Drake and Wallach, 2000; Kranzler and Rosenthal, 2003), to which there may be stigma attached (Evans-Lacko and Thornicroft, 2010; Hartwell, 2004). However, it should be noted that, more recently, research has linked online communication via social media sites, such as Facebook, with an individual's offline presence, so this linking of the online and offline worlds may compromise anonymity (Nguyen et al., 2012). In this study, a mixture of online communication platforms, including social media sites, were suggested as options for participants to choose from for the conduct of their qualitative interviews. Interestingly, no participants who were actively working towards recovery from substance use, and therefore potentially still using substances, chose to take part in these interviews, but it cannot be ascertained whether this lack of involvement was due to issues over anonymity.

There are multiple practical benefits to conducting data collection online, including recruitment of large numbers of participants in a relatively short space of time (Birnbaum, 2004; Gosling et al., 2004; Stetina et al., 2008). However, it should be considered, that in order to reach larger groups of participants online, an array of recruitment strategies and resources still have to be employed which draw upon coordinated efforts and techniques including advertisements, links through other websites and direct emailing (Gordon et al., 2006). Research has highlighted the value of social media in particular in accessing large numbers of participants, through sharing and snowballing online posts (O'Connor et al., 2014). There are also fewer financial and other resource implications associated with this approach to both recruitment and data collection compared with more traditional methods, such as postal questionnaires or face-to-face methods, which may incur transport costs (Lefever et al., 2007; McDonald and Adam, 2003; Wright, 2005).

Due to the benefits afforded by technology and the increasing use of this in social research, this study of online recovery resources for substance misuse used a combination of both quantitative and qualitative online data collection methods. Each of the data collection procedures used in the study, and the findings from these, will now be described in more detail.

Online quantitative survey

Online quantitative survey procedure

The online quantitative survey contained questions about categories of online recovery resources that were decided upon following a meeting of the study team, comprising the research team. Participants could also enter any additional resources that they used which had not been included in the survey, to offer a greater insight into the availability and use of these resources.

The survey questions that enquired as to the types of online recovery resources participants had accessed, were divided into six categories of resources: (1) therapeutic resources; (2) forums; (3) information about substances (such as side effects and legal status); (4) harm reduction; (5) mental health; and (6) resources for family and friends. Different, more specific, online resources were listed within these broader categories, with the option for participants to add additional resources that they had used if they were not included in the lists provided in the survey.

The survey also asked questions about how long participants had used each online resource, what time of day they typically accessed these resources, what devices they used to access these resources, and their recovery status, with these being: 'in recovery' (those who were maintaining abstinence or reduced substance use), 'not working towards recovery' (those who reported no current difficulties with substances), or 'working towards recovery' (those actively working on reducing or stopping their substance use). Of the sample, 12% identified that they were working towards recovery, 56% identified themselves as in recovery, and 32% identified themselves as not working towards recovery. The quantitative data generated by the survey enabled the qualitative interviews to be tailored to individuals (e.g. to ask about specific resources they had reported use of within the survey), and provided the basis on which further lines of enquiry and explanatory questions could be developed within the interviews.

Initially, participants were recruited to an online quantitative survey via snowball sampling, through advertising information about the study on online forums, including Twitter and Facebook via Breaking Free Online's and in2Recovery's pages, which were then shared on other substance misuse organisations and websites. In addition to substance use information websites (e.g. www. dsdaily.org.uk), the study was advertised via conferences and public events with a focus on substance use. Participants who were interested in taking part in the study were provided with a URL to access the online survey though 'Survey Monkey' (www.surveymonkey.co.uk). After excluding participants who identified themselves as being under the age of 18, a total of 130 participants responded to this online survey (51% males, 48% females, 1% not specified). Participants had an average age of 45 years, with a range of 20–67 years.

Ethical considerations for the online quantitative survey

Established ethical guidelines state that participants should give their informed consent, if they are deemed capable, prior to taking part in any research study (British Psychological Society, 2010; Ess and Association of Internet Researchers, 2002). Participants need to be fully aware of what the research will involve and of their rights as a participant, for them to make a decision regarding their participation. Therefore, to explain the purpose and design of the study, participant information concerning the content of the survey was displayed in the advertising material for the study. This information was again reiterated on the first page of the online survey and participants were asked to read the information before going on to complete the survey. This information also clearly stated that participants were free to withdraw from the study if they wanted to, without reason, with this right to withdraw forming a key component of informed consent, as a participant should be allowed to remove their consent to participate if they wish (British Psychological Society, 2010). This ethical consideration is particularly important within healthcare and in clinical populations, and participants should be made aware that withdrawing from a study will not affect the support or treatment that they are currently receiving. In this study, an 'exit this survey' button was made clear to participants, which was at the top of every page of the survey, as participants could exit the survey and return at a later date to complete it if they wished to do so. Participants were also given contact details of the principal researcher (SD) and informed that they could contact her for more information should they need it. Entry into the survey was taken as consent to participate in the study.

An additional ethical consideration was that only participants aged 18 or over could take part in the study, to ensure that no child or minor took part in the research without their principal caregiver's permission. Participants under the age of 18 could be considered a vulnerable group, as they may not be deemed capable of giving their informed consent to take part in research, therefore, applying procedures to mitigate against minors or children participating in research studies is intended to protect them from this potential risk (British Psychological Society, 2010). These age-related exclusion criteria were clearly stated in the advertising materials. However, before commencing with the survey, participants were asked to confirm whether they were aged 18 or over, and so if any participants indicated that they were under 18, their data were excluded from the study. All participants could also only enter the survey once from the same Internet Protocol (IP) address, therefore if participants were excluded from the study, they could not re-enter, or at least not from the same device. Although not foolproof, this acts as an initial safeguard against child or minor participation and repeat attempts at survey entries. Stating date of birth was also a requirement within the survey, with this information being used to identify anyone under the age of 18, so that their data could be deleted.

Reflections on conducting the online quantitative survey

Although the survey was advertised through a variety of means, including conferences and public events related to substance misuse, it appeared that online posts to promote the survey considerably boosted numbers, as participant rates were seen to increase immediately following information about the survey being posted online via websites and forums. To enhance recruitment, such information was posted online periodically during the study, and was included across a range of online resource sites, such as information pages and forums. Permissions were gained from relevant site moderators before this information was shared across online resources, and the posting of this research information was restricted to 'business'-related websites as opposed to 'personal' profiles, to maintain professional boundaries (British Psychological Society, 2012).

Overall, the initial online quantitative survey was beneficial in gaining access to a large sample of participants within a relatively short amount of time. This helped in the exploration of the use of these online resources, and highlighted the links between the use of different kinds of recovery resource use and different phases of the recovery process, which will be discussed in detail later in the chapter. However, it could be seen here that the survey design was impacted by the digital mode of delivery, and each category of recovery resource was allocated its own separate page to improve the layout of information. For this reason, many answers to 'other additional resources' included resources that were listed on succeeding pages, thereby causing repetition in the data. Future researchers may wish to consider this in similar research designs and make clear where answers may overlap.

Online qualitative interview

Online qualitative interview procedure

At the end of the online quantitative survey, participants were asked if they would like to take part in an online qualitative interview about their experiences of using online recovery resources. If they were interested, they were asked to supply their email address so that the principal researcher could then email the participant with further information about the qualitative interview phase, and ask if they would like to take part. If they were happy to take part, the participant was asked when the most convenient time for the interview might be and what the most appropriate means of contact for the interview was, such as via email or instant messenger services. Asynchronous interviews, such as emails, were the preferred choice for most participants, however, reasons behind this were not explored. However, it is likely that these preferences reflected participants' availability during office hours (weekdays from 9 a.m. until 5 p.m.) as this is when the interviews were conducted.

Qualitative interviews were semi-structured and questions were open-ended to elicit further information on participants' use of online recovery resources. General questions forming the basis of the interviews were decided upon by the researcher team. Questions were adapted and personalised to suit each individual participant and were based on their initial quantitative survey responses, for example, asking for more information about their use of the resources they reported accessing in their survey responses. Interviews were text-based and participants were told that they could use abbreviations and 'emojis' in their interview if they wished, however, these were to be elaborated on if required.

Ethical considerations for the online qualitative interviews

Prior to taking part in the interviews, participants were once again sent information about the purpose of the interview to ensure that informed consent to participate was gained from the sample (British Psychological Society, 2010). This information was sent either via email attachment for asynchronous interviews, or was copied into the text of the start of each synchronous interview. Participants were told that any information they shared would remain anonymous, and that any personally identifiable data would be removed from the interviews and not shared with anyone outside of the research team, to comply with ethical standard of confidentiality (British Psychological Society, 2010).

Before interviews were held, participants were also reminded of their right to withdraw from the study at any time, without reason, and that they did not have to respond to a question if they did not want to. However, participants were asked that they made their choice to withdraw or not respond to a question explicit to the interviewer during the interview. This was important as any inactivity during a synchronous interview could be mistaken for a slow response or the participant briefly leaving their electronic device to attend to something else. Similarly, if the participant was to leave the conversation during a synchronous interview, this could be mistaken for problems with the internet connection or the device. Therefore, participants were asked to inform the researcher that they were leaving the interview if this occurred.

As interviews were entirely text-based, this meant that no microphones or web cameras were used. This was done to protect both the interviewer and interviewee, and to increase confidentiality. This also served a practical purpose as no audio transcription was necessary following completion of the interviews as all data would already be text-based, although some minor amendments had to be made to some interview transcripts, for example, to correct spelling errors. This text-based approach also mitigated against any potential internet issues which might impact upon the interview. For example, a slow internet connection resulting in gaps in audio and therefore difficulties understanding what the participant or researcher was saying, potentially leading to miscommunication and frustration. Furthermore, in the case of asynchronous interviews, such as emails, the use of live audio is not possible and so only text could be used to communicate to participants. Therefore, using text across both synchronous and asynchronous interview formats allowed some standardisation to occur between the two interview methods.

Reflections on conducting online qualitative interviews

There were some difficulties experienced with recruitment to the qualitative interview phase of the study, as in some instances, email addresses provided by participants following the online quantitative survey were incorrect. It is therefore recommended that future studies either ask participants to enter their email address twice, to avoid potential accidental typographical errors, or ask participants to confirm their email address by clicking on a link sent to their email address. A further problem experienced, was that participants did not always respond to the emails sent to them, including the initial email following recruitment to the study, and any follow-up emails. In a review by Sheehan (2001) about email survey response rates, it was suggested that unsolicited emails may be less likely to be responded to as they could be perceived as containing viruses, especially if from an unknown sender, or automatically filtered out of an email inbox into a junk folder. Evidence by Mann and Stewart (2000) and Dabbish et al. (2005) further suggest that retention and response rates may be influenced by participants' perceived experiences of the email interview as interesting and important. Furthermore, compared to face-to-face interviews, email interviews can lack a sense of human engagement and connectedness, also potentially reducing response and retention rates (James and Busher, 2006). However, difficulties with recruitment are not specific to online research methods and can be seen throughout social research generally (e.g. Allsup and Gosney, 2002; Howard et al., 2009). Future research may wish to employ incentives to encourage a greater response rate, but should ensure that appropriate ethical concerns are managed, including ensuring that incentives are not disproportionate.

There were some differences between the synchronous and asynchronous interviews regarding the outcomes and practicalities of these online qualitative interview approaches. On the one hand, synchronous interviews were the most similar to face-to-face qualitative interviews as there was an almost immediate response to questions, which resulted in interviews being conversational in tone. Practical benefits of the online modalities through which these synchronous interviews could be conducted, such as instant messenger services, include that the screen displays when the other person is typing, which allows the researcher to give the participant time to respond before asking another question. Other advantages to conducting synchronous online interviews were that topics or interesting insights raised by the participant could easily be probed by the researcher and elaborated upon, and questions could easily be guided by previous answers. More in-depth information was also more likely to be provided by participants using synchronous interviews, such as descriptions of past experiences, to add further context to answers. Nonetheless, there were some difficulties experienced with this synchronous interview approach. For instance, synchronous interviews were difficult to set up, as this involved finding a time when both the researcher and participant were available. This was particularly problematic as interviews could take over an hour to complete. Despite emails being sent to participants to remind them about the interview, some participants also forgot their interview date, which delayed the interview process.

In contrast to synchronous interviews, asynchronous interviews allowed participants to respond to questions at a time most convenient to them. A list of questions was emailed to participants based on the general interview schedule, and was personalised to each participant based on their responses from the initial quantitative survey. Participants would be asked to reply, via email, by copying the questions into their reply and responding under each question, so that questions and their corresponding answers could be matched up. This process was then repeated to probe for further information based on the participants' previous responses. This approach was perceived as easier and quicker for the researcher to initially prepare for compared to synchronous interviews, as asynchronous interviews allowed the full set of interview questions to be sent in one email, rather than having to ask each question in turn during an instant messenger conversation, and then waiting for separate question responses before moving onto the next question. However, the overall time taken to complete an asynchronous interview could be weeks, due to the delay between sending the interview questions to the participants and receiving their answers to the interview questions. Furthermore, although more participants were happy to be interviewed in this way, perhaps due to the ease of responding to questions at a time convenient to them, answers to questions and further probes for more information were particularly brief, and participants did not always go into sufficient detail about their experiences. This may have impacted upon analyses of qualitative data and theme development, as key information surrounding the use of online recovery resources may have been missed.

The flexibility to use both synchronous and asynchronous interviews meant that it was easier to retain participants. For example, if participants missed their scheduled synchronous interview, they were offered the option of completing their answers via an asynchronous email interview. However, as this method of data collection is relatively under-researched, there is limited information to suggest which approach, synchronous or asynchronous, proffers adequate information for qualitative data collection. In this instance, however, it was found that asynchronous interviews generally resulted in short responses and little expansion of ideas, which made analysis of these interviews more difficult compared to synchronous interviews.

Findings from the study

The aim of this study was to explore the uses of online recovery resources for substance misuse, through online data collection methodologies. This mixed-methods study used a quantitative online survey and online qualitative interviews to investigate the range of online substance misuse recovery resources available, and how these resources are used by individuals at different stages of their recovery journeys. As the population of interest for the research was those who were actively using online resources, this study did not consider those who are digitally excluded, and so this research cannot state the overall proportion of those who access online resources compared to those involved in substance misuse recovery who do not access online resources. However, by conducting this research, the availability and potential suitability of online resources were explored, with the aim to facilitate further research in this area.

Evidence from the online quantitative survey of this mixed-methods study suggests that online forums, such as Facebook and Twitter, were the most highly accessed recovery resources by participants. Additionally, these online resources were more likely to be accessed in the evening compared to other times of day, particularly by those who were actively 'in recovery' or 'working towards recovery' from their substance misuse. These findings are supported by data from the online qualitative interview phase of the study, which indicate that the use of online recovery resources allowed participants to actively work on their recovery outside of typical treatment service opening hours, such as evenings and weekends. This is important, as recovery from substance misuse is a long-term, continual process that cannot be constrained by service opening hours, with participants in the qualitative interviews reporting that difficulties with cravings, for example, can be experienced at any time of day. Moreover, some individuals identified that they could not access recovery services within usual opening hours, due to work commitments or child care arrangements, for example. Therefore, these online resources may help to overcome some of these time-bound limitations to accessing offline recovery services.

As the online quantitative survey asked participants about their current perceived stage of recovery, this information was used to examine potential differences between these recovery stage groups in relation to which online recovery resources they accessed. The three recovery stage groups were currently 'working on their recovery' from substance misuse (actively trying to reduce or stop using substances), 'in recovery or abstinent' from substances (maintaining recovery from substance use), or currently 'not working towards recovery' (no perceived difficulties with substances). Between-group analyses revealed that those who were currently 'working towards recovery' and thus taking action to stop or reduce their substance use, were more likely than those who were either 'in recovery' from substance misuse difficulties or 'not working towards recovery', to use therapeutic resources. Online therapeutic resources include psychosocial and behavioural change interventions, or online structured mutual aid groups run by trained facilitators. These therapeutic resources explore the underlying causes behind substance use and facilitate behavioural change and the development of coping skills. One such example would be the use of online cognitive behavioural therapy programmes such as Breaking Free Online, or online mutual aid groups such as SMART Recovery.

Qualitative data confirmed many of the findings from the quantitative survey, and revealed details of some of the specific benefits of the different kinds of online recovery resources reported as being accessed in the quantitative survey. For example, participants reported that benefits of online recovery resources extended beyond being available outside normal treatment service hours, and included several wider benefits compared to the offline realm more generally. Online resources were reported as being particularly useful in overcoming the social anxiety that may be experienced with face-to-face or group therapy within services. Moreover, those who perceive themselves as 'in recovery', and who were therefore less likely to be accessing traditional offline recovery services, reported that they were more likely to use online recovery resources to help them maintain their abstinence from substances, and used these online resources as a relapse prevention tool.

Some participants also reported that they facilitate or contribute material to some online recovery resource sites, and that while these materials are intended to benefit others in their recovery, contributing to developing these online resources also helped participants to maintain their own recovery. This act of contributing to online recovery materials made participants feel like they were 'giving back' to the recovery community. This finding is supported in the mutual aid literature, which emphasises the importance of supporting others as a part of an individual's own ongoing recovery from substance misuse (Borkman, 2008). This suggests that online resources can empower individuals in recovery by giving them a place to develop and share their own ideas and experiences, changing traditional top-down views around treatment, to that which is more peer-led. The online survey also revealed that use of recovery forums was common among survey respondents, with the qualitative interviews indicating that this may be in part explained by the use of online recovery resources as a means of connection with others in recovery from substance misuse. Qualitative interview participants reported that these online resources offered support and friendship, and reduced feelings of loneliness by creating an online community around recovery.

Notwithstanding the benefits of online substance misuse recovery resources reported in the qualitative interviews, the importance of using both online and offline resources was also stressed by most participants, as they felt it was important that those in recovery did not 'isolate' themselves online, but instead accessed other forms of support via offline services. An interaction between the online and offline worlds was also reported throughout the online qualitative interviews. For example, online resources were reported as providing an initial point of contact for offline services, such as a telephone number, or contact details and meeting times of a local offline group, which might at first be found via a website. In contrast, offline resources and groups designed to support the development of digital skills were reported to help facilitate access to technology more broadly, and online recovery resources more specifically. This interaction was also applicable beyond participants who identified in the study as service users, to those participants who had previously been service users and who were now working in the substance use sector as professionals. These participants reported that they use online resources to communicate with some service users who were not able to make it to offline meetings. Therefore, in addition to these online recovery resources being perceived by participants as proffering benefits for those in recovery from substance misuse, participants reported that online resources may be best used in tandem with more traditional offline resources in order to take advantage of each other's relative strengths. Therefore, while there is a clear distinction between the online and offline worlds, perhaps each stand at alternate ends on a continuum of available support, with a combined approach of both methods offering the best outcomes.

Despite the perceived benefits of online recovery resources, participants identified that the principal barrier to accessing these online resources was the lack of available signposting information stating which resources were suitable for participants and where these can be found. Consequently, further work is needed not only to further expand knowledge around the use of these online recovery resources within the substance use sector more generally, but also to explore ways to increase awareness and access to these resources. Online and digital data collection methodologies may help to facilitate further research to achieve these aims.

Overall reflections of using online approaches to research

Overall, the process of using online data collection methods to conduct this research was interesting. It is arguably difficult to access this population of interest; people in recovery from, or still using, substances can be reluctant to participate in such research, as admitting to substance-using behaviour can often incur legal implications. However, online methods may provide a means of participating by maintaining suitable distance between these behaviours and the researcher, as some anonymity can be maintained, as discussed previously. As a result of using these online methods, this research has enabled an exploration of online behaviour around substance use treatment and recovery resources within this 'hidden' population. Furthermore, the use of online data collection methods seemed particularly appropriate to study the use of online substance misuse recovery resources and specifically target people who use these. The focus of this research was particularly novel due to the limited examples in the literature of the use of these online methods of data collection, particularly in relation to qualitative data collection, and specifically within substance misuse. Additionally, the study raised some interesting points of consideration with regard to developing strategies to adhere to ethical considerations when conducting such online, digital research.

Further work is planned to follow up this research with an international sample of participants, as the current study was restricted to UK recovery community members, with the aim to use the information gathered about different online recovery resources to create a signposting document for those personally experiencing or working with individuals with substance use difficulties. The lack of any signposting resources to these kinds of online recovery resources for not only service users, but also their family and friends, was reported in the qualitative interviews conducted, which means that people are not always able to access the most appropriate online support, if any. To complete this additional research and develop these signposting resources, the use of online data collection methods will be essential to reach participants from across the globe easily and inexpensively.

The novelty of this online approach to conducting research was apparent when arranging qualitative interviews with participants, as many preferred to talk face-to-face or over the telephone, rather than over the internet. This may reflect participants' familiarity with these other methods as a means of communication. Participants who wished to use offline methods of communication were reminded of the aims of the research, to use online methods to explore the use of online resources, and were asked if they were happy to proceed with an online interview. All of these participants were then happy to use online methods to continue with the research. Also, while it may be reasonable to assume, as this study did, that participants actively using online resources would have a degree of digital skill, it was perhaps naïve to infer confidence in using these online resources, as a few participants reported difficulties particularly when using applications such as instant messenger services. It would be interesting to investigate the preferences of participants with regard to using online or offline data collection methods, and explore how these preferences are influenced. Future research could consider using both modalities to ensure that data collection is in line with these individual preferences.

Currently there is limited guidance in the literature on how to conduct these types of online data collection approaches to research, specifically using real-time online qualitative interviews. Furthermore, ethical guidelines on the use of digital methods are still undergoing development. Ethical guidelines provided by organisations such as the Association of Internet Researchers (Ess and Association of Internet Researchers, 2002; Markham and Buchanan, 2012) and the British Psychological Society (British Psychological Society, 2013) provide some information on the ethical ideals that must be upheld within research, such as 'autonomy' and 'responsibility'. Largely these reflect the ethical considerations that are also relevant to non-digital research. However, there is a lack of practical solutions for how these ethical guidelines should be adhered to within online research. For example, how can one ensure that informed consent has been given? This could be as simple as asking the participant if they understand what they will have to do as part of the study, if they understand their ethical rights, and if they still want to continue with the study. Then again, if the aim of the research is to explore pre-published blog posts or forum comments, gaining informed consent may be more difficult, especially as contact information is not typically shared and many people operate on online forums under pseudonyms to protect personal information and identities, which can make contact challenging. It might even be unclear as to whether informed consent is needed, as blog and forum posts are already in the public domain. It would appear that applying common sense is the most appropriate method to conducting online research within the digital domain. For example, Markham and Buchanan (2012) recommend that ethics should always consider the rights of the participant, the restrictions of the 'venue' or site, and if in doubt, consult and collaborate with other researchers. There are also concerns about where to go for ethical approval for industry research that is not affiliated with a university or health service, which needs to be made clearer.

Conclusion

Social science researchers are increasingly making use of online and digital technologies as a means of collecting data. However, while these approaches may serve some practical benefits, there is limited information both on how best to conduct this research, and on the specific ethical guidelines that should be considered during this process. This study, exploring the use of online treatment and recovery resources within substance use, serves as an example of how an online mixed methodology design can be used to investigate data, and some of the practical and ethical considerations encountered during this process. Specifically addressed within this study was the use of an online quantitative survey and follow-up online qualitative interviews, to investigate online recovery resources use, with findings suggesting the importance of an interaction between online and offline resources to support recovery from substance misuse, and the use of online spaces to revolutionise treatment by giving agency to those in recovery. While the ethical issues surrounding these forms of data collection are discussed, overall, it may be unrealistic to develop specific ethical parameters for every type of data collection method, and every online tool that can be used to facilitate this. Therefore, a common-sense approach is suggested, using prior ethical knowledge within the constraints of the rules and regulations of specific websites. An increased confidence in the ability to conduct this online research, safely and appropriately, may encourage further study in this area and increase the practical knowledge within the literature of how to incorporate these methods into research.

References

Allsup, S. J., and Gosney, M. A. (2002). Difficulties of recruitment for a randomized controlled trial involving influenza vaccination in healthy older people. *Gerontology, 48*(3), 170–173.

Best, D., and Laudet, A. (2010). *The potential of recovery capital.* London: RSA.

Birnbaum, M. H. (2004). Human research and data collection via the Internet. *Psychology, 55*(1), 803–832.

Borkman, T. (2008). The twelve-step recovery model of AA: A voluntary mutual help association. In L. A. Kaskutas and M. Galanter (Eds.), *Recent developments in alcoholism* (pp. 9–35). New York: Springer.

British Psychological Society. (2010). *Code of human research ethics.* Leicester: British Psychological Society.

British Psychological Society. (2012). *eProfessionalism: Guidance on the use of social media by clinical psychologists.* Leicester: British Psychological Society.

British Psychological Society. (2013). *Ethics guidelines for internet-mediated research.* Leicester: British Psychological Society.

Buckley, P. F. (2005). Prevalence and consequences of the dual diagnosis of substance abuse and severe mental illness. *The Journal of Clinical Psychiatry, 67,* 5–9.

Budd, T., Collier, P., Mhlanga, B., Sharp, C., and Weir, G. (2005). *Levels of self-report offending and drug use among offenders: Findings from the Criminality Surveys.* London: Home Office.

Butler, T., Indig, D., Allnutt, S., and Mamoon, H. (2011). Co-occurring mental illness and substance use disorder among Australian prisoners. *Drug and Alcohol Review, 30*(2), 188–194.

Campbell, D. T., and Fiske, D. W. (1959). Convergent and discriminant validation by the multitrait-multimethod matrix. *Psychological Bulletin, 56*(2), 81–105.

Chou, C. (2001). Internet heavy use and addiction among Taiwanese college students: An online interview study. *CyberPsychology and Behavior, 4*(5), 573–585.

Cloud, W., and Granfield, R. (2008). Conceptualizing recovery capital: expansion of a theoretical construct. *Substance Use & Misuse, 43*(12–13), 1971–1986. https://doi. org/10.1080/10826080802289762

Creswell, J. W. (2013). *Research design: Qualitative, quantitative, and mixed methods approaches*. London: Sage.

Curasi, C. F. (2001). A critical exploration of face-to-face interviewing vs. computer-mediated interviewing. *International Journal of Market Research, 43*(4), 361–375.

Dabbish, L. A., Kraut, R. E., Fussell, S., and Kiesler, S. (2005). Understanding email use: Predicting action on a message. Paper presented at the Human Factors in Computing Systems: Proceedings CHI'05.

Drake, R. E., and Wallach, M. A. (2000). Dual diagnosis: 15 years of progress. *Psychiatric Services, 51*(9), 1126–1129.

Elison, S., Humphreys, L., Ward, J., and Davies, G. (2013). A pilot outcomes evaluation for computer assisted therapy for substance misuse: An evaluation of Breaking Free Online. *Journal of Substance Use, 19*(4), 1–6.

Elison, S., Ward, J., Davies, G., Lidbetter, N., Dagley, M., and Hulme, D. (2014). An outcomes study of eTherapy for dual diagnosis using Breaking Free Online. *Advances in Dual Diagnosis, 7*(2), 52–62.

EMCDDA. (2016). *The internet and drug markets, EMCDDA Insights 21*. Luxembourg: Publications Office of the European Union.

Ess, C., and Association of Internet Researchers. (2002). Ethical decision-making and Internet research: Recommendations from the AoIR ethics working committee. Retrieved from http://aoir.org/reports/ethics.pdf

Evans-Lacko, S., and Thornicroft, G. (2010). Stigma among people with dual diagnosis and implications for health services. *Advances in Dual Diagnosis, 3*(1), 4–7.

Fazel, S., Bains, P., and Doll, H. (2006). Substance abuse and dependence in prisoners: a systematic review. *Addiction, 101*(2), 181–191.

Foster, G. (1994). Fishing with the net for research data. *British Journal of Educational Technology, 25*(2), 91–97.

Gordon, J. S., Akers, L., Severson, H. H., Danaher, B. G., and Boles, S. M. (2006). Successful participant recruitment strategies for an online smokeless tobacco cessation program. *Nicotine and Tobacco Research, 8*(Suppl. 1), S35–S41.

Gosling, S. D., Vazire, S., Srivastava, S., and John, O. P. (2004). Should we trust web-based studies? A comparative analysis of six preconceptions about internet questionnaires. *American Psychologist, 59*(2), 93–104.

Gruber, T., Szmigin, I., Reppel, A. E., and Voss, R. (2008). Designing and conducting online interviews to investigate interesting consumer phenomena. *Qualitative Market Research: An International Journal, 11*(3), 256–274.

Hartwell, S. (2004). Triple stigma: Persons with mental illness and substance abuse problems in the criminal justice system. *Criminal Justice Policy Review, 15*(1), 84–99.

Hester, R. K., Lenberg, K. L., Campbell, W., and Delaney, H. D. (2013). Overcoming Addictions, a Web-based application, and SMART Recovery, an online and in-person mutual help group for problem drinkers, part 1: Three-month outcomes of a randomized controlled trial. *Journal of Medical Internet Research, 15*(7), e134.

Hewson, C. (2007). Gathering data on the Internet: Qualitative approaches and possibilities for mixed methods research. In A. N. Joinson, K. McKenna, T. Postmes, and

U.-D. Reips (Eds.), *Oxford handbook of internet psychology* (pp. 405–428). Oxford: Oxford University Press.

Howard, L., de Salis, I., Tomlin, Z., Thornicroft, G., and Donovan, J. (2009). Why is recruitment to trials difficult? An investigation into recruitment difficulties in an RCT of supported employment in patients with severe mental illness. *Contemporary Clinical Trials, 30*(1), 40–46.

Ison, N. L. (2009). Having their say: Email interviews for research data collection with people who have verbal communication impairment. *International Journal of Social Research Methodology, 12*(2), 161–172.

James, N. (2007). The use of email interviewing as a qualitative method of inquiry in educational research. *British Educational Research Journal, 33*(6), 963–976.

James, N., and Busher, H. (2006). Credibility, authenticity and voice: Dilemmas in online interviewing. *Qualitative Research, 6*(3), 403–420.

Joinson, A. N. (2001). Self-disclosure in computer-mediated communication: The role of self-awareness and visual anonymity. *European Journal of Social Psychology, 31*(2), 177–192.

Kranzler, H. R., and Rosenthal, R. N. (2003). Dual diagnosis: Alcoholism and co-morbid psychiatric disorders. *The American Journal on Addictions, 12*(s1), s26–s40.

Lawn, W., Barratt, M., Williams, M., Horne, A., and Winstock, A. (2014). The NBOMe hallucinogenic drug series: Patterns of use, characteristics of users and self-reported effects in a large international sample. *Journal of Psychopharmacology, 28*(8), 780–788.

Lefever, S., Dal, M., and Matthiasdottir, A. (2007). Online data collection in academic research: Advantages and limitations. *British Journal of Educational Technology, 38*(4), 574–582.

Mann, C., and Stewart, F. (2000). *Internet communication and qualitative research: A handbook for researching online.* London: Sage.

Markham, A., and Buchanan, E. (2012). Ethical decision-making and internet research: Recommendations from the AoIR ethics working committee (version 2.0). Association of Internet Researchers.

McCabe, S. E. (2004). Comparison of web and mail surveys in collecting illicit drug use data: A randomized experiment. *Journal of Drug Education, 34*(1), 61–72.

McCabe, S. E., Boyd, C. J., Couper, M. P., Crawford, S., and d'Arcy, H. (2002). Mode effects for collecting alcohol and other drug use data: Web and US mail. *Journal of Studies on Alcohol, 63*(6), 755–761.

McDonald, H., and Adam, S. (2003). A comparison of online and postal data collection methods in marketing research. *Marketing Intelligence and Planning, 21*(2), 85–95.

Meho, L. I. (2006). E-mail interviewing in qualitative research: A methodological discussion. *Journal of the American Society for Information Science and Technology, 57*(10), 1284–1295.

Morley, K. I., Lynskey, M. T., Moran, P., Borschmann, R., and Winstock, A. R. (2015). Polysubstance use, mental health and high-risk behaviours: Results from the 2012 Global Drug Survey. *Drug and Alcohol Review, 34*(4), 427–437.

Mumola, C. J., and Karberg, J. C. (2006). *Drug use and dependence, state and federal prisoners, 2004.* Washington, DC: US Department of Justice, Office of Justice Programs, Bureau of Justice Statistics.

Murray, C. D., and Harrison, B. (2004). The meaning and experience of being a stroke survivor: An interpretative phenomenological analysis. *Disability and Rehabilitation, 26*(13), 808–816.

Murray, P. J. (1995). Research data from cyberspace interviewing nurses by e-mail. *Health Informatics Journal, 1*(2), 73–76.

Neale, J., Allen, D., and Coombes, L. (2005). Qualitative research methods within the addictions. *Addiction, 100*(11), 1584–1593.

Nguyen, M., Bin, Y. S., and Campbell, A. (2012). Comparing online and offline self-disclosure: A systematic review. *Cyberpsychology, Behavior, and Social Networking, 15*(2), 103–111.

O'Connor, A., Jackson, L., Goldsmith, L., and Skirton, H. (2014). Can I get a retweet please? Health research recruitment and the Twittersphere. *Journal of Advanced Nursing, 70*(3), 599–609.

PHE. (2014). *New psychoactive substances: A toolkit for substance misuse commissioners*. London: PHE.

Seymour, W. S. (2001). In the flesh or online? Exploring qualitative research methodologies. *Qualitative Research, 1*(2), 147–168.

Sheehan, K. B. (2001). E-mail survey response rates: A review. *Journal of Computer-Mediated Communication, 6*(2).

Stetina, B. U., Jagsch, R., Schramel, C., Maman, T. L., and Kryspin-Exner, I. (2008). Exploring hidden populations: Recreational drug users. *Cyberpsychology: Journal of Psychosocial Research on Cyberspace, 2*(1).

Winstock, A. R. (2015). The Global Drug Survey 2015 findings. Retrieved from www.globaldrugsurvey.com/the-global-drug-survey-2015-findings/

Wright, K. B. (2005). Researching Internet-based populations: Advantages and disadvantages of online survey research, online questionnaire authoring software packages, and web survey services. *Journal of Computer-Mediated Communication, 10*(3)

Yarosh, S. (2013). Shifting dynamics or breaking sacred traditions?: The role of technology in twelve-step fellowships. Paper presented at the Proceedings of the SIGCHI Conference on Human Factors in Computing Systems, New York.

Young, S., Persichitte, K., and Tharp, D. (1998). Electronic mail interviews: Guidelines for conducting research. *International Journal of Educational Telecommunications, 4*(4), 291–299.

5 Exploring breast cancer bloggers' lived experiences of 'survivorship'

The ethics of gaining access, analysing discourse and fulfilling academic requirements

Cathy Ure

Introduction

Breast cancer is a subject area that generates significant online interest. In January 2016, a Google search using the term 'breast cancer blogs' suggests over 15 million blogs, generated by media outlets, charities, healthcare organisations and individuals affected by the disease, are accessible on the internet. This chapter reflects on the ethical challenges arising from a study, carried out for an MSc-level dissertation, which used personal blogs written by women living with and beyond breast cancer. The study aimed to explore how women blogged about their experiences of breast cancer 'survivorship' through the analysis of blogged discourses used to position 'self' in relation to 'survivorship' and living with and beyond breast cancer. It was prompted by a growing awareness of the increasing number of women living beyond breast cancer (Maddams et al., 2012); the proliferation of online communication bringing women diagnosed with breast cancer together through informal 'social' networks (Attai et al., 2015; Bender et al., 2011; Katz et al., 2015); and challenges arising from the concept of 'survivorship' (Doyle, 2008; Feuerstein, 2007; Jagielski, Hawley and Griggs, 2012; Khan, Rose and Evans, 2012) and what it meant to women living with and beyond breast cancer.

Why research blogs?

Today, approximately 550,000 women are living with or beyond breast cancer in the UK. Due to earlier diagnosis, improvements in treatment and an ageing population, this number is anticipated to increase threefold by 2040 (Maddams et al., 2012, 2009) While it is good news that breast cancer survival is improving, recent empirical evidence concludes women have unmet emotional, physical and psychosocial needs post treatment (Aaronson et al., 2014; Burg et al., 2015; Eccles et al., 2013; Maher and McConnell, 2011). Against this background, experiences of long-term 'survivorship' are increasingly of interest to healthcare professionals, policy-makers and researchers and yet, women's illness narratives posted online remain an untapped data source for understanding the 'lived experiences' (Gualtieri and Akhtar, 2013; Keim-Malpass et al., 2013) of women living with and beyond breast cancer. In a systematic review of the uses, benefits and limitations of Social Media for Health Communication, Moorhead et al. (2013) reported that between January 2002 and February 2012, 13 articles relating to blogging and health communications had been published in peer-reviewed articles. Only one was related to cancer (Chung and Kim, 2007) and none were conducted in relation to breast cancer or used discourse analysis.

Interested in the idea of advancing knowledge through the exploration of 'illness' blogs, I was also compelled by Hookway's (2008) argument that blogs offered substantial benefits for social scientific research in that they provided similar, but far more extensive opportunities than their 'offline' parallel of qualitative diary research. Hookway (2008) argues that blogs offer practicality in terms of sourcing data; they have the capacity to 'shed light on social processes across space and time' (p. 93) and they provide insight into everyday life. Personal blogs are naturalistic data in textual form. They provide immediate text for analysis, which is free from the influence of a researcher and therefore produces experiential discourse that has not been shaped by an outside influence. The issues blogged about, perspectives taken and emotions expressed in personal breast cancer blogs are written as an expression of personal experience and seemed an obvious environment to explore in order to understand women's experiences of 'survivorship'. In addition, blogs provide a publicly available, low-cost and instantaneous technique for collecting substantial amounts of data that is unhindered by geographical limitations (Hookway, 2008). I felt retrospective blog analysis was an approach which enabled an investigation into the way breast cancer bloggers experience 'discourse, meaning and reality' (Bearden, 2008). It enabled exploration of how women living beyond breast cancer represent their identities and the benefits achieved from living their breast cancer experiences online. Gumbrecht (2004) describes the blog as a 'protected space' for communication and self-presentation (cited in Schmidt, 2007, p. 1412), which strives to 'balance staying private and being public' (Schmidt, 2007, p. 1413). This suggests blog writing as a performance (Goffman, 1959); an idea built upon by Hookway (2008), who argues that 'blogging might be conceptualized as a disembodied form of "face-work" concerned with the art of self-representation, impression management and potential for self-promotion' (p. 96). I anticipated that the investment made in the personal construction of a blog would result in breast cancer bloggers sharing more candidly and honestly about their own lived experiences than would be the case in an interview situation. Blogs were also a reflection of experience over time and not subject to a narrative developed within a limited interview period. More critically, blogs are written either implicitly or explicitly for an audience. It is the presence of an audience together with the opportunity for dialogue and joint content production, between the blog author and the blog reader, which makes blogs an exciting, untapped social research resource that can provide rich insight into the ongoing experiences of living with breast cancer. In contrast, using more traditional qualitative interview techniques, such as focus groups or interviews would change the nature of the knowledge of women's experiences of 'survivorship' discourses as they would be shaped by the questions or areas of investigation raised by the researcher. In addition, as a researcher naïve to the experience of living with cancer or chronic illness, I was concerned this might unwittingly present barriers rather than enabling a candid sharing of what 'living with and beyond cancer' means on a daily basis.

Interpretivist epistemology: the approach taken to understanding meanings of 'survivorship'

Documet et al. (2012) report that literature exploring what it means to be a breast cancer 'survivor' is limited. In a broader study of cancer 'survivorship' and discourses of identity, Little et al. (2002) identified that 'surviving' or living with a previous diagnosis of cancer changes the sense of personal identity (p. 171). The authors argue that understanding these changes is necessary to understand 'what it is to be a cancer survivor'. Despite establishing this need, Park, Zlateva and Blank (2009) commented that 'little is known about post-cancer identities' (p. 430) and it remains an emerging field of study.

Twombly (2004) argued that the term 'cancer survivor' was originally used as 'a motivating psychosocial term' to encourage people to 'learn to fight' cancer. It was 'designed to empower patients to make decisions about their care and to push for better research and treatment' (p. 1414). Using the term 'patient' was not 'consistent with the newer view of an informed and active participant in care, which is what the term 'survivor' was seen to imply' (p. 1415). A 'survivorship' narrative therefore emerged 'as part of our culture' which was positioned as producing 'changes in personal identity' (Little et al., 2002, p. 170). For many who had cancer, this was seen to involve the 'integration of a new, and perhaps permanent identity' (Zebrack, 2000, p. 238) – that of 'cancer survivor'. However, positioning everyone receiving a cancer diagnosis as 'survivor' has been seen to be controversial. Twombly (2004) reported that the President of the National Breast Cancer Coalition in the USA argued that 'defining everyone who has ever had breast cancer as a survivor paints more of a pretty picture of breast cancer than exists' (p. 1415). It also implies that those affected by the disease 'readily embrace the identity of survivor' (Kaiser, 2008, p. 79). As the 'survivorship' discourse has become culturally embedded, those affected by a diagnosis become positioned by pre-existing discourses.

In order to understand how women living with and beyond breast cancer position 'self' in relation to 'survivorship' and living with and beyond breast cancer, I felt an interpretivist approach using discursive analysis of blogged texts would enable insight to be developed through exploring meanings, nuances and the depth of discourses which demonstrate the complexities and limitations of common discourses used relating to 'survivorship'. This interest in the performative (Burr, 2003; Goffman, 1959) nature of breast cancer 'survivor's' blog writing gave rise to some interesting ethical challenges which will be discussed in this chapter. Critical discursive analysis assumes that linguistic material is action-orientated, that is, that language performs certain social functions, such as justifying or questioning or accusing (Breakwell et al., 2012. Through this approach it is possible to examine how women construct accounts of living beyond breast cancer and 'survivorship' and what these accounts have to say about the representations of cancer 'survivors' in the wider social context. The analysis of data focuses on what is said and how it is said. I set out to identify the dominant forms of representations constructed by the repertoires (Potter and Wetherell, 1987), the ideological dilemmas experienced (Billig et al., 1988) and what kinds of subject positions (Davies and Harré, 1990) were commonly available with a focus on power relations, agency and structure and authority (Salmons, 2016).

The ethical entanglements of collecting blog data for analysis

What has become clear is that while important contributions are being made in grappling with ethical issues coming out of online research from professional bodies (BPS, 2007, 2013) and from member-based academic associations (AoIR, 2002, 2012), there remain gaps in the literature explicitly describing the practical processes of 'ethical' decision-making and the actions taken when conducting such research. Henderson, Johnson and Auld (2013) describe a 'stark silence' (p. 548) when it comes to ethical issues addressed in social media research studies with 'relatively few researchers' writing about the ethical research practices, decisions and dilemmas involved in using social media as part of a research process (p. 546). This leaves a sizeable gap in the literature and fails to support undergraduate and postgraduate learning about both the complexity of and potential solutions to supporting the ethical conduct of research in this field. In my own area, I was surprised to see both limited attention given to exploring the blogs of women living with breast cancer and to discover there had been very different approaches taken to using content generated online by women detailing their experiences of breast cancer. Some research studies accessed blogs without seeking informed consent, that is to say blogs were considered to be public, with no particular ethical considerations raised (de Boer and Slatman, 2014; McNamara, 2007). In studies of women's narratives of their breast cancer experiences, Pitts (2004) and McNamara (2007) considered women's blogs as purposefully written for a public audience. They deemed consent was not necessary and used the pen names used by bloggers to identify and cite extracts used in analysis. A hybrid approach has also been adopted whereby those bloggers who had an email address published on their blog were asked for permission to include their blogs for analysis whereas a larger group of bloggers who did not have an email address linked to their blog were not asked for permission (Keim-Malpass et al., 2013). These examples show the ethical parameters for collecting information in online public spaces are ambiguous (AoIR, 2012) and researchers debate what is appropriate ethical practice. There still remains, after over 20 years debate, no consensus among social scientists regarding what is private and what is public online (Stevens et al., 2015).

Given the approaches taken to accessing blogs previously it is perhaps unsurprising that when initially outlining my research proposal for this study, I was encouraged to be expedient, given the relatively short timeframe available to complete a dissertation research project. I could consider blogs to consist of 'open data' if they were not password-protected by their authors, an approach commonly used. Given the timeline for this project, this was tempting as it removed barriers to beginning the data collection process. However, some debate ensued as to whether a blog analysis study 'needed' to be submitted to the University Ethics Review Panel. As we have seen, some researchers do not seek ethical approval from their institutions as they argue the data is already 'public data'. In contrast, some researchers argue that social media data is in the public domain but still seek institutional ethical approval (Attard and Coulson, 2012; Coulson, Buchanan and Aubeeluck, 2007). Exploring these different approaches created time for investigation and reflection, and enabled the use of 'reflexivity as a resource' (Guillemin and Gillam, 2004) about my own axiological beliefs which would underpin my approach to the analysis of breast cancer blogs. In trying to determine the 'right approach' to take, I began to draft an application for ethical approval and found this to be an extremely useful process for considering whether I was researching secondary data or data from 'human participants' (BPS, 2007, 2009, 2013). At the same time, I read and searched for blogs written by individuals who met my 'search criteria'. I tried to put myself in the shoes of the blogger as I shaped my ethics application and in doing so I was constantly faced with the question of what does it mean to ethically 'do the right thing' (Bliss and Rocco, 2013) when conducting blog analysis?

Is blog data secondary data already existing in the public domain? Or is the subject at the heart of this study the key – the women living beyond breast cancer? If so, any research using 'human participants' requires ethical approval to meet both university requirements and those of the British Psychological Society. Given the ambiguity created by the 'private-public debate' and taking on board the viewpoint of Henderson et al. (2013) which argues that researchers cannot rely on ethical research committees to be our 'ethical compass' due to their own 'struggle to deal with emerging technologies and their implications' (p. 546), I chose to focus on the 'subject' at the heart of this research project – the women living with and beyond breast cancer. Having begun to immerse myself in the writings of the breast cancer blogging community, I could recognise that bloggers may consider their publicly accessible blogs to be 'private' even though they would have accepted the terms of the End User Licence Agreements employed by web service providers which effectively makes them 'public' to all (BPS, 2013). It seemed that gaining institutional ethical approval was not only 'the right thing to do' but was key, given my focus on hearing and presenting women's voices in relation to 'survivorship'. How ethical would it be to report on women's discourses relating to breast cancer 'survival' through surveillance rather than engagement? Pragmatically, the university's ethical approval also offered credibility for when I would seek bloggers' permission to analyse their blogs. This led to an ethics application being submitted and approved without correction.

The ethical entanglements of conducting critical discursive analysis on blog data

One of the challenges of conducting discursive analysis of blog posts is the need to be able to quote in full from blog posts to enable interpretation of the data to be transparent. Key tenets of the ethical use of internet-mediated research include confidentiality and anonymity (Beninger et al., 2014; BPS, 2007, 2013). These tenets create challenges for discursive researchers of online content given the ease with which quotes from online sources can be 'Googled' to trace their origins (BPS, 2007; Eysenbach and Till, 2001). While the BPS encourages researchers to paraphrase or use 'composite characters for analysis' (BPS, 2007, p. 4) to ensure anonymity, this approach is not appropriate for a discursive psychological methodology. Given that I would need to use direct quotes in the analysis and write-up of this study, the BPS guidelines indicated that written consent for use of quoted publicly available data was required (BPS, 2009). In my mind, I needed to address this issue in the earliest stages of contact with potential participants. There is, however, limited discussion in empirical papers outlining how discourse analysts of health-related blogs have determined their strategy for quoting blogged texts or how this has been addressed with bloggers. For example, a study analysing discourses relating to mothers' blogs of the medicine use of their children with ADHD (Clarke and Lang, 2012) quoted blog texts in full but took care to remove any identifying data. Another explored parents' blogged discussions of childhood depression, in which pseudonyms were used and blogged texts were quoted in full (Clarke and Sargent, 2010). Neither explained their rationale or discussed the ethical implications inherent in quoting blogged texts in full. A lack of methodological papers providing insight into how to conduct and report 'ethically' on a discursive analysis of personal health blogs exists.

Ultimately, I drew upon Sharf (1997, 1999) who used discourse analysis to explore communication processes in an online breast cancer support group. Prior to including any quotes in her final paper, she contacted the relevant individuals to ask for their consent. I determined that given my tight timelines for the study, coupled with a desire to be transparent in the research processes I was using, it would make more sense to ask for permission at the outset as to whether the blogger would permit text to be quoted without further permissions being required, or whether they would wish to be contacted 'post-analysis' should I wish to include a quote from their blog within the final write-up. Consequently, on the consent form, three questions specifically addressed the use of blog material (Table 5.1).

Challenges of identifying a sample

The sheer number of blogs posted in relation to breast cancer on the internet is overwhelming. Gualtieri and Akhtar (2013) comment that qualitative blog research could offer 'a rare insight' into patient experience but currently blogs

Table 5.1 Consent form questions relating to use of blog texts for analysis and write-up

I give my consent to the use of my blog for discourse analysis.	YES	NO
I give my consent for the use of quoted text from within my blog in the write-up to this study, without requiring further permissions from myself.	YES	NO
I may give consent for the use of quoted text from within blog in the write-up to this study, however, permission for the specific text to be included will be required.	YES	NO

remain largely unused due to an absence of a 'repository' of patient blogs. For this project, a significant amount of time was spent identifying blogs which met the research criteria. These criteria stated that: (1) blogs had to be publicly available with no login or passwords required; (2) blogs had specifically to address 'survivorship' or living beyond cancer; and (3) blogs had to relate to the blogger's personal experience of breast cancer with age at diagnosis and the diagnosis itself stated. The blogs needed to be regularly updated, with the most recent update being within the last month. Contact details were required in order to request permission for use. To ensure analysis was conducted in relation to the experience of 'survivorship' sometime distant from date of diagnosis, only blogs that were started before 1 January 2011 were then included in the sample and blog rolls were found to be the most efficient method using a modified snowball approach to identifying blogs that met all criteria.

The slow process involved in identifying potential blogs for analysis helped shape the ethical approach taken to later stages of this project. The data required in order to identify whether the blog met the research criteria were often not accessible from the first glance at an individual blog. All writers construct their blogs differently and while some may open at a home page with the relevant data included in their introductory blog; the majority did not. Consequently, a great deal of time was spent lurking online (Setoyama, Yamazaki and Namayama, 2011). Reading blog posts was often an emotional process and one which made me consider whether I was developing para-social interactions (Giles, 2002) with blog authors. It also caused me to reflect upon my role as an 'outsider' (Dwyer and Buckle, 2009) and student researcher entering the breast cancer blogging community and how this might be perceived. The feeling of identification and empathy with the extended narratives of women living three years plus since diagnosis; together with the recognition that many were networked together through a very active global breast cancer social media-focused community, meant that I chose to adopt an approach to seeking participation in my study which focused, as best it could, on being considerate of individual needs and the potential impact on the wider breast cancer community. I was sensitive to entering the breast cancer community from a position of relative 'naïvety' – that is, as an outsider. I was also sensitive to the ethical dilemma of potentially intruding into a 'life lived' and being an unwelcome visitor. Consequently, I felt that approaching all of my identified sample group, which appeared to some extent 'connected' online, with a blanket request to access blog discourses was perhaps inappropriate and potentially unethical. I was conscious that a request for inclusion in a study where 'lived experiences' of breast cancer were analysed raised ethical issues for myself as a researcher, given that I might not have the scope to use an individual's blog in my analysis, should the blog corpus be vast. I had a very strong sense that, if given consent, an 'ethical' approach would necessitate the analysis of all blogs to which I was given access.

Discourse analysis is a time-consuming and demanding methodology (Potter and Wetherell, 1987) whereby the researcher is required to read and reread large bodies of transcripts, in this case, blogs. Gaining access to a 'manageable' number of blogs, rich in naturalistic data, related to 'survivorship' therefore seemed a key priority for ethical handling of this study. I therefore elected to email a small number of bloggers on a rolling basis (three at a time) informing them of my study and asking for permission to analyse their blog posts. Conscious of the breadth and depth of information shared in the blogs in my sample, I was perhaps naïvely concerned with being overwhelmed by data and with how to appropriately steward personal blogged narratives often addressing sensitive issues. An absence of previous studies highlighting approaches to identifying blogs for analysis and thereafter seeking permission from blog authors meant an inductive approach to blog searching and ethical decision-making in relation to blog analysis was required, as issues relating to 'ethics in practice' (Guillemin and Gillam, 2004) emerged. Questions – post project – that remain unanswered include whether approaching a wide number of bloggers simultaneously would have been an ethical approach to take, given the data analysis approach being undertaken. Or whether 'blog solicitation' (Hookway, 2008, p. 14) through the posting of advertisements about the study through social media channels would have resulted in contributions, discussion within the wider breast cancer community and greater uptake. It might certainly have been a more time-efficient process to use. Ultimately, through taking the approach I did, quite a different scenario presented itself than was originally anticipated.

Gaining 'informed' consent: practicalities and epistemological challenges

Bloggers meeting the research criteria were contacted requesting informed consent to analyse the discourses employed. I contacted bloggers via their email addresses provided on their blog. In line with recommendations subsequently made by Beninger et al. (2014), the email stated from where I had gained the bloggers' contact details; outlined the purpose of the study (Box 5.1) and requested permission to analyse the discourse within their blog, specifically in relation to the concepts of 'survivorship' and 'living beyond cancer'.

A study information sheet and consent form were included and the right to withdraw from the study at any time was clearly established. In order to support the legitimacy of the project and to encourage transparency (Beninger et al.,

---

Box 5.1 Taken from the initial email contact

I have been following your blog with interest and am writing to let you know about a research study I am currently leading which may be of interest to you.

[...] My dissertation explores the use of discourses around breast cancer survivorship and living beyond cancer, which is a subject you have discussed within your blog. I am interested in using the naturalistic texts of blogs to understand how women who have had, or who have breast cancer represent online the concept of 'survivorship'.

I would like to be able to use content from your own blog within my study. This necessitates nothing further from yourself, other than your permission to do so. I have attached with this email further details of the study and a consent form for you to sign electronically if you give permission for me to use some aspects of your blog. It is important to consider all the information related to this study prior to giving consent. Mull it over for 24 hours. However, if you do give permission, you can withdraw that permission at any time during the study without needing to provide any explanation of your decision to do so.

The purpose of this study is to gain greater knowledge of the ways in which women discuss their experiences of living beyond cancer as it is an area which is currently under-researched. It can potentially add to the body of health-related knowledge, which is developing, relating to how cultural discourses can influence perceptions of self, which can be both helpful and unhelpful.

2014) I provided a link to my profile page on my University Department's blog and my Twitter username.

Ultimately, using my 'rolling' approach to gain consent was extremely time-consuming and usually unsuccessful. In total, ten bloggers were emailed details of the study over a period of approximately six weeks, as I waited for a response before emailing other bloggers. One blogger responded positively; one blogger refused consent as they were personally engaged in 'survivorship' research. Another declined to become involved unless 'I could find a way to cure cancer'. Five did not respond. Two bloggers responded positively one month later and unfortunately after the analysis was well underway. The blog corpus for the study was therefore extracted from one US blog posted by one blogger, who requested 'proper credit' for inclusion of her blogged texts.

Ethical guidelines relating to internet research explicitly discuss the requirement to ensure the anonymity and confidentiality of authors of texts used (AoIR, 2002, 2012; BPS, 2013). In this instance, the blog author provided full consent on condition that 'proper credit' was provided. This was an 'ethically important moment' (Guillemin and Gillam, 2004). In establishing her authorial rights, the blogger was able to ensure her own voice was heard and acknowledged, however, this approach created a key tension in relation to conducting 'ethics in practice'. In many ways, this 'condition' was a very positive response. First, I had consent to use blogged materials and, second, this removed challenges I would have had to negotiate in relation to the use of quotes to support discursive findings. This 'condition' made the process of analysis and write-up appear more straightforward.

In addition, I was extremely fortunate to have received consent from this particular individual. She was a prolific blogger who focused on building a supportive relationship with those who read her blog. On average, there were 33 comments posted following each blog analysed, which included her own responses to every comment made. While this made the data extremely rich, it raised new ethical challenges, unaddressed in much of the research literature. What are the ethical considerations that should be extended to those commenting on this particular blog? Are they knowingly engaging in a public act of communication by choosing to post a brief response to a blog post? Are the same ethical considerations given to blog authors applicable to those posting short comments in response to the blog post? This is an area of ambiguity, and limited attention, in current internet research guidelines. As I began my analysis, I argued that as consent was already provided by the blog author, further consents from blog commenters were not required, notwithstanding the practical challenges of seeking consent from a wide body of people involved 'by association' in a research project. I therefore included comments posted to the blogs within the corpus of data and used pseudonyms to protect the individual identities during coding, analysis and write-up.

Later, issues relating to disseminating the findings of my study made me reflect on the 'rights of privacy' of blog commenters. I had argued the case to include blog comments as permission to use the blog had been granted and I worked under the assumption that my dissertation would be read by my supervisory team and external examiner only. In terms of learning gained from this project, it may be useful for academics to encourage all postgraduate dissertation students, using digital methods, to start out on their dissertation path assuming they are writing for peer review and publication. This would demand greater scrutiny of all decisions related to internet-mediated research throughout the research process. There is also a gap within the procedural ethics processes in exploring the challenges of ethical dissemination of online research findings which should be addressed. Interestingly, although my blog author was specific in requesting 'full credit' for inclusion of her own blogs in the research project, she did not make any comment relating to the use of the comments on each blog. While my participant information sheet stated that 'the information this study will collect relates to how women who have had breast cancer use discourses to describe the lived experience of living beyond cancer', it did not specifically state that comments posted by others to the blog would be analysed as part of the corpus of data. On reflection, blog analysts would be minded to be explicit at the outset with blog writers about exactly which data they will use for analysis.

The BPS (2013) details the requirement for gaining 'valid consent' (p. 8) when conducting internet-related research. This involves verifying the characteristics of participants to ensure they say who they are. This was achieved through email discussion related to the research project before the consent form was returned. In addition, details about the study were provided, including the nature of involvement for participants; possible associated risks and the right to with-draw (BPS, 2013). Despite obtaining 'valid consent', my study raised issues relating to the principle of 'informed consent' and how this is understood and achieved. This study, as is the case with many studies, did not progress in the way anticipated at the outset. Bloggers were reluctant to give consent to use their blogged texts resulting in a 'case study' of one US blogger and her online con-versations with blog commenters. While this was unanticipated, I had accounted for this situation in my ethics application:

> For this study, whilst ideally research should continue until no new data emerges (Howitt, 2010), it is difficult to pinpoint whether one blog – rich in the original blogged discourse and co-created dialogue created between the blogger and their audience – will form the data set or whether up to half a dozen will be utilised.

In these circumstances, what were the ethical implications of using one blog? I had university ethics approval for conducting this study using a singular blog if the blogged discourse was rich and included co-created dialogue. But the use of one blog raised the question, what are the responsibilities on researchers to verify 'ongoing consent'? Kaiser (2009) commented that discussions about informed consent are rarely ongoing. She argued that 'once the consent form is signed, researchers lack a standardized way of returning to the issue of data use with respondents' (p. 1634). In this particular case, I did not go back to the blogger at the outset of the analysis process. Institutional deadlines were drawing near and I had limited opportunities to deliver without accessing blogs without consent. In essence, the power of the researcher stepped forward as I chose to complete the analysis and dissertation write-up. As the write-up moved on, I was unclear how to go about a debrief. The literature fails to address debriefing in social media-related studies or the sharing of discursive analysis of online texts. While I had not com-municated that I would share my findings at the outset of the study – something again which blog analysts would be minded to do – my axiological beliefs led me to forwarding my dissertation in full to the blogger in order to be transparent about the sampling process, the recruitment process, the epistemological approach and my findings. Sharing my findings were important to check that 'informed consent' was still secure (Beninger et al., 2014). Given the epistemological approach of dis-cursive analysis, this felt, at the time, a risk. What would happen if the blog author rejected the findings; disagreed with the methods used and withdrew permission to use the blogged texts? As Kaiser (2009) reflects: 'our respondents might not like how we use their data or how we choose to portray them' (p. 8). However, having spent a number of months collecting data and becoming deeply immersed in it, sharing the outcomes with the author who had been so generous in sharing her own work, and to whom the work pertained, seemed 'the right thing to do'. It felt like I had handed 'power' back to the blogger.

The blogger responded by email predominantly focusing on my interpre-tations and findings. It was a fruitful discussion which helped deepen my understanding still further about the nuances affecting how 'survivorship' discourses can be perceived and how researchers present findings. Although this sharing of views was ultimately positive, it began from a position of challenge relating to the analytical approach used. While my participant information sheet, consent form and original email had specifically stated that a discursive analytical approach would be taken to explore the discourses of 'survivorship', it became apparent that my blogger had not understood what that approach meant 'in practice'. This raises significant ethical questions about the nature of 'informed consent' which I continue to reflect upon. Do we as researchers hide behind technical language which assumes understanding on the part of our participants because 'informed consent' is given? Do we as researchers need to develop approaches to involve participants (when we can), which includes a sharing of knowledge from the outset, whereby we explain and justify our research methodologies before seeking involvement? And, if so, how do we achieve this as researchers working in online environments with 'social' digital data? These issues need to be explored further.

The challenges of an 'ethical' dissemination

Interest in my research findings led to encouragement to disseminate my work outwith my university department. 'Good practice' regarding anonymity restricted my ability to share content which drew on the conversations between the blogger and her blog commenters. Anonymity could not be guaranteed. Given the blogger was cited openly in the broader work, minimal investigation would bring forward the identity of anyone contributing comments to a particular blog post. In essence, the approach taken by the blogger to be publicly credited removed the opportunity to use others' comments within the analysis, in a public setting. Onward dissemination therefore became restricted to findings based purely on the bloggers' blogged materials, and arguably upon public dissemination the findings appear less rich than the breadth of work that formed the dissertation.

Throughout the project and during dissemination, one of my principal concerns related to decisions that could create 'potential harm' (BPS, 2013, p. 1). This is challenging when working with personal health blog data, discursively analysed. Guillemin and Gillam (2004) explain that the potential harms to participants involved in qualitative research 'may be subtle' and often arise from 'the nature of the interaction between the researcher and the participant' (p. 272). The need to ensure 'trust' is maintained within the research relationship is therefore key. To support this aim, I shared my thinking with the blogger regarding onward dissemination; checked I had support for disseminating the findings which I felt could be 'publicly displayed' and also raised the issue of why I felt it was inappropriate and unethical to use commenters' posts when I disseminated my research findings. My focus was on ensuring the protection of the relationships the blogger had nurtured carefully with her blog readers over many years which I was keen not to affect through the possibility of deductive disclosure. This reflexive approach to dissemination was welcomed and supported by the blog author.

Conclusion

In this chapter, I have sought to account for how an inductive approach to addressing issues relating to 'ethics in practice' was used to address challenges arising from an analysis of breast cancer blogs written by women living with and beyond the disease. Procedural ethics processes present opportunities for those conducting research on 'social' online data to integrate reflexivity into the ethical practices that lie at the foundations of their research approach. This reflexive ethical approach requires researchers to 'constantly take stock of their actions and their role in the research process and subject these to the same critical scrutiny as the rest of their "data"' (Mason, 1996, p. 6). As a discursive analyst of blogged texts, at each 'ethically important moment' I reflected upon whether I was doing 'the right thing' and I continue to do this as the research carried out continues to be drawn upon. Challenges to be addressed include understanding what 'informed consent' is in the digital era. What is being analysed when we talk about blog analysis and how do we convey transparently the epistemological approaches underpinning our investigations? We also need to consider how do we build research 'partnerships' and attend to the ongoing dynamics within connected online communities? What is best practice in relation to providing a debrief of research conducted exploring the online social construction of health-related issues? Of particular interest from this study was the difficulty in identifying a sample of blogs and gaining access through informed consent. This signals that social science researchers should be mindful that blog content may not be considered publicly available data, free for researchers to use, by their authors. It is therefore the responsibility of the researcher to determine how to act ethically in a rapidly evolving space where 'good practice' and 'accepted practice' are two different concepts.

References

Aaronson, N., Mattioli, V., Minton, O., Weis, J., Johansen, C., and Dalton, S. et al. (2014). Beyond treatment: Psychosocial and behavioural issues in cancer survivorship research and practice. *European Journal of Cancer Supplements, 12*(1), 54–64. http://dx.doi.org/10.1016/j.ejcsup.2014.03.005

Association of Internet Researchers. (2002). Ethical decision-making and internet research: Recommendations from the AoIR ethics working committee. Retrieved from http://aoir.org/reports/ethics.pdf

Association of Internet Researchers. (2012). Ethical decision-making and internet research. Retrieved from http://aoir.org/reports/ethics2.pdf

Attai, D., Cowher, M., Al-Hamadani, M., Schoger, J., Staley, A., and Landercasper, J. (2015). Twitter social media is an effective tool for breast cancer patient education and support: patient-reported outcomes by survey. *Journal of Medical Internet Research, 17*(7), e188. http://dx.doi.org/10.2196/jmir.4721

Attard, A., and Coulson, N. (2012). A thematic analysis of patient communication in Parkinson's disease online support group discussion forums. *Computers in Human Behavior, 28*(2), 500–506. http://dx.doi.org/10.1016/j.chb.2011.10.022

Bearden, K. M. (2008). Rare and tragic: Young women diagnosed with advanced breast cancer; a discourse analysis. Thesis submitted to Flinders University, Adelaide, Australia.

Bender, J., Jimenez-Marroquin, M., and Jadad, A. (2011). Seeking support on Facebook: A content analysis of breast cancer groups. *Journal of Medical Internet Research*, *13*(1), e16. http://dx.doi.org/10.2196/jmir.1560

Beninger, K., Fry, A., Jago, N., Lepps, H., Nass, L., and Silvester, H. (2014). Research using social media; users' views. *NatCen Social Research*. Retrieved from www. natcen.ac.uk/media/282288/p0639-research-using-social-media-report-final-190214. pdf

Billig, M., Condor, S., Edwards, D., Gane, M., Middleton, D., and Radley, A. (1988). *Ideological dilemmas. A social psychology of everyday thinking*. London: Sage.

Bliss, L., and Rocco, T. (2013). *Mind the gap: Qualitative researchers and mixed methods research*. Retrieved 27 January 2016, from http://digitalcommons.fiu.edu/cgi/viewcontent.cgi?article=1025andcontext=sferc

Breakwell, G. M., Smith, J. A., and Wright, D. B. (2012). *Research methods in psychology* (4th edn). Los Angeles: Sage.

British Psychological Society. (2007). Report of the Working Party on Conducting Research on the Internet Guidelines for ethical practice in psychological research online. Retrieved from www.bps.org.uk/sites/default/files/documents/conducting_research_on_the_internet-guidelines_for_ethical_practice_in_psychological_research_online.pdf

British Psychological Society. (2009). *Code of ethics and conduct: Guidance published by the Ethics Committee of the British Psychological Society*. Leicester: The British Psychological Society.

British Psychological Society (2013). Ethics Guidelines for Internet-mediated Research. INF206/1.2013. Leicester: British Psychological Society. Retrieved from: www.bps. org.uk/publications/policy-andguidelines/research-guidelines-policydocuments/research-guidelines-poli

Burg, M., Adorno, G., Lopez, E., Loerzel, V., Stein, K., Wallace, C., and Sharma, D. (2015). Current unmet needs of cancer survivors: Analysis of open-ended responses to the American Cancer Society Study of Cancer Survivors II. *Cancer, 121*(4), 623–630. http://dx.doi.org/10.1002/cncr.28951

Burr, V. (2003). *Social constructionism*. London. Routledge.

Chung, D., and Kim, S. (2007). Blogging activity among cancer patients and their companions: Uses, gratifications, and predictors of outcomes. *Journal of American Society for Information Science*, *59*(2), 297–306. http://dx.doi.org/10.1002/asi.20751

Clarke, J., and Lang, L. (2012). Mothers whose children have ADD/ADHD discuss their children's medication use: An investigation of blogs. *Social Work in Health Care, 51*(5), 402–416. http://dx.doi.org/10.1080/00981389.2012.660567

Clarke, J., and Sargent, C. (2010). Childhood depression: Parents talk with one another on the net. *Social Work in Mental Health, 8*(6), 510–525. http://dx.doi.org/10.1080/15332985.2010.481997

Coulson, N., Buchanan, H., and Aubeeluck, A. (2007). Social support in cyberspace: A content analysis of communication within a Huntington's disease online support group. *Patient Education and Counseling, 68*(2), 173–178. http://dx.doi.org/10.1016/j.pec.2007.06.002

Davies, B. and Harré, R. (1990). Positioning: The discursive production of selves. *Journal for the Theory of Social Behaviour, 20*(1), 43–63.

de Boer, M., and Slatman, J. (2014). Blogging and breast cancer: Narrating one's life, body and self on the Internet. *Women's Studies International Forum, 44*, 17–25. http://dx.doi.org/10.1016/j.wsif.2014.02.014

Documet, P.I., Trauth, J.M., Key, M., Flatt, J., and Jernigan, J. (2012). Breast cancer survivors' perception of survivorship. *Oncology Nursing Forum, 39*(3), 309–315. doi:10.1188/12.ONF.309-315

Doyle, N. (2008). Cancer survivorship: Evolutionary concept analysis. *Journal of Advanced Nursing, 62*(4), 499–509. http://dx.doi.org/10.1111/j.1365-2648.2008.04617.x

Dwyer, S. C., and Buckle, J. L. (2009). The space between: On being an insider-outsider in qualitative research. *International Journal of Qualitative Methods, 8*(1), 54–63.

Eccles, S., Aboagye, E., Ali, S., Anderson, A., Armes, J., and Berditchevski, F. et al. (2013). Critical research gaps and translational priorities for the successful prevention and treatment of breast cancer. *Breast Cancer Research, 15*(5), R92. http://dx.doi.org/10.1186/bcr3493

Eysenbach, G., and Till, J. (2001). Ethical issues in qualitative research on internet communities. *BMJ, 323*(7321), 1103–1105. http://dx.doi.org/10.1136/bmj.323.7321.1103

Feuerstein, M. (2007). Defining cancer survivorship. *Journal of Cancer Survivorship, 1*(1), 5–7. http://dx.doi.org/10.1007/s11764-006-0002-x

Giles, D. (2002). Parasocial interaction: A review of the literature and a model for future research. *Media Psychology, 4*(3), 279–305. http://dx.doi.org/10.1207/s1532785xmep 0403_04

Goffman, E. (1959). The presentation of self in everyday life. In C. Calhoun, J. Gerteis, J. Moody, S. Pfaff, and I. Virk (eds) *Contemporary sociological theory* (3rd edn). Oxford: Blackwell.

Gualtieri, L., and Akhtar, F. (2013). Cancer patient blogs: How patients, clinicians, and researchers learn from rich narratives of illness. In *Information Technology Interfaces (ITI), Proceedings of the ITI 2013 35th International Conference* (pp. 3–8). Catvat: IEEE.

Guillemin, M., and Gillam, L. (2004). Ethics, reflexivity, and "ethically important moments" in research. *Qualitative Inquiry, 10*(2), 261–280. https://doi.org/10.1177/1077800403262360

Henderson, M., Johnson, N., and Auld, G. (2013). Silences of ethical practice: dilemmas for researchers using social media. *Educational Research and Evaluation, 19*(6), 546–560. http://dx.doi.org/10.1080/13803611.2013.805656

Hookway, N. (2008). 'Entering the blogosphere': Some strategies for using blogs in social research. *Qualitative Research, 8*(1), 91–113. http://dx.doi.org/10.1177/1468794 107085298

Howitt, D. (2010). *Introduction to qualitative methods in psychology*. Harlow: Pearson Education.

Jagielski, C., Hawley, S., Corbin, K., Weiss, M., and Griggs, J. (2012). A phoenix rising: Who considers herself a "survivor" after a diagnosis of breast cancer?. *Journal of Cancer Survivorship, 6*(4), 451–457. http://dx.doi.org/10.1007/s11764-012-0240-z

Kaiser, K. (2008). The meaning of the survivor identity for women with breast cancer. *Social Science and Medicine, 67*(1), 79–87. http://dx.doi.org/10.1016/j.socscimed.2008.03.036

Kaiser, K. (2009). Protecting respondent confidentiality in qualitative research. *Qualitative Health Research, 19*(11), 1632–1641. http://doi.org/10.1177/1049732309350879

Katz, M., Utengen, A., Anderson, P., Thompson, M., Attai, D., Johnston, C., and Dizon, D. (2015). Disease-specific hashtags for online communication about cancer care. *JAMA Oncology, 1*. http://dx.doi.org/10.1001/jamaoncol.2015.3960

Keim-Malpass, J., Baernholdt, M., Erickson, J., Ropka, M., Schroen, A., and Steeves, R. (2013). Blogging through cancer. *Cancer Nursing, 36*(2), 163–172. http://dx.doi. org/10.1097/ncc.0b013e31824eb879

Khan, N. F., Rose, P. W., and Evans, J. (2012). Defining cancer survivorship: A more transparent approach is needed. *Journal of Cancer Survivorship, 6*(1), 33–6. doi:10. 1007/s11764-011-0194-6

Little, M., Paul, K., Jordens, C. F. C., and Sayers, E.-J. (2002). Survivorship and discourses of identity. *Psycho-oncology, 11*, 170–178.

Maddams, J., Brewster, D., Gavin, A., Steward, J., Elliott, J., Utley, M., and Møller, H. (2009). Cancer prevalence in the United Kingdom: Estimates for 2008. *British Journal of Cancer, 101*(3), 541–547. http://dx.doi.org/10.1038/sj.bjc.6605148

Maddams, J., Utley, M., and Møller, H. (2012). Projections of cancer prevalence in the United Kingdom, 2010–2040. *British Journal of Cancer, 107*(7), 1195–1202. http://dx. doi.org/10.1038/bjc.2012.366

Maher, J., and McConnell, H. (2011). New pathways of care for cancer survivors: adding the numbers. *British Journal of Cancer, 105*, S5-S10. http://dx.doi.org/10.1038/ bjc.2011.417

Mason, J. (1996). *Qualitative researching.* London: Sage.

McNamara, K. (2007). Blogging breast cancer: Language and subjectivity in women's online illness narratives. Retrieved on 15 January 2014 from http://hdl.handle. net/10822/551596

Moorhead, S., Hazlett, D., Harrison, L., Carroll, J., Irwin, A., and Hoving, C. (2013). A new dimension of health care: Systematic review of the uses, benefits, and limitations of social media for health communication. *Journal of Medical Internet Research, 15*(4), e85. http://dx.doi.org/10.2196/jmir.1933

Park, C. L., Zlateva, I., and Blank, T.O. (2009). Self-identity after cancer: 'survivor', 'victim', 'patient' and 'person with cancer'. *Journal of General Internal Medicine, 24*(Suppl. 2), 430–435. doi: 10.1007:s11606-009-0993-x

Pitts, V. (2004). Illness and internet empowerment: Writing and reading breast cancer in cyberspace. *Health (London), 8*(1), 33–59. http://dx.doi.org/10.1177/13634593040 38794

Potter, J., and Wetherell, M. (1987). *Discourse and social psychology: Beyond attitudes and behaviour.* London. Sage.

Salmons, J. (2016). *Doing qualitative research online.* London. Sage.

Setoyama, Y., Yamazaki, Y., and Namayama, K. (2011). Benefits of peer support in online Japanese breast cancer communities: Differences between lurkers and posters. *Journal of Medical Internet Research, 13*(4), e122. http://dx.doi.org/10.2196/ jmir.1696

Schmidt, J. (2007). Blogging practices: An analytical framework. *Journal of Computer Mediated Communication, 12*, 1419–127. doi: 10.1111/j.1083-6101.2007.00379.x

Sharf, B. D. (1997). Communicating breast cancer on-line: Support and empowerment on the internet, *Women and Health, 26*(1), 65–84. doi: 10.1300/J013v26n01_05

Sharf, B. D. (1999). Beyond netiquette: The ethics of doing naturalistic discourse research on the internet. In S. Jones (Ed.), *Doing internet research: Critical issues and methods for examining the net.* (pp. 243–257). Thousand Oaks, CA: Sage. doi:10.4135/97814522 31471.n12

Stevens, G., O'Donnell, V. L., and Williams, L. (2015). Public domain or private data? Developing an ethical approach to social media research in an inter-disciplinary project. *Educational Research and Evaluation: An International Journal on Theory and Practice, 21*(2), 154–167. doi: 10.1080/13803611.2015.1024010

Twombly, R. (2004). What's in a name? Who is a cancer survivor? *Journal of the National Cancer Institute, 96*(19), 1414–5.

Zebrack, B. J. (2000). Cancer survivor identity and quality of life. *Cancer Practice, 8*(5), 238–42.

6 Text research on online platforms
Heuristic steps and pitfalls

Tom Van Nuenen

Introduction

This chapter will discuss basic heuristic steps for explorative and unsupervised computational text research in current online environments – a form of 'corpus-assisted discourse studies' (Partington, Morley and Haarman, 2006). We will examine several popular methods for researchers to gather, prepare, sort and analyse online data, and offer suggestions to fix the vacillation between so-called 'distant' and 'close' reading strategies – not for the purpose of prediction or classification, but for a straightforward textual interpretation. We will engage with the questions of scope, prioritisation, transformation and representation that come with such an interpretative back-and-forth. The chapter opens with a discussion of the context and broader epistemological questions of online text analysis before investigating a case study, taken from the relatively new digital contexts for travel writing. In what follows, we will outline several procedures for scraping, pre-processing and analysing an online data repository using Python – although no actual code will be depicted and no prior exposition to Python is needed. We will see a number of caveats and issues arise in the process, most of which are typical of online text mining, and we will discuss the merits and deficiencies of this approach.

Method: data analytics and text mining

Computational methods in the humanities have produced a field that has come to be known in the past few years as digital humanities (DH). The field had been around for decades before its recent rise to popularity: it was previously known as the humanities computing, and dates back to least to Father Roberto Busa's work on concordances in the 1940s.[1] The practice of computationally gathering and analysing large corpora of texts (sometimes called 'text mining') grew steadily out of this first attempt (cf. Flowerdew, 1997; Baker, 2004, p. 1). Text mining temporarily de-emphasises individual occurrences of features or words in favour of a focus on the larger system or corpus and its aggregate patterns and trends. As a method, it has become increasingly useful due to the rapid growth in production of personal information and public sharing in Web 2.0 contexts, as well as the broader advent of big data infrastructures and the rise of databases and processes that John Durham Peters (2013) calls 'logistical media' – that is, media whose content is not so much narratival or representational as it is organisational. Peters notes the current 'heightened popular attention to media technologies that function in a different register than the content-driven mass media' (2013, p. 40): the importance of metadata for both end users and analysts (Who wrote this? When? Where?) is one example of this.

In light of these recent societal changes the mainstream humanities have started picking up on the digital humanities. Its response has never been void of criticism. Andrejevic et al. (2015) recently summarised the epistemological trend, brought about by big data analytics, that is now increasingly apparent in the humanities at large. The authors point to research strands such as New Materialism, Object-Oriented Ontology or New Medium Theory. The popularity of these perspectives, they add, implies a shift away from discursive or ideologically-minded approaches: what these new approaches offer instead is an 'analysis of the circulation of affects and effects rather than of meanings, content or representations' (Andrejevic et al., 2015, p. 382). These machine-centric ontologies, in which human experience is considered less significant than the historical media processes of collecting, storing and retrieving data, in fact reinforce the political goals of the big businesses owning today's biggest datasets (cf. Galloway, 2013, p. 347). The authors proceed to rightfully question the move away from discursive and political approaches to the data that society produces. Yet, '[an] adherence to the horizon of meaning is a strategic critical resource in the face of theoretical tendencies that reproduce the correlational logic of the database by focusing on patterns and effects rather than on interpretations or explanations' (p. 382).

In other words, digital methods, data mining and distant reading all fit in with an era of information capitalism involving proprietary platforms that engage in mass customisation, targeting and personalisation. This means that we must approach digital tools for text research as techno-economic constructs, enabling certain types of knowledge and subjectivity, instead of ostensible 'post-ideological' tools that help us gauge reality instrumentally. Any aggregate analytical attempt should embark from and stay focused on the historical, experiential, imaginary and ideological functions of discourse. This inherently brushes against the type of 'real-time' data analyses in which text mining serves the purpose of predicting trends (Asur and Huberman, 2010; Bollen, 2011; Lidman, 2011; Mischne and Glance, 2006). Additionally, the result of increasingly complex models and techniques renders the divide between digital humanists and their analog colleagues even bigger.

Data analytics, alternatively, can be used more modestly, as a form of data exploration. As Matthew Jockers (2013) emphasises, computational text analysis allows us to support or challenge existing theories and assumptions, while calling our attention to general patterns and missed trends in order to better understand the context in which individual texts, words or features arise. In the process of distant reading, as opposed to close reading, the reality of the text undergoes a process of deliberate reduction and abstraction, and the distance in distant reading is considered not an obstacle but a specific capacity for know-ledge (Moretti, 2005, p. 1). Computational results may be used to provoke a dir-ected close reading, and this is where we get to hybrid methods in which close and distant reading methods coalesce (see, for instance, Ramsay, 2011, and the methods adopted by Awan et al., 2011; Procter et al., 2013; Veinot, 2007).

What might be gained by a computationally aided text analysis? Most funda-mentally, it allows one to trace connections, patterns and other discursive 'hints' in databases that could not be made by humans, due to their scope. However, in online environments, we often find ourselves dealing with unstructured data (Ampofo et al., 2015) that does not conform to a stringent formal schema or type: this means that a procedure of hypothesis testing to distinguish between these forms of data is often not possible. Rather, we may want to discover themes or discourses in a corpus of texts that allow us insight into the ideologies, attitudes, sentiments or discursive logic inherent in language. We will consider the possibilities for such an approach in a specific case study: that of con-temporary forms of online travel writing.

Case study: online travel writing

Travel writing, in the literary arena, has traditionally had close connections with both fiction and autobiography. It is a notably broad genre, involving a breadth of stylistic, formal or generic forms, such as novelistic characters and plot line, poetic descriptions, historical information, essayistic discursiveness, or autobio-graphical elements. This multifariousness offers the writer 'a way to show the effects of his or her own presence in a foreign country and to expose the arbi-trariness of truth and the absence of norms' (Blanton, 2002, p. 27). The hap-hazard formal boundaries of the genre mirror the kinds of experiences it describes: many definitions of travel stress the open-endedness and instability that belong to its practice – and thus also to the stories written about it. Many writers (cf. Mayes, 2012; Raban, 2011) underline the explorative, wayward and imaginary dimensions of travel, and the authorial position associated with its recounting. Well rehearsed as this perspective on travel authorship is, we might add that by far the most popular form of travel writing nowadays occurs in a different context (and with a different purpose), namely online. Here, we find new forms of representing travel, such as travel blogs and travel review and recommendation platforms. These environments have yielded genres of travel writing in their own right, which have as of yet not been sufficiently indexed and analysed.

The methodological deficit of not considering online genres of travel writing exemplifies an established pattern in the literary analysis of travel writing. Travel writing was for a long time no certified topic of scholarly attention, unlike, as Kuehn and Smethurst note, its 'more prestigious cousins' such as the novel, poetry or drama (2015, p. 1). This changed in the 1980s, when the counter-traditional wave in the humanities famously declared the end of grand narratives, and started engaging with minor and marginalised texts. The current chapter proceeds further in that direction, offering a transdisciplinary approach to digital environments and the everyday-life discourses one finds therein. Silverman (2006) has called such discourses 'naturally occurring data', defined as opposed to manufactured or provoked data, i.e. data that is not dependent on the researcher's intervention. If it is clear that many people nowadays make sense of the world through the lens of tourism, its discourse should be sought after in everyday small talk rather than in some separate field of activity (Edensor, 2001), where the 'everyday' does not equate to the trivial or inconsequential, but to innocuous texts in which the ideologies, identities and symbols of tourism reverberate. Travel writing, in other words, is in need of more 'folkloristic' endeavours that study forms that would not have been possible pre-Internet.

In the context of travel and tourism research, text mining methods have been applied to understand tourist motivations, behaviours and sentiments. Magnini et al. (2011), for instance, have used such methods to analyse the primary sources of customer delight by considering 743 travel blog entries in which phrases such as 'delightful surprise' were used. However, numerous humanities scholars have expressed their concerns with these kinds of digital methods and the possibilities they might bring to the table. boyd and Crawford summarise these concerns by warning that computational analysis and data mining may 'narrow the palette of research options' (2011, p. 1), as the researcher may become ensnared in the positivist tactic of counting, deducing and staving: *Erklären*, instead of *Verstehen*, in Dilthey's famous terms. The question then becomes how we can read into discourse *as* discourse, instead of inferring psychological motivations from these writings.

This question becomes more pressing as many types and genres of media we find online cannot easily be read as individual texts. Yet travel blogs, reviewing and recommendation services (TripAdvisor, Airbnb), and even apps such as Tinder are expressions of travel in their own right. On their own, these anecdotal, short pieces of text might not involve the same kinds of explicit social engagement that we find in many types of traditional travel writing. Yet ideological and socio-political structures do shape these discourses, and we can consider them though a distant reading approach – especially since the scale of content being created warrants some degree of suspicion about the kinds of close reading that are traditionally used to understand travel writing. These are new and digitally native genres in algorithmic culture, and as Mahnke and Uprichard (2014) note, we need to explore the possibilities of 'algorithming the algorithm', that is, making use of it through its own language.

For instance, we might consider forum entries on Lonely Planet's travel forum Thorn Tree. The forum, which has been running since 1996, hosts a plethora of interaction between (prospective) travellers about certain places: its aim is for travellers to 'exchange travel information, advice, hints and tips' (see www. lonelyplanet.com/thorntree/). In order to index these entries we will be looking at unsupervised methods, that is, methods that draw inferences from data sets without assigning documents to classes (Manning et al., 2009, p. 349). This means that the researcher uses algorithms that find hidden patterns or groupings in data 'by themselves'. This is the opposite of supervised methods, which make use of labelled data in which the aim is to replicate a categorical distinction that a human supervisor imposes a priori. Unsupervised methods involve no assumptions on the researcher's part about what will be found in the data – it is data-driven. This makes such methods extremely well suited for explorative research, for trying out different data sortings and transformations to tease out patterns in the corpus.

The dynamic unpacking of multiple representations and the sortation of textual data already implies a hermeneutic movement. It implies that the researcher needs to bring an affinity, or sensitivity, or a *hunch*, to the table, in order to recognise a meaningful pattern as it emerges. This also implies selecting a specific corpus of data to index: taking a random sample of content from Thorn Tree will be unlikely to yield the most interesting results. In most cases, the researcher will come to the data with a specific topic of interest in mind, as well as preformed theoretic considerations. For instance, we may take an interest in a specific geographical context, Greece, as it is a hugely popular European tourist destination and may involve discursive content about its recent social, political and economic turmoil (most saliently, the Syrian refugee crisis and the country's debt issues).

A familiar epistemological issue arises here. Is this type of inquiry, in which we filter natural discourses based on certain theoretical assumptions, a form of confirmation bias? It is worth revisiting Foucault, who emphasised the gaps within and, more broadly, the epistemic affordances of discourse. Discourse, after all, refers to a particular linguistic matrix that the researcher may lay bare. Similarly, the Foucauldian episteme – the total set of relations that determine a historical form of discourse – is not some 'system of postulates that governs all the branches of knowledge [*connaissance*]', but rather 'a constantly moving set of articulations, shifts, and coincidences that are established only to give rise to others' (Foucault, 1972, p. 191). We ought, in other words, to take a nominalist stance and doubt the generic integrity of any *forms* of discourse that we may exhume in our endeavours. We can speak of literary discourse, political discourse, and so on, but it is much harder to talk about literature or politics as definite types. All forms of utterance are permeable: no set of utterances can be thought of as a delimited, structured field. To Foucault, this is also related to the role of the author, who is a function of discourse instead of an authority or originator. Instead of trying to *confirm* anything, thus, what these sortations offer is rather a technique to try out specific lenses, prisms or perspectives on a certain form of discourse. The theoretical sophistication of the argument, and the (de)merits of the specific type of sortation, will ultimately determine the intersubjective validity of the analysis.

On the practical end, there is an issue of ephemerality in analysing online data. Most of those texts are not systematically or linearly structured, and their existence is highly unstable. Scrap Thorn Tree, too, is continuously updated, both in terms of its layout and content. This leads to oft-discussed questions about performing research within the temporality of the on-going transformation of the Internet – 'Internet Time', as Karpf (2012) calls it. Longitudinal studies on social media, for instance, are always behind the times, as people may access these media through different interfaces and devices over time (p. 647; see also Mirzoeff, 2009). The lack of a stable methodological form for examining these stochastic and ephemeral environments might also explain, at least in part, the lack of scholarly research into these forms. However, while online text research aimed at *Verstehen* may be condemned to studying already vanishing cultural networks and patterns, we should emphasise that it might be a misguided ideal to want to compensate for the continuous reshuffling of media, platforms, or ways of talking. The aim of discourse analysis, after all, is to see the structure, the patterns, and the underlying historical tendencies of these seemingly disparate fluctuations. Thus, the question not so much becomes how to constantly update data, but when to open and close the proverbial shutter – something we will attend to further on.

Scraping and pre-processing

Web scraping, or web harvesting, is a form of data extraction from a web server using software techniques. While out-of-the-box tools for such scraping purposes do exist, many tasks will benefit from a purposefully written script that takes out exactly those elements from a website that the researcher needs, and leaves everything else 'untouched'. For instance, when scraping Thorn Tree, one might primarily be interested in the content of the posts themselves, as well as certain kinds of metadata, such as the user names and the posting date.

We can retrieve large collections of online data in two main ways: through a website's back end or data access layer, by making use of an API (Application Programming Interface), or, alternatively, through its front end or presentation layer – which is the user interface – by 'scraping' the website. An API refers to a set of routines, protocols and tools, drawn up by the owner of a web service, that provides access to the features or data of the service to (some of) its users. Gaining access to server-side information through a company-provided API, if possible, is highly recommended, as it constitutes a lawful form of data collection sanctioned by its legal owner. The first question when encountering any web platform is thus whether an API is available. In the case of Thorn Tree, no API is offered. Yet, like many other platforms, Thorn Tree owns all of the content created by its users,[2] and using a scraper without written permission is not allowed in its terms of service. Here, the researcher is at risk of breaching the website's terms of use, and the issue of copyright versus 'fair use' comes into play, especially when copyrighted content is directly reproduced in the academic paper. In the legal frameworks of many countries, there is a difference between the legality of scraping (which may constitute a breach of contract with the service provider but does not constitute an illegal act), and the legality of publishing scraped content (which is a form of copyright breach). These legal specifics depend on state and federal law, and are continuously changing along with the Internet itself. Any researcher wishing to undertake a scrape will thus have to tread lightly and will typically have to clear it with their university's ethical board.

The issue that must then be faced is one of ethics. How do we decide upon the sufficiency and admissibility of scraping this kind of personally created and privately owned data (instead of public domain data that literary scholars are often dealing with)? The Ethics Working Committee of the AoIR (Association of Internet Researchers) has published two major reports to assist researchers in making ethical decisions in their research, which we might take as a point of departure. They highlight a number of key guiding principles that have to be taken into account when performing Internet research, most of which are process- and context-dependent (Markham and Buchanan, 2012). One question pertains to the privacy of subjects. Surely, much text mining research would be impossible if traditional degrees of human consent were constantly required. This has led some to argue that studies on computer-mediated communication are 'more akin to the study of tombstone epitaphs, graffiti, or letters to the editors. Personal? Yes. Private? No.' (Rafaeli, as quoted in Sudweeks and Rafaeli, 1996, p. 121). The AoIR[3] report notes that any kind of Internet research should take heed of the vulnerability of the subjects existing behind or within even seemingly impersonal research data and avatarial representations. Research should weigh the rights of the subjects under scrutiny against the social benefits of research, and meditate on what the individual or cultural definitions and expectations of 'public' and 'private' expressions are. This ethical reflexivity, finally, should be maintained through all stages of the research project (Markham and Buchanan, 2012).

A few things might be noted about the privacy of the subjects on Thorn Tree. First, while a considerable amount of them write under a synonym, they could easily be traced if they were to be cited directly through a literal Google search. Yet when it comes to user posts on this forum, we might note that the kinds of discourse on offer will in most cases not contain vulnerable information about the users themselves. Further, as users agree to the publication of their reviews, asking for individual consent seems unnecessary.

If the researcher decides upon proceeding with the data gathering, there are some well-known open source Python packages readily available, such as BeautifulSoup or Scrapy. These are essentially pre-programmed collections of code (mostly functions and classes) that the researcher may download to simplify the task of scraping a website. BeautifulSoup,[4] for instance, provides functions for the user to find specific HTML or CSS elements in the website's code, and then scrape the content 'within' those elements. The user then simply writes a loop using these functions, which starts on a user-defined search query (for instance, the main forum page for Greece[5]) and accesses all the pages in the search results, while retrieving the content for each entry. One notable best practice for scraping is to spread out the requests to the server when writing a scraping script, so that the server does not overload. The data is typically saved into a manageable file format, such as a .csv (Comma Separated Values) or .xml (Extensible

Markup Language) file, which can be accessed with another script in the pre-processing stage.

It should be noted that scraping involves a number of caveats. First, scraping scripts are highly unstable, as websites tend to be updated continually and even a single change in the HTML format of a page can destabilise a script. Second, scripts will often automatically 'click through' subsequent pages of a website (for instance, by finding the 'next page' tag in the HTML of a page). The researcher should therefore implement a method for detecting duplicates in the scraped entries. Blogs or platforms may be organised in unexpected ways, and duplicate posts are fairly common. Since many scraping scripts are imperfect, we need to check whether there are any duplicates in the downloaded list of text files. One way of programmatically doing this is through using a hash table, which in this case attributes the byte size of every text file in our collection to a unique identifier. When two identifiers are the same, we can remove the duplicates.

Another issue pertains to the syntactic 'noise' inherent in social media texts, with lexical variants and acronyms being regularly used in such discourses (Java, 2007; Becker et al., 2009; Preotiuc-Pietro et al., 2012; Yin et al., 2012; Eisenstein, 2013; Baldwin et al., 2013). These can be normalised (automatically converted based on a small algorithm, e.g. 'smh' for 'shaking my head'), but this does not seem necessary for our current purposes: in the top 1,000 most-frequent words of our corpus, no such variants could be found. We can then index the size of the corpus we are dealing with. Our corpus has a total word count of 3,173,974 words: this is certainly not 'big data', in that it does not pertain to 'datasets whose size is beyond the ability of typical database software tools to capture, store, manage, and analyze' (Manyika et al., 2011). We might, however, call it 'bigger data', which both in terms of its amount and form (i.e. many different authors) might be approached differently than from a typical close reading perspective. Many types of independent humanities research will deal with corpora of roughly this size, instead of the relational databases that are usually called big data: it is argued that these 'bigger datasets' still benefit from digital tools.

If we filter our corpus by year (a valuable form of sortation if we are interested in the development and change of topics through time), we can see that the sizes of the subcorpora per year are strikingly different (see Table 6.1).

If we want to compare word counts between subcorpora, we would need to normalize the counts to account for these different sizes. Further, since 2004 and 2006 contain such a radically low word count, they might best be discarded from the analysis altogether. We may also note that the word count in 2015 goes down significantly, as the analysis was run in August of that year. Regardless, it seems that the number of posts on Thorn Tree has peaked in 2007, and has since been decreasing.

The next stage may involve differing types and degrees of data transformation. For instance, the researcher may want to remove stop words from the corpus, or choose to 'compress' the data by stemming, lemmatising, or POS

Table 6.1 Word count frequencies per subcorpus

Subcorpus	Frequency
2004	836
2006	5,178
2007	612,004
2008	383,107
2009	328,044
2010	333,016
2011	408,032
2012	388,796
2013	276,664
2014	249,757
2015	188,540

(part of speech) tagging the data. By lemmatising all the words in a corpus, for instance, one ends up with a significantly smaller number of word types. If we then agree that such types of reduction do not impede upon the themes that are discussed in the data, they can assist in teasing out macroscopic patterns in a large corpus. For instance, one might want to analyse a corpus based upon the usage of nouns, which are argued to be especially suitable for capturing thematic trends (Jockers, 2013, p. 131). In this stage, as well as the ones succeeding it, trying out different types of transformations is key: textual corpora behave in unexpectedly different ways and since we are not looking to corroborate a hypothesis but simply tease out discursive patterns in a text, we might, for instance, try a filter for verbs (to distinguish types of behaviour) or pronouns (to find patterns of gender). Such POS tagging can further be applied to compare grammatical functions of certain words (such as checking whether the word 'travel' is used dominantly as a verb or a noun – the latter of which could possibly indicate a thematic calibration).

Analysis and representation: word counts

With the corpus transformed, the next question is how we can start exploring the corpus for trends and patterns. First, the researcher may be interested in a measure of difference between the subcorpora (which, in our case, are composed of the years in which posts were posted). These differences can be calculated in several ways: popular varieties include Euclidian distance, and cosine similarity. First, we want to count all the words in all the files and represent them in what is called a document-term matrix. We can create one easily through the Python package, *Scikit-learn*, which offers a series of options for what is called vectorisation[6] (i.e. the conversion of a collection of text documents to a matrix of token counts). We can then calculate the distance between subcorpora by comparing the word frequencies associated with each subcorpus. The Euclidean distance between two vectors in the plane derives from geometry, where it is the length of the hypotenuse that joins two vectors. There are Python packages that can calculate Euclidian distances (Scikit-learn is one of them), which take as an input the document-topic matrix.

Additionally, the texts will often be normalised through TF-IDF (Term Frequency – Inverse Document Frequency) transformation. Term Frequency measures the number of times a term (or word) occurs in a document (similar to the document-term matrix). These may additionally be normalised to take the difference in size of our subcorpora into account, by dividing the word frequency by the total number of words in that document. Inverse Document Frequency, then, is a way to weigh down terms that occur frequently throughout the entire corpus (articles, prepositions, certain pronouns, and so on), and to weigh up less-frequently occurring terms (as we suspect these words to be more 'telling' of a certain document or subcorpus). To calculate the IDF score, we simply divide the total number of documents by the number of documents in which a certain word occurs, and then take the logarithm of that quotient. Finally, we multiply the normalised TF and IDF scores per word to acquire their TF-IDF score.

Next, we can calculate the cosine distances between these TF-IDF scores, in order to see if there are any notable subcorpora (which, in our case, are made up of years) in terms of word usage. Cosine similarity is a mathematical technique for measuring the angular similarity between two vectors, i.e. geometric structures with both length (called magnitude) and direction. Essentially, now that we have transformed our collection of words into a collection of numbers, it becomes possible to calculate the differences between these numbers. Of course, such a bag-of-words approach will ignore many important aspects of sentence structure dependencies between words, roles played by the various arguments in the sentence, and so on (see also Mihalcea et al., 2006).

Scikit-learn offers a function to calculate cosine distances, though we need to 'flip' the measure in order to calculate cosine difference instead of similarity (to do so, we simply deduct the cosine similarity from 1). We can proceed to visualise the distances between the subcorpora using these quotients. To do so, we need to assign a point in a plane to each subcorpus, in which the distance between the points is proportional to the pairwise distances; this is called multidimensional scaling (MDS). Scikit-learn offers a function that yields precisely such a distance matrix, and we can proceed to visualise it using Pyplot, a well-known plotting package for Python. As we can see, the resulting graph shows that the language in the blogs are about equally distant from each other; no one year stands out in terms of word usage (Figure 6.1).

If, however, we add a corpus of 60,000 similar texts from the forum of TripAdvisor – also detailing trips to Greece, 2014 – we see that the difference in word usage with Thorn Tree is significant. In short, there does seem to be a generic integrity to the types of forum exchanges based on the platform (Figure 6.2).

Next, the researcher may perform a very broad review of the notably frequent words in the corpus to index prevalent themes. One package that is very often used for such purposes, besides Scikit-learn, is NLTK[7] (Natural Language Toolkit), offering functions for tokenising, collocations, stemming, and so on.

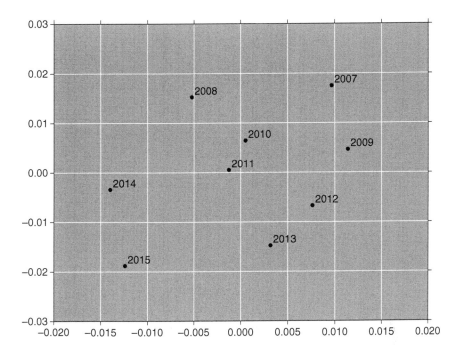

Figure 6.1 Cosine distances between subcorpora using TF-IDF for Thorn Tree.

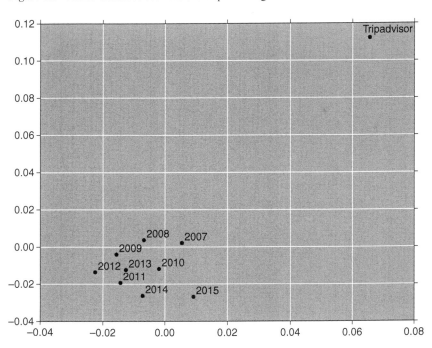

Figure 6.2 Cosine distances between subcorpora using TF-IDF for TripAdvisor.

Such an analysis, which bases itself on straightforward word counts and, in steps, branches out to their linguistic contexts, is deceptively simple. It is a heuristic method, involving trial and error: it needs to take into account the plurality of modalities, meanings and functions of the words it considers; it needs to decide whether to sort the words by lemma or lexeme; it needs to accept that many normalised keywords will not be analytically interesting. Yet the method allows a pointed cross-examination of a totality of texts that would be impossible to achieve otherwise.

It turns out that the most-used word in the corpus is, perhaps unsurprisingly, 'Athens' (with 14,645 tokens), followed by the words 'would' and 'time'. What do these words mean? To find this out, we can look at the clusters and concordances of these words: that is, the context in which they arise. Some simple operations can give the researcher a better image of the corpus at hand; for instance, we can iterate through the corpus randomly and manually sift through a number of concordances, so that the researcher does not favour a certain subcorpus by starting alphabetically. The auxiliary verb 'would' appears most frequent in the semantic function of communicating desire or inclination, with the trigram 'would like to' (1,171 instances). In this specific context, sifting through the corpus shows that the word commonly refers to the intentions of prospective visitors to certain places, leading to a question that brings them to the forum. 'Time', which acts as a verb only sporadically (268 times) and almost solely as a noun (11,135 times), appears most frequently in the trigram 'time of year' (576 instances), which points towards preferable or undesirable times of year in which a trip should be undertaken.

We could imagine being more specifically interested in one certain topic: for instance, relating the two recent socio-economic crises in Greece – the government debt and the Syrian refugees, respectively – to the language of tourism and the accounts of travellers to the country. To find this out, we could do a manual search for words that could be of interest, such as 'refugee' or 'economic'. This is where lemmatisation or stemming can prove useful since, for instance, entering the lemma will also yield the instances of related terms such as the plural 'refugees'. First, we may want to check the top words in the corpus to see if any words come up that may appear indicative of our topic of interest. In our example we will find that even the top 100 words, with stopwords removed, do not include any words that indicate socio-political talk. This means we should look for those words ourselves. We could look, for example, at the relative frequency (compared to the total amount of words in the subcorpus in which it arises) of the word 'refugee' in the lemmatised corpus. In terms of time, this yields a very clear image (Figure 6.3).

The next step can be to see what the lexical context of this word looks like, in other words, in what context they arise. Sifting through such concordance search results randomly has the heuristic benefit of allowing the researcher to read, line after line, the sentences surrounding the search term, so that she can focus on discursive patterns. For instance, randomly going through the Thorn Tree corpus yields the following first posts:

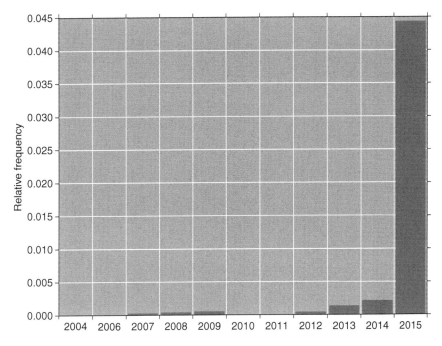

Figure 6.3 Relative frequencies of 'refugee', normalised to total number of words in the subcorpus.

> … as I can judge from a distance the refugees are given food and a place to sleep.…

> … at this time of year there are no refugees in the Cyclades.…

> … they might think me one of the refugees or someone trying to get into.…

> … get a grip for heaven's sake, they're refugees, illegal immigrants.…

We can already see several usages of the word arise: the first is that of the citizen journalist who reports on the treatment of refugees; the second refers to practical matter of when one might expect refugees in the Cyclades islands; the third involves a tourist who worries about being mistaken for a refugee; and the fourth is voiced by a user who emphasises the illegality of refugees. As we can see, such a randomised concordance reading can give an insight into the breadth of the content of the comments on the forum, the clashing of ideologies and the social effects of language.

Analysis and representation: topic modelling

Another popular method to distil topics from a large collection of files is through topic modelling. Topic modelling programs automatically extract topics from texts, taking a single text or corpus and searching for patterns in the use of words, attempting to inject semantic meaning into vocabulary. A topic, to the program, is a list of words that occur in statistically meaningful ways. Topic modelling is unsupervised – that is, the program running the analysis does not know anything about the meaning of the words in a text. Instead, it is assumed that any piece of text is composed by an author by selecting words from possible 'baskets' of words – the number of which is determined by the user – where each basket corresponds to a topic or discourse.[8] From this assumption it follows that one could mathematically decompose a text into the probable baskets from whence the words came. The tool goes through this process over and over again until it settles on the most likely distribution of words into baskets, resulting in the titular topics.

There are many different topic modelling programs available; in this chapter we use the well-known package of MALLET (McCallum, 2002). The topic models it produces provide us with probabilistic data sortations, which we may argue are indicative of certain discursive gravitational points and latent structures behind a collection of texts. The researcher can then contextualise these structures using a relevant theoretic framework. The Mining the Dispatch project of the University of Richmond, for instance, uses MALLET to explore 'the dramatic and often traumatic changes as well as the sometimes surprising continuities in the social and political life of Civil War Richmond'.[9] Another example can be found in the work of historian Cameron Blevins, who uses MALLET to 'recognize and conceptualize the recurrent themes' in Martha Ballard's diary.[10]

Engaging in topic modelling, like most digital tools, is a matter of trial and error; of trying different scopes and focus points so as to find patterns in the data. As such, it is vital to perform many different analyses, for instance, making use of the lemmatised corpus, or the noun-filtered corpus, as well as different sizes of topic models (e.g. one iteration with ten topics, one with 50, one with 100). A first thing to be noted is that topic models based on multi-user-generated data (instead of representing a comparison between single authors, as is often done in literary studies) yield very few clear patterns, even when we sort the data chronologically. This undoubtedly mirrors the heteroglossia of the many voices on offer. However, some significant patterns may be found: in our case, it turns out that a 100-topic, noun-based model of the corpus yields one topic that immediately 'makes sense' (Figure 6.4).

What we see here is a rather straightforward topic that associates certain types of weather with months of the year (the X-axis 'corpus segment' refers to all of the documents in the corpus, which are ordered chronologically). We can see that the discourse about the weather (involving both keywords for summer as for winter) peaks in certain points: looking closer, we then learn that this is in winter, when weather conditions are unfavourable. This mirrors the earlier

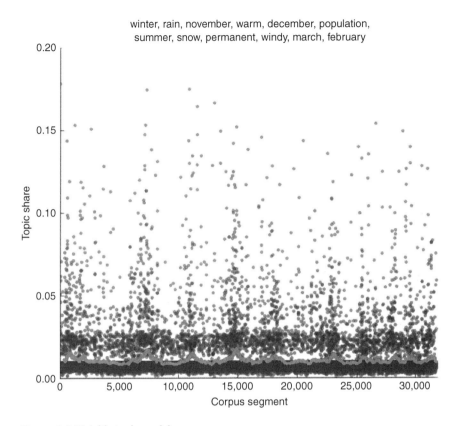

Figure 6.4 Notable topic model.

finding where the frequent word cluster 'time of year' indicated a typically tour-istic interest in the seasonal aspect of time and when to visit a place.

We could now offer some further suggestions based on this image: Thorn Tree users appear to speak of the weather more frequently as it becomes less favourable. We might then proceed with a sentiment analysis to corroborate those findings, or start reading the stories taking place in winter from up close. We may also note that the words 'permanent' and 'population' also appear in this topic, seemingly unrelatedly. We can quickly find, however, that the word 'permanent' is most commonly associated with the word 'population' in the corpus. And 'permanent population', when regarding its broader context, proves to appear in the context of Greek islands, such as Crete and the Cyclades. It appears that the topic of the weather is most salient on the Greek islands. It is an unsurprising finding, as those islands typically form the backdrop for beach holi-days, with the associated expected types of weather – but the way of tracking this issue through topic modelling is promising regardless.

Discussion

In the above we have outlined several strategies to sort and analyse online textual data, for the purpose of answering straightforward questions about the formation of corpora and the discursive patterns therein. It was shown that different sortations and representations allow for different epistemological moves. An important element of this type of analysis has thus far been kept implicit: it is a method involving, time and again, forms of disappointment. We will not always find meaningful patterns of relations in bigger datasets, and even if we do, they will not necessarily lead to fruitful and productive close reading and interpretation. The data set we have used here is an example: for instance, we have found very little evidence of socio-political discourse in the corpus, and the patterns that did arise could be explained by rather trivial circumstances. We could leave it at that but, as we noted before, text mining in the humanities should not become a matter of hypothesis confirmation. What this lack of meaning implies is not that the method is unfit or the narratives it looks at are uninteresting, rather, that certain tools will be found better suited for certain datasets. 'Shooting with many guns' means that many shots will not hit the mark, and communicating these misfires should be an integral part of writing papers that leverage digital methods.

Some words might be spent, then, on the function that Digital Humanities (DH) tools may have in the broader field of the humanities. In general terms, DH is a field that is perhaps best not to be distinguished by its tools, but rather by the questions that these tools bring about. Digital methods allow us many avenues of insight into the same problems the humanities have always struggled with. As the use of digital tools becomes increasingly popular and accessible, we need to establish ethical guidelines on a case-by-case basis that deal with the novel issues that each project finds itself facing. We should also take at heart the criticism from the likes of Stanley Fish: digital strategies should not just follow whatever surprising statistical facts may appear, without due contextualisation. Beyond such issues of ethics and data dredging, the problem-solving approach that DH internalises could foster not a reduction, but a multiplication of both knowledge and discussion.

Notes

1 Busa was a Jesuit scholar who lemmatised the works of Thomas Aquinas. His *Index Thomisticus*, originally published in the 1970s, can today be found online: www. corpusthomisticum.org/it/index.age. All online sources were retrieved on 8 January 2017.
2 See www.lonelyplanet.com/legal/website-terms/
3 The Association of Internet Researchers.
4 See www.crummy.com/software/BeautifulSoup/
5 See www.lonelyplanet.com/thorntree/forums/europe-western-europe/greece
6 See http://scikitlearn.org/stable/modules/generated/sklearn.feature_extraction.text.Count Vectorizer.html
7 See www.nltk.org/

8 As Ted Underwood (2012) notes, 'The notion that documents are produced by discourses rather than authors is alien to common sense, but not alien to literary theory.'
9 See Nelson (n.d.).
10 See Blevins (2010).

References

Ampofo, L., Collister, S., Loughlin, B., and Chadwick, A. (2015). Text mining and social media: When quantitative meets qualitative and software meets people. In P. Halfpenny and R. Procter (Eds.) *Innovations in Digital Research Methods.* London: SAGE.

Andrejevic, M., Hearn, A., and Kennedy, H. (2015). Cultural studies of data mining: Introduction. *European Journal of Cultural Studies, 18*(4–5), 379–394. doi:10.1177/1367549415577395.

Asur, S., and Huberman, B.A. (2010). Predicting the future with social media. Paper presented at the International Conference on Web Intelligence and Intelligence Agent Technology Conference, York University, Toronto, Canada.

Awan, A.N., Hoskins, A., and O'Loughlin, B. (2011). *Radicalisation and media: terrorism and connectivity in the new media ecology.* London: Routledge.

Baker, P. (2004). Querying keywords: Questions of difference, frequency and sense in keywords analysis. *Journal of English Linguistics, 32*(4), 346–359. doi: 10.1177/0075424204269894.

Baldwin, T., Cook, P., Lui, M., Mackinlay, A., and Wang, L. (2013). How noisy social media text, how different social media sources? Paper presented at the Association for Computational Linguistics 6th International Joint Conference on Natural Language Processing, Nagoya, Japan.

Becker, H., Naaman, M., and Gravano, L. (2009). Event identification in social media. In *Proceedings of the 12th International Workshop on the Web and Databases*, Providence, USA.

Blanton, C. (2002). *Travel writing: The self and the world.* New York: Routledge.

Blevins, C. (2010). Topic modeling Martha Ballard's diary. Retrieved from www.cameronblevins.org/posts/topic-modeling-martha-ballards-diary/.

Bollen, J. (2011). Computational economic and finance gauges: polls, search, and Twitter. Paper presented at the Behavioral Economics Working Group, Behavioral Finance Meeting, Palo Alto, CA.

boyd, d. and Crawford, K. (2011). Six provocations for Big Data. Paper presented at the Oxford Internet Institute conference, A Decade in Internet Time: Symposium on the Dynamics of the Internet and Society, University of Oxford. doi: 10.2139/ssrn.1926431.

Edensor, T. (2001). Performing tourism, staging tourism. *Tourist Studies, 1*(1), 59–81.

Eisenstein, J., O'Connor, B., Smith, N.A., and Xing, E.P. (2010). A latent variable model for geographic lexical variation. Paper presented at Association for Computational Linguistics' Conference on Empirical Methods in Natural Language Processing, Cambridge, MA.

Eisenstein, J. (2013). What to do about bad language on the internet. In *Proceedings of the 2013 Conference of the North American Chapter of the Association for Computational Linguistics: Human Language Technologies,* pp. 359–369, Atlanta, GA, USA.

Flowerdew, J. (1997). The discourse of colonial withdrawal: A case study in the creation of mythic discourse. *Discourse and Society, 8*(4): 453–477.

Foucault, M. (1972). *The archaeology of knowledge.* New York: Pantheon.

Galloway, A.R. (2013). The poverty of philosophy: Realism and post-Fordism. *Critical Inquiry, 39*(2): 347–366.

Java, A. (2007). A framework for modeling influence, opinions and structure in social media. Paper presented at the AAAI 22nd Annual Conference on Artificial Intelligence (AAAI-07), Vancouver, Canada.

Jockers, M. L. (2013). *Macroanalysis*. Urban, IL: University of Illinois Press.

Karpf, D. (2012). Social Science Research methods in Internet time. *Information, Communication & Society, 15*(5), 639–661. https://doi.org/10.1080/1369118X.2012.665468.

Kuehn, J., and Smethurst, P. (2015). *New directions in travel writing studies* Basingstoke: Palgrave Macmillan.

Lidman, M. (2011). Social media as a leading indicator of markets and predictor of voting patterns. Master's thesis, Umeå University.

Magnini, V.P., Crotts, J.C., and Zehrer, A. (2011). Understanding customer delight: An application of travel blog analysis. *Journal of Travel Research, 50*(5), 535–545. doi:10.1177/0047287510379162.

Mahnke, M. and Uprichard, E. (2014). Algorithming the algorithm. In R. König and M. Rasch (Eds.), *Society of the query reader: Reflections on Web search* (pp. 256–270). Amsterdam: Institute of Network Cultures.

Manning, C. D., Raghavan, P., and Schütze, H. (2009). *An introduction to information retrieval*. Cambridge: Cambridge University Press.

Manyika, J., Chui, M., Brown, B., Bughin, J., Dobbs, R., Roxburgh, C., and Hung Byers, A. (2011). Big data: The next frontier for innovation, competition, and productivity. Retrieved from www.mckinsey.com/business-functions/business-technology/our-insights/big-data-the-next-frontier-for-innovation.

Markham, A. and Buchanan, E. (2012). Ethical decision-making and internet research recommendations from the AOIR Ethics Working Committee (Version 2.0). Retrieved from http://aoir.org/reports/ethics2.pdf.

Mayes, F. (2002). *The best American travel writing*. Boston: Houghton Mifflin Company.

McCallum, A.K. (2002). MALLET: A Machine Learning for Language Toolkit. Retrieved from http://mallet.cs.umass.edu.

Mihalcea, R., Corley, C., and Strapparava, C. (2006). Corpus-based and knowledge-based measures of text semantic similarity. Paper presented at the AAAI 21st national conference on Artificial intelligence (AAAI-06), Boston, MA.

Mirzoeff, N. (2009). *An introduction to visual culture*. New York: Routledge.

Mischne, G. and Glance, N. (2006). Predicting movie sales from logger sentiment. Paper presented at the AAAI Spring Symposium on Computational Approaches to Analyzing Weblogs, Palo Alto, CA.

Moretti, F. (2005). *Graphs, maps, trees: Abstract models for a literary history*. London: Verso.

Nelson, Robert K. (n.d.). Mining the dispatch. Retrieved from http://dsl.richmond.edu/dispatch/pages/intro

Partington, A., Morley, J. and Haarman, L. (2004). *Corpora and discourse*. Bern: Peter Lang.

Peters, J.D. (2013). Calendar, clock, tower. In J. Stolow (Ed.), *Deus in machina: Religion and technology in historical perspective* (pp. 25–42). New York: Fordham University Press.

Preotiuc-Pietro, D., Samangooei, S., Cohn, T., Gibbins, N., and Niranjan, M. (2012). Trendminer: An architecture for real time analysis of social media text. Paper presented at the ICWSM Workshop on Real-Time Analysis and Mining of Social Streams, Dublin, Ireland.

Procter, R., Vis, F., and Voss, A. (2013). Reading the riots on Twitter: Methodological innovation for the analysis of big data. *International Journal of Social Research Methodology, 16*(3): 197–214.

Raban, J. (2011). Why travel? In *Driving home: An American journey*. New York: Pantheon.

Ramsay, S. (2011). *Reading machines*. Urbana, IL: University of Illinois Press.

Silverman, D. (2006). *Interpreting qualitative data: Methods for analysing talk, text and interaction* (3rd edn). London: Sage.

Sudweeks, F., and Rafaeli, S. (1996). How do you get a hundred strangers to agree? In T.M. Harrison and T. Stephen (Eds.), *Computer networking and scholarly communication in the twenty-first-century*. New York: State University of New York Press.

Underwood, T. (2012). Topic modeling made just simple enough. Retrieved from http://tedunderwood.com/2012/04/07/topic-modeling-made-just-simple-enough/.

Veinot, T. (2007). The eyes of the power company: Workplace information practices of a vault inspector. *The Library Quarterly, 77*(2): 157–180.

Yin, J., Lampert, A., Cameron, M., Robinson, B., and Power, R. (2012). Using social media to enhance emergency situation awareness. *IEEE Intelligent Systems, 27*(6): 52–59.

7 Tinder matters

Swiping right to unlock new research fields

Jenna Condie, Garth Lean and Donna James

Start where you are.

(Gibson-Graham, 2011)

Swiping (ourselves) right into research

There is no one story to tell about Tinder, the popular location-aware mobile application (app) designed primarily (but not necessarily) for dating, and how it mediates our social encounters with others. There is so much to say. Do we start with the psychology of mobile dating (e.g. Sumter, Vandenbosch, and Ligtenberg, 2017) or with Tinder's touchscreen and user design (e.g. Werning, 2015)? How can we respond to the networked possibilities and new intimacies that mobile dating apps afford (e.g. Hobbs, Owen, and Gerber, 2016) as well as the problematic behaviours being witnessed and materialised (e.g. Mason, 2016)? Starting is difficult because it matters how we frame our 'knowledges-in-the-making' (Wilson, 2009) and 'what stories we tell to tell other tell stories with' (Haraway, 2016: 12). When the world is hot, fast, urban and young (Mirzoeff, 2015), how can research on Tinder make a difference?

There is an urgent need to think, research, and write in ways that acknowledge the assemblages; the complex entanglements of technology, people (including ourselves), place and power. When you use Tinder, you are present in hybrid ways, 'matching' with people in close geographical proximity. You are intimately knotted with technology and its tentacles of networked connectedness with other social media, such as Facebook, Instagram, Snapchat, and Spotify, as well as other dating platforms such as Grindr, Bumble, and Happn. In the quest to maintain/gain a high user base, Tinder is a ever moving target with an evolving interface designed for enhanced user experience and appeal: it is a business generating profit from our most intimate relations of all. Through gamified, simplified, digital practices (the most 'iconic' being the swipe mechanism), Tinder enables partner finding at speed, and in turn contributes to a commodification of people (Werning, 2015) that raises public concern (e.g. Sales, 2015). Who has value in the '24/7 singles bar in your pocket' (Azani, 2015)? In Tinder's marketing materials, a homogeneous, heteronormative ideal is presented where 'older, gender-variant, homosexual, low socio-economic status (SES), and rural-dwelling people are absent … and featured actors are predominantly white' (Duguay, 2017: 358). Indeed, these marketing messages echo the hierarchies of gender, sexuality and race that location-aware dating apps (re)produce (Callander, Holt, and Newman, 2012; Callander, Newman, and Holt, 2015; Mason, 2016). Messy and muddled, complex and consuming, Tinder is completely inseparable from the people who use it. Without us, there is no Tinder. We therefore need to orientate towards the question: what are we becoming with Tinder?

So we start where we are, 'as specific located beings' (Gibson-Graham, 2011: 2), drawing upon personal experiences of using Tinder (mainly in Australian and European contexts) and the experiences of our research participants who have used Tinder and other location-aware apps (e.g. Backpackr, Grindr and Couch Surfer) while travelling across the world. Our first research study aimed to discover how people use location-aware social apps, including those designed primarily for dating (i.e. Tinder), during travel. Our methods were the usual suspects: an online qualitative survey and follow-up qualitative interview (via email). But we had essentially 'swiped [ourselves] right' into researching screened and technologically-mediated travel experiences in times of the 'mobile' and the 'digital'. We had witnessed the prevalence of travellers on Tinder searching for tour guides, friends, lovers, local knowledges and momentary companions; people that our main location in the cosmopolitan, densely populated, global city of Sydney in Australia brings close. We sought out the social commentaries of travel bloggers discussing the phenomena of 'Tinder travel' and 'Tinder tourism', who recommend the app and others like it as way-finders and knowledge-generators for those in places new and unknown (e.g. Davis, n.d.; Sinders, 2015). We consumed Tinder's video advertisements, attentive to the use of travel as the key narrative to sell its premium service Tinder Plus (see Tinder, 2014), which enables users to change their geo-location and therefore swipe and match with others ahead of arriving in their destination. Tinder is designed for the mobile, digital, agential one.

We knew/know a lot about Tinder outside of, and without, our formal data collection tools. How do we account for our experiences of feeling what it is like to swipe through a sea/catalogue of others: to match, to chat, and to meet with people as friends and/or as dates and/or something unexplained, in places new and old, on the move and while at home? We questioned/question the ethics of our simultaneous Tinder use and research and the composite of the two (see Condie, Lean, and Wilcockson, forthcoming). We are very much part of the 'research-assemblage' (Fox and Alldred, 2013) finding that the more immersed you are (the more 'Tindering' you do), the more acute the nuances, traces, and implications of the technology become. We swiped ourselves right into the thick of it and remain there (albeit in different guises) to stay close to the practices and doings of Tinder and other location-aware mobile dating and travel apps. Tinder is heteronormative (Duguay, 2017), and so are we: we are white, working-to-some other class, heterosexual, urban-dwelling academics. The politics of location are present in the work that we do and the knowledges we produce (Braidotti, 2013).

We focus on Tinder here, as opposed to providing a broader analysis of the plethora of apps within a saturated mobile dating/travel app market, given its prevalence with public and (our) personal realms and to 'make trouble' with the 'thick, ongoing presence' with 'all sorts of temporalities and materialities' (Haraway, 2016: 2). Tinder is how we entered the 'field'. One of us opened the field for another, then another, and also for others researching Tinder and location-aware dating apps with us as part of the 'Travel in the Digital Age' (TinDA) team at Western Sydney University, Australia. Our 'I's' are epistemo-logically inescapable and relationally dependable in our knowledge-making practices. This is particularly pertinent to the research context of mobile dating apps, where the personalised web and its algorithmic culture actively shape what you experience and who you encounter, which shapes everything thereafter. Although, our tellings here are more than reflective in that we seek to defract[1] (Barad, 2003) and document the differences that we generate in our knowledge practices (Wilson, 2009). Where reflection produces the same (e.g. like a reflected image in a mirror), diffraction deals with the effects of difference like 'the interactions of ripples from more than one stone dropped into a pool at once' (Kara, 2017: 291). We cannot disentangle ourselves from the 'field' into which we were already becoming Tinderer-researchers, as 'we do not obtain knowledge by standing outside of the world; we know because "we" are of the world'(Barad, 2003: 829). We start where we are to consider the possibilities and implications of location-aware mobile dating/travel apps for reworking social relations, mobilities, belongings, and humankind.

Becoming with Tinder: new materialism for social inquiry

To know Tinder better, we are engaging and playing with ideas and concepts that can be roughly housed together under the banner of 'new materialism'. Our new materialist engagement started after our first 'Travel in the Digital Age' (TinDA) research study of how people use location-aware social apps during travel, which has a qualitative research design, primarily consisting of online surveys (see www.tindaproject.com/participate/) and interviews. Our research methods of choice predate the conceptual considerations in this chapter, however, we seek to align and develop our theoretical-methodological entangle-ments here. To do so, we draw upon snippets of data from our TinDA projects, which include data generated through the qualitative online survey and inter-views with people who have used Tinder during travel, as well as interviews with women about their everyday experiences of using Tinder.

New materialist work seeks to 'stretch prevailing modes of subjectivity in a new direction' (Connolly, 2013: 400) by decentring the human and recognizing the agency of the material world. Karen Barad proposes an 'ethico-onto-epistemology'[2] of 'agential realism' (Barad, 2007), which offers a 'posthuman' *understanding of intra-activity that joins the human and non-human so that* '"[h]umans" are neither pure cause nor pure effect but part of the world in its open-ended becoming ... neither has privileged status in determining the other'

(Barad, 2003: 821–822). The term 'intra-action' is used as opposed to 'inter-action' to move beyond the conception that two entities (e.g. human/non-human) were previously distinct. With a new materialist framework in play, technology (smartphones and software) performs with its humans/users and these perform-ances take place somewhere. Attention turns to the much broader and more complex 'research-assemblage' of 'the bodies, things and abstractions that get caught up in social inquiry' (Fox and Alldred, 2015: 400), which includes the researchers as knowledge-makers too. Widely discussed and gaining traction within science and technology studies and gender studies (Schadler, 2016), new materialism relates to, and takes seriously, the struggles and strengths of fem-inist, postcolonial, anti-racist and queer theory in the breaking down of binaries and the examination of the boundary-making practices we engage in when 'worlding worlds' (Haraway, 2016).

The binary constructs often used in social analyses of technology and behaviour create categories and reinforce boundaries that can (and should) be considered differently, radically even. When we use Tinder, we are not in another place or another world. We are in the same realm. We do not just use Tinder. We are Tinder in that, without us, there would be no Tinder: no profiles to swipe through, no people to match and chat with. New materialist social inquiry encourages awareness and bewareness of where we place the 'agential cuts' and challenges the use of binary constructs that reinforce boundaries – human/non-human, home/away, digital/material, online/offline, male/female – to situate people, place and location-aware apps in a web of relations and 'intra-actions' (Barad, 2003). For example, Warfield (2016: 2) draws on Barad's 'agen-tial cut' to advance understandings of the selfie phenomenon, to show how the separation of 'the photo from the body, the technology, and the expressed sense of self' limits our knowledge around the 'gendered apparatuses of bodily pro-duction'. By making techno-scientific practices visible with a new materialist lens, people and technology (Tindering-Tinderers) become inseparable as the human is decentred and agency is located within 'intra-activity'. What also becomes more visible with ethico-onto-epistemological attention are the techno-scientific practices of knowledge production, where research is compiled in a 'research-assemblage' of 'micropolitics' and 'machines' (Fox and Alldred, 2015): the data collection machine, the data analysis machine, the report writing machine, the researcher-machine. In turn, the boundaries of what could and should be included in research are confused within new materialist inquiries that seek to make the behind-the-scenes workings of knowledge production both knowable and accountable. What is it that we are doing? What do our data do and produce?

In her *Cyborg Manifesto*, Haraway (1991) writes that we should take pleasure in the confusion of boundaries, as such confusion leads to a responsibility for their construction. The ethical commitment to take responsibility for the (research) stories we tell, the data we produce, and the technoscientific practices we engage in when worlding knowledges aligns closely with the more radical philosophies of feminism, anti-racism, postcolonial, and queer theory. Tinder matters and we need to get to its materialities to focus on its 'social production' rather than 'social construction' (Fox and Alldred, 2013).

> Because everyone's on Tinder, like it's so fucked up in this society like we're more connected than we have ever been before, but we're more disconnected. And it's like no one knows how to form relationships, like I don't even know how people get into relationships anymore, like, genuinely, how does that happen?
>
> (Jessica, 28)

Tinder has agency to act and produce and our research participants tell us so. As Jessica asks, how do we get into relationships now Tinder is here? Why do relationships matter and to whom? How do people move from swiping right, chatting, and dating, to long-term relationships with wedding bells and babies? Who do such questions matter the most to? There is no linear process to be tracked and a straightforward answer to conclude. What becomes is 'a branching, reversing, coalescing and rupturing flow' (Fox and Alldred, 2013: 401). Our research inquiry has branched into many research inquiries as new people come on board, projects emerge, and as our participants push us towards new questions and queries. We are decentring our focus on humans/users to acknowledge that there are many *things* in play and being assembled: other people, apps, devices, locations, distances, times, infrastructures, economies, geographies, histories, and desires that contribute to these ongoing processes of change. The profit-driven agenda behind location-aware social apps also requires consideration in our research – who wins and who loses? It is therefore not enough to locate agency with people or with technology as

> in the historical era of advanced postmodernity, the very notion of 'the human' is not only de-stabilized by technologically mediated social relations in a globally connected world, but it is also thrown open to contradictory redefinitions of what exactly counts as human.
>
> (Braidotti, 2006: 197)

What counts as human when we are seemingly struggling to form relationships without the loving arms of technology?

Within the emerging (rush of) research on Tinder, anthropocentric approaches to studying the Tinder phenomena seemingly prevail where agency – the ability to act – is located firmly within the person. Psychological studies in particular place agency with the Tinder user to the neglect of the technology's agentic capacity to act in the processes of relations and becomings. The focus might be on the user's motivations and gratifications for using Tinder (Sumter, Vandenbosch, and Ligtenberg, 2017); how our personality traits predict our Tinder use (Timmermans and De Caluwé, 2017) and anti-social Tinder 'trolling' behaviours (March, Grieve, Marrington, and Jonason, 2017); or how men and women differ in their mobile dating (Abramova, Baumann, and Krasnova, 2016; Sevi, Aral, and Eskenazi, 2017). These studies place an 'agential cut' (Barad, 2007) between the human and the non-human, the subject and the object, the man and the woman, where one is considered to be causing or marking an effect on the other. The focus is on motivations, personality traits, and individual differences (including gender) and the measurement of these socio-cognitive/biological entities, which results in 'essentialised' (Fuss, 1989), 'finalised' (Bakhtin, 1984) and 'othered' (Braidotti, 2013) accounts of the human. While 'the subject' and our subjectivities are far from redundant in a post-humanist, new materialist mode (ibid.), we need to think differently about subjectivities and what it means to be human with technology. Technology and its ability to act with people in the productions and performativities of bodies, things and power, should not be overlooked or ignored.

Tinder as a 'cyborg' research tool

If subjectivities need to be rethought in times of technological entanglement, so too do the research methods we use. Our 'Tinder Travel' study and the research inquiries that have spun from it, are predominantly qualitative by design. In the hierarchy of qualitative research methods, qualitative surveys and interviews have taken precedence, directing our attention towards 'human actions, experiences and reflections' and potentially away from the matters and 'the relations within assemblages, and the kinds of affective flows that occur between these relations' (Fox and Alldred, 2013: 402). The methodological risks of employing a qualitative research design that centres human experiences are that we produce oversimplified, depoliticised, dislocated representations of reality. How do the research methods we use, our 'social science apparatus' (Ruppert, Law, and Savage, 2013), need to change in times of the 'digital'? Is there something right under our noses?

In a review of new materialist research, Fox and Alldred (2013) found a preference for qualitative research designs, particularly ethnography, sometimes with an auto-ethnographic component, as well as in-depth qualitative interviewing. They note that qualitative research designs are likely favoured due to their capacity to produce contextualised understandings of social phenomena. It is perhaps unsuprising that discursive forms of data generation continue in new materialist work, given the power that language has been granted through social research practices where even materiality is turned into 'a matter of language or some other form of cultural representation' (Barad, 2003: 801). Still, surveys and interviews that privilege language or discourse and a 'dialogical epistemology' (Cooper and Condie, 2016) enable researchers to 'get at' digitally mediated practices. As participants recount their Tinder experiences, their digital practices and 'doings' (Barad, 2003), the becomings and flows (Fox and Alldred, 2013), can be known:

> I worked in tech so I also had little bug bears about the way it [Tinder] worked. Like you use iMessage or a text and it comes through instantly,

whereas with Tinder a message just sits there and be like err, I'm gonna be 5 minutes now before you have the next message and I was like, this is no way to have a conversation when I'm trying to make friends with this person.

(William, 29)

Fox and Alldred (2013) propose that new materialist researchers need to systematically 'dredge' all sorts of empirical data sources to know about the affects of bodies and things, to then piece together and identify the social relations and formations in motion. We can ask participants questions about Tinder but we can also look at it ourselves. Tinder is an acutely visual platform, which begs to be seen. Using dialogical research methods alone potentially limits access to the visuality of Tinder. According to Tinder (2014), its users are swiping through a collective 1.6 billion profiles per day where the primary focus of the app's interface are photographs. So many people are looking at the visual images of so many others. Gaining ethical approval to look at Tinder, to analyse profiles, or to ask participants to use Tinder as part of their interviews, is more difficult than gaining approval for the 'arm's length' and 'eyes averted' surveys and interviews. Auto-ethnographical approaches are notable within new materialist research (Fox and Alldred, 2013) and can add much to the research stories we tell about human-technology assemblages of contemporary dating and partner seeking, including Tinder's ever pressing visuality:

I sign back up to Tinder to practice what we preach about Tinder matters and the potentialities for social research methods. I'm now very partnered and disclaim this in my bio with 'here for research purposes only'. Tinder sets my search criteria to men aged 23–43, ten years either side of my age, and within 80 kilometres of me and my phone. The first profile up is a blonde-haired, blue-eyed, white man in a white polo shirt with a tattooed sleeve, seven years my junior and only 3 kilometres away. I'd put my money on him being British. I try to get back to my settings page but the app's design has changed since I was last here. I can't get out of the swiping function. Tinder's forcing me to see his pictures, to see him. I click top left, then top right and end up at the 'recommend to a friend' or 'report' options. If I'm not careful, I'm going to end up superliking the very first profile I see.

Drawing upon our own experiences enables us to emphasise the nuances of human-technological performances with Tinder as well as the complexities of being there as a Tinderer-researcher. Kara (2017) notes that auto-ethnographic methods can be productive in terms of researcher creativity, which for us, has instigated more visual methodological strategies to embrace the discursive-materiality of location-aware technologies. For example, we now ask interview participants to draw their mobile dating experiences on maps of the Greater Sydney Region to tease out and visualise the spatialised relations of place, identity, and the classed, gendered, sexualised and racialised social encounters made possible within the Tinder assemblage. There is also something to be gained in terms of outing and accounting for our research practices. We can start to trace our 'knowledges-in-the-making' (Wilson, 2009) to share with others working and interested in this field.

'Entering the field' has long been discussed as a complex set of processes and negotiations, often involving gatekeepers who open the field for us in the early stages of research (Gobo, 2008). Yet now it takes just a few downloads, clicks, sign-ups, and swipes to unlock new research spaces that offer opportunities and possibilities for a deep engagement with the 'thick, ongoing present' (Haraway, 2016) and the hybrid entanglements of humans, technologies, and places. To experience Tinder is to know it is alive and lively and dynamic. Drawing a boundary between researcher and Tinderer is haphazard. When you are active in the 'field' and reside there for a while, you get a strong sense of the ongoing processes, and the twists and turns of your life circumstances intra-acting with the apps in unpredictable ways. Only when you remain there and engage in the discursive-material practices of swiping, matching, chatting, and meeting, do the capabilities of Tinder as a research tool become visible. Notably so as a medium through which to learn about, and join in with, other people and practices within a place:

> At home alone in a new city (and single), I plucked up the courage to download Tinder. The risks were still that someone I knew – a new acquaintance, colleague or student even – could discover me on Tinder. Being on Tinder presented 'trouble' for my 'identity work' but much less work than it would have done in my hometown. Troubles aside, Tinder was full of insights about my new town and the people here – who they are, where they are from, why they are here, what they like, where they go, what they want, what they do, and how they live in this city.

There are many themes of significance in the above retrospective telling of a researcher's entering of our new research field. Briefly, the story aims to highlight that location and place are central to how you use Tinder and who you can be there; there is a closeness or nearness to Tinder in terms of encountering known people (the implications of which are tied to the app's facilitation of casual sex and its associated stigma that is more pronounced for women); and that Tinder provides a specific position from which to witness people in place and the lives lived there. Where you are shapes who you are and how you 'be' with Tinder. It has taken us a while to engage more deeply with ethnographic practices such as participant observation and auto-ethnographic methods to know Tinder better. We articulate elsewhere (Condie, Lean and Wilcockson, forthcoming) that our moves towards research designs that centre other people's experiences and avoid our own, might reflect our discomfort with 'being there' (Pink et al., 2015) in an ethnographic sense. Our initial research focus on travel, as opposed to 'everyday' or even 'home' use, also works to create distance from ourselves and our ordinary daily lives. We produce an 'agential cut' between 'home' and 'away', a boundary that is not very clear-cut at all with technology.

The above story of joining Tinder invokes the concept of the *flâneur* or *cyber-flâneur*, literary figures that 'walk worlds' (Wilson, 2009). Shaw points out:

> If you are in any way involved in the analysis of urban culture, you, at some point, are forced to confront the extraordinary persistence of the *flâneur* as a figure that haunts both modern and postmodern concepts of urban subjectivity.
>
> (2015: 1–2)

There is plenty to say about urban life with Tinder but who gets to say it? Given the privilege associated with the *flâneur* as someone with a masculine freedom to explore urban life without the threat and risk of being 'out of place', Shaw turns to Haraway's (1991) notion of the cyborg, which is perhaps a granddaughter of the *flâneur* (Shields, 2006). Wilson (2009: 500) extends the notion of cyborgs for ontological hybridity (as a hybrid of machine and organism) to argue for cyborg epistemologies that 'enact hybrid ways of knowing'. By staying close to the phenomenon, as 'cyborging' (Kitchin, 1998), hybrid, entangled researchers, can we better understand 'how the social is materialized in and saturated with device' (Ruppert, Law, and Savage, 2013: 24) as well as witness the geographies of 'cyber-urban' (Forlano, 2015) spaces that are becoming with location-aware mobile apps?

The location-awareness of modern dating technologies differentiates what we now have from past iterations (e.g. online dating websites). As Tinder simply cannot work without knowing where you are (your geo-location), it is rather ironic that anthropocentric, psychologised research on location-aware mobile dating apps skirts around location by decontextualising the social encounters made possible by them. Even though our skin acts as a 'corporeal boundary', humans 'are figured by and in steady interconnection with their environment, and they cannot be perceived and described without it' (Schadler, 2016: 506). Our focus on travel has enabled us to prioritise the location-awareness of contemporary dating/travel apps and forced us to think in terms of flows, movements, processes and situatedness. The exchange between TinDA project interviewer Scarlett and research participant Jennifer (aged 25) provides an example of how humans and their swiping practices are figured and embedded within where they are:

SCARLETT [INTERVIEWER]: Would you say you use Tinder as casually [for casual sex] as you did travelling at home?

JENNIFER: Na [no], not really.

SCARLETT [INTERVIEWER]: Why not, do you think?

JENNIFER: Sometimes I'm scared, well, here I'm more strategic because of where I work, in case they're [other Tinder users] a client from work. Because a lot of people have come up [as profiles on Tinder] and I'm like na

[no], just swipe left and keep going because they are clients. I'll look to see if we've got mutual friends and I don't mind the people. And because I'm here permanently, I go to a lot more effort, you know, stalk them first, whereas overseas I just kept swiping, it didn't even matter.

Jennifer articulates how the social stigma of online dating and casual sex persists (David and Cambre, 2016; Duguay, 2017) but arguably fades further away from home. So too does risk it seems, although our research participants indicate that digitally mediated social encounters are gendered and in order to trust someone to meet them, women do a lot more work to 'stalk' and stay safe. Embracing more spatialised understandings of the human (Tucker, 2011) positions Tinder and Tinderers as locational, relational, temporal, mobile, discursive, and material. In new materialist social inquiry, the mobilities and ongoing processes can be attended to for a situated understanding of Tinder that is sensitive to our lives of 'code and place' (Forlano, 2015).

A most compelling example of how the smartphone and Tinder reassemble 'social science apparatus' (Ruppert, Law, and Savage, 2013) comes from anthropologist Anya Evans (2017) and her research examining the politics of space in the Occupied Palestinian West Bank. The impossibilities of engaging with geographical proximate but socially separated groups are sidestepped with Tinder, a space 'not restricted by the occupation's enforced ethnic separation, placing Palestinians, Israelis, and IOF soldiers on a relatively equal playing field of access' (Evans, 2017). Evans' (2017) ethnographic field notes can be interpreted with Barad's (2007) notion of diffraction in that they do more than reflect, they document the ripple effects of being there on her knowledge-making and the ethical entanglements of doing research in the romantic and sexual spaces of Tinder.

The aim to defract rather than reflect brings to the fore our initial research questions to understand how people use location-aware social apps such as Tinder during travel. Why do we want to know this? What differences are we trying to make in the knowledge machine? What figurations can we produce to do justice? What participants have told us so far is entangled with our theoretical engagements with feminist new materialism. We do not all travel with Tinder equally. By bearing witness to the thick present of our research field, we are moving towards more urgent questions around travel and consumption, the impacts of for-profit motives on intimate relationships, as well as the persistence of colonialism, patriarchy, and racism present within human-technology-place relations. Tinder is far from trivial and we can think and do differently and seriously in feminist new materialist mode.

Tomorrow's relations

As researchers, we must not shy away from the responsibilities of knowledge-making. We must confront the present in all its complexities to consider what we are becoming with technology. A new materialism framework where matter matters, and Tinder matters, where 'neither discursive practices nor material phenomena are ontologically or epistemologically prior' (Barad, 2003: 822) can embrace the complexities and responsibilities of knowing, being and doing. Tinder matters in that it makes and remakes social relations and cultural practices.

Tinder provides more than snapshots into contemporary social life and its networked intimacies: it is a way-finder, knowledge-generator, friendship-giver, sex-sorter, game-changer, time-passer, soul-destroyer, esteem-giver, self-depressor, sushi-train, love-machine. We make Tinder and Tinder makes us. What are we becoming in times of technological entanglement? What is human-technology doing to our relationships and intimacies? By being willingly entangled in Tinder, we hope to develop research questions and inquiries that matter and take response-ability for the research stories we tell.

From our ethico-onto-epistemologies to our hybrid research tools, the techno-scientific academic practices we engage in have consequences for the knowledge we produce. A research focus on travel and travelling has both enabled us and required us to decentre human experiences and to encompass location, place, gender, technology, app design and all of the other things. Given the rapidity of global change, new materialist ethico-onto-ontologies are providing many researchers with the necessary frameworks with which to understand digital technologies in different and radical ways. It is important to question the boundary-making practices of research where we produce knowledge that assumes a boundary between the human and the non-human, the subject and the object, the online and the offline, as well as home and away. An anthropocentric approach to researching location-aware technologies does not do justice to the affective capacities of technology, and the situatedness of everyday, ordinary, digitally mediated lives. When the 'field' is an app on your phone that is in your hand, in your home and every place else you go, the rules of research need rewriting.

Acknowledgements

With thanks to Scarlett McCarthy and Rosy Dennington who produced datasets for Travel in the Digital Age (TinDA) as part of their Psychology Honours theses in 2016. We would also like to thank those who have participated in our research, and attendees of the Feminist Scholars Digital Workshop 2017, who provided feedback on this chapter.

Notes

1 'Diffraction is a mapping of interference, not of replication, reflection, or reproduction' (Barad, 2003: 803).
2 Barad (2007) introduces 'ethico-onto-epistemology' to intertwine questions of ethics, knowing (epistemology) and being (ontology) that have been improperly separated in research practices.

References

Abramova, O., Baumann, A., and Krasnova, H. (2016). Gender differences in online dating: what do we know so far? A systematic literature review. In 49th Hawaii International Conference on System Sciences (HICSS). IEEE Xplore Retrieved from http://ieeexplore.ieee.org/abstract/document/7427665/

Bakhtin, M. (1984). *Problems of Dostoevsky's Poetics*. Trans. C. Emerson. Minneapolis: University of Minnesota Press.

Barad, K. (2003). Posthumanist performativity: toward an understanding of how matter comes to matter. *Signs: Journal of Women in Culture and Society*, 28(3). Retrieved from http://citeseerx.ist.psu.edu/viewdoc/download?doi=10.1.1.466.5231&rep=rep1&type=pdf

Barad, K. (2007). Meeting the universe halfway: quantum physics and the entanglement of matter and meaning. In *Quantum Physics and the Entanglement of Matter and Meaning*. Durham, NC: Duke University Press. https://doi.org/10.1086/597741

Braidotti, R. (2006). Posthuman, all too human towards a new process ontology. *Culture & Society*, 23, 7–8. https://doi.org/10.1177/0263276406069232

Braidotti, R. (2013). *The Posthuman*. Cambridge: Polity Press.

Callander, D., Holt, M., and Newman, C. E. (2012). Just a preference: racialised language in the sex-seeking profiles of gay and bisexual men. *Culture, Health & Sexuality*, 14(9), 1049–1063. https://doi.org/10.1080/13691058.2012.714799

Callander, D., Newman, C. E., and Holt, M. (2015). Is sexual racism really racism? Distinguishing attitudes toward sexual racism and generic racism among gay and bisexual men. *Archives of Sexual Behavior*, 44(7), 1991–2000. https://doi.org/10.1007/s10508-015-0487-3.

Condie, J., Lean, G., and Wilcockson, B. (forthcoming). The trouble with Tinder: The ethical complexities of researching location-aware social discovery apps. In K. Woodfield (ed.), *The Ethics of Internet-Mediated Research and Using Social Media for Social Research*. Bingley: Emerald Books.

Connolly, W. (2013). The 'new materialism' and the fragility of things. *Millennium*. Retrieved from http://journals.sagepub.com/doi/abs/10.1177/0305829813486849

Cooper, A., and Condie, J. (2016). Bakhtin, digital scholarship and new publishing practices as carnival. *Journal of Applied Social Theory*, 1(1), 26–43. Retrieved from http://socialtheoryapplied.com/journal/jast/article/view/31

David, G., and Cambre, C. (2016). Screened intimacies: Tinder and the swipe logic. *Social Media + Society*, 2(2), 1–11.

Davis, A. P. (n.d.). What I learned Tindering my way across Europe. Retrieved June 19, 2016, from www.travelandleisure.com/articles/tinder-while-you-travel

Duguay, S. (2017). Dressing up Tinderella: Interrogating authenticity claims on the mobile dating app Tinder. *Information, Communication & Society*, 20(3), 351–367. https://doi.org/10.1080/1369118X.2016.1168471

Evans, A. (2017). Tinder as a methodological tool. Retrieved May 2, 2017, from http://allegralaboratory.net/tinder-as-a-methodological-tool/

Forlano, L. (2015). Towards an integrated theory of the cyber-urban. *Digital Culture & Society*, 1(1). https://doi.org/10.14361/dcs-2015-0106

Fox, N., and Alldred, P. (2013). The sexuality-assemblage: Desire, affect, anti-humanism. *The Sociological Review*. Retrieved from http://onlinelibrary.wiley.com/doi/10.1111/1467-954X.12075/full

Fox, N., and Alldred, P. (2015). New materialist social inquiry: Designs, methods and the research-assemblage. *International Journal of Social Research.* Retrieved from www. tandfonline.com/doi/abs/10.1080/13645579.2014.921458

Fuss, D. (1989). *Essentially Speaking: Feminism, Nature and Difference.* London: Routledge.

Gibson-Graham, J. K. (2011). A feminist project of belonging for the Anthropocene. *Gender, Place & Culture*, 18(1), 1–21. https://doi.org/10.1080/0966369X.2011.535295.

Gobo, G. (2008). Doing ethnography. Retrieved from https://books.google.com.au/ books?hl=en&lr=&id=VCr2_eA-ngEC&oi=fnd&pg=PR7&dq=%22entering+the+field %22+%22ethnography%22++Giampietro+Gobo&ots=b3Y7Eg6RvE&sig=Pz0U6s3Jh 5NCb0bm-cblnCHwjwQ

Haraway, D. (1991). Cyborg Manifesto: Science, technology, and socialist-feminism in the late twentieth century. In *Simians, Cyborgs and Women: The Reinvention of Nature.* New York: Routledge.

Haraway, D. (2016). *Staying with the Trouble: Making Kin in the Chthulucene.* Durham, NC: Duke University Press.

Hobbs, M., Owen, S., and Gerber, L. (2016). Liquid love? Dating apps, sex, relationships and the digital transformation of intimacy. *Journal of Sociology*, 1–16. https://doi. org/10.1177/1440783316662718

Kara, H. (2017). Identity and power in co-produced activist research. *Qualitative Research.* Retrieved from http://journals.sagepub.com/doi/abs/10.1177/1468794117 696033

Kitchin, R. M. (1998). Towards geographies of cyberspace. *Progress in Human Geography*, 22(3), 385–406. https://doi.org/10.1191/030913298668331585

March, E., Grieve, R., Marrington, J., and Jonason, P. K. (2017). Trolling on Tinder® (and other dating apps): Examining the role of the Dark Tetrad and impulsivity. *Personality and Individual Differences*, 110, 139–143.

Mason, C. (2016). Tinder and humanitarian hook-ups: The erotics of social media racism. *Feminist Media Studies.* https://doi.org/10.1080/14680777.2015.113733

Mirzoeff, N. (2015). *How to See the World.* New York: Pelican.

Pink, S., Horst, H., Postill, J., et al. (2015). *Digital Ethnography: Principles and Practice.* London: Sage.

Ruppert, E., Law, J., and Savage, M. (2013). Reassembling social science methods: the challenge of digital devices. *Theory, Culture & Society*, 30(4), 22–46. https://doi. org/10.1177/0263276413484941

Sales, N. J. (2015). Tinder and the dawn of the 'dating apocalypse.' *Vanity Fair.* Retrieved from www.vanityfair.com/culture/2015/08/tinder-hook-up-culture-end-of-dating

Schadler, C. (2016). How to define situated and ever-transforming family configurations? A new materialist approach. *Journal of Family Theory & Review*, 8(4), 503–514. https://doi.org/10.1111/jftr.12167

Sevi, B., Aral, T., and Eskenazi, T. (2017). Exploring the hook-up app: Low sexual disgust and high sociosexuality predict motivation to use Tinder for casual sex. *Personality and Individual Differences.* Retrieved from www.sciencedirect.com/science/ article/pii/S0191886917303112

Shaw, D. (2015). Streets for cyborgs: The electronic *flâneur* and the posthuman city. *Space and Culture.* Retrieved from http://journals.sagepub.com/doi/abs/10.1177/12063 31214560105

Shields, R. (2006). *Flânerie* for cyborgs. *Theory, Culture & Society*, 23(7–8), 209–220. https://doi.org/10.1177/0263276406069233

Sinders, C. (2015). I used Tinder to get travel tips instead of sex. Retrieved June 19, 2016, from http://fusion.kinja.com/i-used-tinder-to-get-travel-tips-instead-of-sex-1793851426

Sumter, S., Vandenbosch, L., and Ligtenberg, L. (2017). Love me Tinder: Untangling emerging adults' motivations for using the dating application Tinder. *Telematics and Informatics*. Retrieved from www.sciencedirect.com/science/article/pii/S07365853163 01216

Timmermans, E., and De Caluwé, E. (2017). To Tinder or not to Tinder, that's the question: An individual differences perspective to Tinder use and motives. *Personality and Individual Differences*, 110, 74–79. https://doi.org/10.1016/j.paid.2017.01.026

Tinder. (2014). Tinder Plus. Retrieved December 12, 2016, from https://vimeo.com/ 111080451

Tucker, I. (2011). Psychology as space: Embodied relationality. *Social and Personality Psychology Compass*, 5(5), 231–238. https://doi.org/10.1111/j.1751-9004.2011. 00347.x

Warfield, K. (2016). Making the cut: An agential realist examination of selfies and touch. *Social Media + Society*, 2(2), 1–10. https://doi.org/10.1177/2056305116641706

Werning, S. (2015). Swipe to unlock. *Digital Culture & Society*, 1(1), 55–71. https://doi. org/10.14361/dcs-2015-0105

Wilson, M. W. (2009). Cyborg geographies: Towards hybrid epistemologies. *Gender, Place & Culture*, 16(5), 499–516. https://doi.org/10.1080/09663690903148390

8 Remote ethnography, virtual presence

Exploring digital-visual methods for anthropological research on the web

Shireen Walton

Introduction

Digital technologies have developed methodological, epistemological and onto-logical scope for social scientific research. Digital technologies and landscapes shape not only *which* aspects of social life can be engaged with, but also *how* and *where*. For anthropologists – who are primarily in the business of studying social lives and phenomena – nascent theoretical and methodological digital pathways hold much contemporary currency; both within the discipline, and its ability to speak to and engage with other epistemological traditions. Emergent digital and visual methods in particular are opening up innovative avenues for conducting ethnographic research *with* (and not just *about*) participants. At the same time, while 'new' media are giving rise to novel methodological avenues, they also grow out of older technologies and epistemologies. Technology-linked visual research has been a part of the discipline of anthropology from the outset. Beginning in the nineteenth century, photography and film have been used to record ethnographic information, generating 'scientifically' posited data in the field, about 'others'. Margaret Mead and Geoffrey Bateson (1942) had famously used photography to try to objectively capture what they called the 'spirit' of the Balinese character, namely, by producing and compiling photographic 'docu-ments' of Balinese cultural customs and practices. Following the reflexive turn in anthropology in the 1980s, and a greater engagement with subjectivity, visual anthropology began experimenting with alternative epistemologies in research and representation. Participatory video-making with indigenous groups during the 1990s forms a salient example within this milieu (Ginsburg 1991, 1994; Turner 1991). Such practices, and their more recent conceptual and technolo-gical manifestations, lend themselves to what Pink (2006) envisaged as the future of visual anthropology in a *digital* age: a public anthropology capable of making critical interventions.

Today, in a contemporary world saturated by social networks and global flows of digital images, research on and using the digital yields a range of potential research sites and methods, and epistemological and ontological frameworks – as a growing corpus of digital anthropological/ethnographic liter-ature illustrates (Boellstorff, Nardi, Pearce and Taylor 2012; Horst and Miller

2012; Underberg and Zorn 2013; Pink et al. 2015). However, digital methods are still not often the first port of call for anthropologists. For the most part, this can be put down to the discipline's characteristic method of studying 'others' *un*digitally; through long-term fieldwork engagement in everyday lives and practices of people in remote physical settings. The notion of field-based research was first established by Polish anthropologist Bronislaw Malinowski (1922), who, based on his long-term research in the Trobriand Islands, established the view that being in the field for a significant period of time was the main method by which anthropologists could understand and represent peoples and cultures, authentically. For Malinowski, fieldwork provided a methodological corrective to what had preceded it, namely, the Victorian practice of ethnology and representing others remotely, based on travel/colonial literature and other secondary media. This dominant methodological perspective is based on a dual epistemological and ontological presumption, which places virtue in presence, and by the same token, is inherently distrustful of remote enquiry. The strength of Malinowski's legacy has arguably left anthropology slow to adapt – and fully commit methodologically – to the digital, relative to other social science disciplines. A main issue in this regard stems from the assumption that conducting research *on* the digital *via* the digital negates the researcher's presence, and thereby negates the authenticity of her research. Conceiving of the digital landscape as an anthropological field site thereby generally remains a poorer supplement for being there 'for real', where not being there *physically*, equates to not being there *at all.* Indeed, even in cases where digital anthropology comprises the overarching epistemological and methodological framework of the research – such as in the study of digital technologies and ICTs in a said physical location – there is still the underlying expectation that one will go to the physical field site for a sustained period of time studying digital practices and cultures *in situ.*

Two main ontological and epistemological challenges posed by conducting anthropological research not just *on* the digital, but *within* the digital landscape therefore relate to two basic assumptions about anthropological practice more generally, which will remain the overarching epistemological anchor of my discussion in this chapter. These pertain to: (1) the field or locus of research; no longer necessarily a geographical place or society, but conceivable as a virtual network of social relations in flux; and (2) the researcher's embodied participation in their research; no longer contingent upon physical presence, but capable of being undertaken remotely and digitally, online. In this chapter, I explore these two principal features, both of which comprise the epistemological basis of my anthropological research studying popular photography in/of Iran – physically in the country, in the UK, and remotely, online. As I will detail in the chapter, the topic of my research and the methodology developed to study it were, from the outset, connected to the epistemological and ontological approaches that I encountered and subsequently developed throughout the project; namely, transferring the ethnographic tradition to online digital environments, and the personal, professional and ethical implications of doing this.

I will normatively suggest that topic-specific research quandaries and established ethical schema should reflexively inform methodological choices made in digital research (as in non-digital research). In particular, I will anchor my discussion in the potential 'problem' of my restricted physical presence in Iran as an anthropologist, revealing how by engaging with digital methods, what might be traditionally perceived as an obstacle to 'authentic' anthropological research can actually render visible and inform the adoption of other suitable methodological choices and trajectories carved out from within the digital landscape itself. Following from my own research in/on Iran, I conclude by suggesting that methodological potentials in digital and visual anthropology offer broader insights into ways of designing and conducting ethically rigorous qualitative digital research via mobile digital technologies and the web, particularly where transnational, Internet and image-related work is concerned. To begin my discussion, I now give an overview of the topic of my research: photoblogging in Iran, before linking this with how I generated research questions, developed my methodological apparatus and ethical framework, and made certain choices on studying the practice in Iran, the UK and online.

Photoblogging in/of Iran: context, questions, and quandaries

My PhD research investigated the on- and offline practices of Iranian popular photographers, with a special focus on photobloggers (individuals/groups who blog predominantly with photographs rather than text). Photoblogging is a popular hobby the world over, involving the often-daily posting of digital photographs on photography-orientated blogs (Cohen 2005). Its emergence in the early 2000s coincided with the development of the camera phone, which popularised amateur photography, making it even more mobile. In more recent years, photoblogs have been integrated into social networking sites and broader mobile media ensembles. In Iran, photoblogging is largely carried out by middle-class Iranian men and women in their twenties and early thirties, though many Iranian photobloggers also live outside Iran, partaking in the associated practices and activities in virtual Iranian photoblogging communities. While there is much technical and visual commonality in the practice across the globe, photoblogging, like social media at large, is also locally distinct. For many Iranian photobloggers, inside and outside of the country, Iran itself appears to be a chief visual subject of their photography; photographs are purposefully taken in and across Iran on digital cameras and camera phones in order to be shared with global viewers online. My study reveals how photoblogging has emerged as a popular means of consciously (and some less consciously) exploring and debating various visual and symbolic aspects of Iranian culture, everyday life and experience. Digital photographs shown on photoblogs convey the traditions, folklore, religious practices, material culture, food, history and ethnic diversities of Iran in rural and urban contexts – all which serve as visual testaments of everyday life in a much-misunderstood country. As I have discussed elsewhere (Walton 2015), much of this showing reflects a desire on behalf of the photographers to visually alter perceptions of Iran and Iranians as the 'enemy other' of the West and vice versa, propagated in official and mainstream visual/media narratives of the country in Iran and in 'the West' since the Islamic Revolution of 1979. More specifically, this cultural polarisation was seen during certain key moments of social and political conservatism and economic hardship brought about by sanctions imposed upon Iran, as was seen in the post-9/11 international climate from 2001, and particularly under the Ahmadinejad administration in Iran (2005–2013). As a result of these broader political tensions, many Iranians feel that the monolithic representations constructed during these eras have 'dehumanised' the image of their country and crudely simplified understandings of Iranian people the world over. The anonymous photographer behind one of the most popular photoblogs 'Life Goes on in Tehran' (LGOIT), and one of my main research participants, summarises a central point about the practice of photoblogging as follows:

> I knew early on that the most effective approach to humanizing Iranians was to show the daily life in my immediate surrounding ... photoblogging is my medium of choice if for no other reason than the fact that it involves a camera and the Internet. Even a tiny barely functional camera phone provides the means to capture what I wanted to show to the world: the truth about Iran.
>
> (Online interview, LGOIT, 2012)

Here LGOIT conveys the broader significance of photoblogging in Iran, highlighting the overall importance placed on mobile digital technologies (such as camera phones) by Iranian photobloggers such as himself, as appropriate vehicles for deploying alternative systems of capturing and representing a certain everyday 'truth' about Iran 'from below'.[1] Here, as he puts it, even a 'tiny barely functional camera phone' is suitable for facilitating the kind of popular cultural self-representation LGOIT seeks to capture and communicate to viewers via the Internet. Historically speaking, photography has always been mobile, and linked with epistemological questions. Pinney (2008) shows how as photographic technology became increasingly miniaturised and increasingly mobile in the early twentieth century, its *habitus* changed – it was no longer dependent upon official support or the same levels of financial investment as in the nineteenth century. LGOIT's remarks above reflect these broader theoretical observations about changes in analogue photography, but at the specific historical juncture wherein *digital* photography became increasingly *mobile* in the early 2000s with the advent of camera phone photography. As my study more broadly reveals, photobloggers emphasise these novel socio-technological potentials, while drawing on the documentary realism of mobile digital technology, in order to 'set the record straight' about Iran through their practices. On another note, photoblogs also serve as alternative low-cost/free exhibition venues for showing Iranian photography beyond official galleries and public museums inside and outside of Iran, and their respective politics, policies and restrictions. Given the relationship introduced above between nascent mobile digital technologies and their facilitating of an epistemological shift in ways of seeing Iran, at this point, I will turn to discuss how I became interested in the topic of Iranian photoblogging. Here, as I will describe below, early theoretical observations and methodological/ethical considerations influenced the development of both my research questions, and how I chose to set about answering them.

Developing the research questions

My introduction to Iranian photoblogging came about in 2011, when I was conducting research as part of a master's project in social anthropology on the visuality of Iranian blogs. My master's project stemmed from two personal observations at the time: (1) the thriving online cultural life in the Iranian blogosphere, detailed most comprehensively in a seminal study on the subject by Sreberny and Khiabany (2010); and (2) my observations of the striking locality to the digital, visual and online cultural practices that I had observed among Iranians inside and outside of Iran during the presidential election protests in Iran in June 2009. From the symbolic use of the colour green to signify reformist banners, graffiti and make-up, to the more general popular photography and film-making activities taking place on the streets by the new citizen journalists, in what scholars and journalists alike have since called the 'Twitter Revolution' (Sreberny and Khiabany 2010; Mottahedeh 2015). The protests of 2009 in Iran seemed to render digital/visual communication a new *modus operandi* for both domestic and transnational Iranian communication, as has been duly observed by scholars (Dabashi 2010; Khatib 2013; Khosronejad 2013). Given points (1) and (2), I was surprised, at the time, to find that literature on Iranian online visual-cultural production beyond studies of 2009 green wave activism was scarce, nigh on altogether absent. My interest in studying cotemporary Iranian visual culture online developed further in line with these observations, coupled with a growing personal interest in and broader awareness of the socio-political commentaries and acute aesthetic sensibilities of Iranian contemporary art, photojournalism and New Wave Iranian Cinema (Balaghi and Gumpert 2002; Tapper 2002; Naficy 2011). Beyond the official domains of art production and activism, what could be said of the nascent popular digital visual cultures witnessed on the Iranian social web? This I set out to investigate. Through a casual and almost haphazard online search of 'Iranian photoblogs', I came across the photoblog *Life Goes on in Tehran* (LGOIT). Intrigued by the title, I investigated a little further, and soon discovered it to be an intriguing combination of art praxis and what it more prosaically was: a blog. Curiously here, aesthetic sensibility and cinematography loomed large. These elements were evident in the design; including the choice of images, the unique horizontal scrolling layout of the image galleries, and the witty and subtle politics of the captions (Figure 8.1).

The overall *mise-en-scène* of the photoblog formed the impression that something at once global in form, and yet intimately Iranian – and with unmistakable use of western cultural references and aesthetic markers – seemed to have

Figure 8.1 'Life Goes on in Tehran', April 2009 album.
Source: http://lifegoesonintehran.com/25_April_2009.html.

popular global appeal, judging by the photoblog's global fan base and comment streams (Figure 8.2).

This led me to deduce that perhaps Iranian photoblogs deserved further critical attention than had (and still have) been observed by scholars. Online environments, for Iranians, seemed to be not just a profoundly social arena as they are elsewhere across the globe, but also appeared to be a place for articulating something of a shared subjectivity and experience in local/global contexts, while providing a space for taking photography and transnational visual communication seriously.

For my master's study I proceeded to investigate LGOIT as a case study, based on online interviews conducted with its publicly anonymous creator. These interviews fed into my wider visual analysis of images on the site, and discourse analysis of samples of posted comments. Back then in 2011, the literature on digital ethnography was sparse, and my approach during my master's project was thus largely one of experimentation, trial and error. Nevertheless, I conducted my research within the established ethical code of conduct in anthropology, which chiefly considers the protection of research participants and their data, along with the researcher's ethical conduct in the field – however physical or virtual. Both the analyses and methods of enquiry I conducted at this early stage set an important methodological and ethical precedent for the rest of my doctoral project, namely, that online data collection is only one part of the process of excavating and generating meaning in digital research. Hookway's (2008) ethical discussion of conducting qualitative research on blogs highlighted a useful distinction, early in on my research process, between what he terms the 'trawling' and 'soliciting' of blogs; the former being a passive form of browsing the presented web material, and the latter an active form of enquiry involving deeper strategies, such as making contact with the blogger, and soliciting

LIFE GOES ON IN **TEHRAN**

Mission Statement: To show that regardless of what any president would have you imagine, despite what any media outlet would have you believe, life goes on in Tehran and elsewhere in Iran.

About: A personal monthly photo blog by a former Los Angeles resident who moved to Tehran. Featuring photos taken using a camera phone.

2014 Update: While this website will serve as a slice of [my] life in Tehran between 2007 and 2010, all activity is hereby moved to our Facebook Page. New photos from Iran will post to Facebook via my Instagram account.

Furthermore, all photos tagged by *anyone* with #LGOIT will be automatically featured on our Facebook page under the Instagram tab. So if you live in Iran, go ahead and tag your photos with #LGOIT and show the world that Life Goes On In Tehran...

Figure 8.2 'Life Goes on in Tehran' home page.
Source: http://lifegoesonintehran.com.

meaning beyond the surface of the visible/publicly available content. That such a qualitative distinction exists between the two I had already suspected from investigating the existing literature on 'virtual ethnography' (Hine 2000, 2008), and from my theoretical training in classical ethnography and visual anthropology. The epistemological basis of these three areas, which treated both virtual data and images as social objects – worthy of (material) cultural analysis, between processes of production, circulation and consumption – in effect, made the process of translating established theoretical and methodological approaches in anthropology and sociology to the digital context, theoretically reasonably straightforward. Specifically, the qualitative/ethnographic researcher's commitment to contextualising the social 'object/subject' of enquiry would involve an equally rigorous process of contextualisation in the broader (and offline) social and political networks and subjects' lifeworlds. As an anthropologist, above all, the process would require getting to know the people with whom one is conducting research over a length of time. These established social scientific principles, I suspected, would hold as equally true in online research and data collection as in offline practices, though the precise carrying out of these processes would inevitably involve a certain amount of ontological, conceptual and experiential reorientation, as I discovered, and will discuss.

Having conducted a preliminary study of a small sample of Iranian photoblogs purely online, I developed my research questions for a larger, transnational enquiry into the practice in my doctorate. This would involve further in-depth case studies of photobloggers' lives, movements and practices, and include a larger sample of what in the end totalled 250 photoblogs. I initially conceived of the project as being carried out for the most part in Iran, while conducting digital ethnography, online, simultaneously. In the original conception of the project, I had planned to spend time 'being there' with Iranian photographers in person in major cities such as Tehran and Esfahan, where their practices appeared to be particularly prevalent. Prior to the official start of my fieldwork term, I had established some core research questions based on my previous study, namely, how Iranian photoblogging was signalling the development of a new popular documentary/art form in Iran, and the impact of these 'new' types of images on local and global social imaginaries, particularly regarding Iran's relationship (cultural, political and ideological) with the West. From the UK, I solicited preliminary contacts in Iran and began to prepare the logistics of my trip. The form the ethnography eventually took, however – involving one month in Iran, and the remaining 11 months in London, Oxford and online – relates to certain constraints that I then faced at the specific political 'moment' that I began to undertake my research in October 2012. I will reflexively account for these below, showing how these issues raised certain epistemological and ontological issues, which informed the methodological strategies I adopted to perform digital-visual athropology online.

The autumn of 2012 was a particularly heightened moment of political tension between the conservative administration of President Mahmoud Ahmadinejad in Iran and the western countries. In addition, in America, Republican Party campaigns during the US presidential election in November 2012 were, along with various political figures in Israel, threatening to coerce Iran into a war over their suspected nuclear programme, contributing to an overall tense international political climate. Concurrently, the Iranian Embassy in London and the British Embassy in Tehran were closed, following a violent attack on the latter the previous year in November 2011, thought to be carried out by members of Iran's volunteer *Basij* militia, in connection with UK-imposed sanctions on Iran. As a result of these fraught international and domestic political climates, travelling to Iran, particularly for British citizens, became a significant point of contention. The Foreign and Commonwealth Office (FCO) in London had warned against all travel to Iran for British citizens, and this warning was, in turn, presented to me, a sole British passport holder, by the Health and Safety and Central University Research Ethics Committee (CUREC) bodies of my university, who both advised against, and could not officially sanction my proposed fieldwork in Iran. Determined to continue pursuing my research, I solicited advice from personal contacts in Iran, and eventually managed to obtain a visa for travel from the Iranian consulate in Paris, aided no doubt by my being half-Iranian. This personal dimension, I believe, had made me somewhat prioritised in administrative processes since I had much of the required documentation for obtaining a visa in hand, and familial connections in place. I proceeded to spend one month in Iran between October and November 2012. I fully engaged with my own subjectivity during my visit, where inevitably personal and biographical aspects seeped into my observational frame, as I set about learning all that I could about Iran from Iranians while physically present in the country. I had never before visited the country, and spoke the Persian language familiarly, but with a certain modesty stemming from having learnt it in a haphazard manner in a familial context in the UK. Regardless of my subjective attachment to the country, my second-generation diasporic sensibility and sense of remove from Iran itself and Iranian culture *in situ*, meant that in effect (and particularly in hindsight), my psychological experience of physically travelling there was ultimately not unlike that of the classical anthropologist travelling to the land of 'others', in order to learn something of culture and social practices by way of comparison. In Iran, I was able to meet with local photographers I had connected with online from the UK, and undertook some rudimentary fieldwork activities involving semi-structured interviews, gallery visits, and participating in what are locally known as 'photo tours' (*safarhā-ye akkāsi*): social occasions linked to group travel and photographic activities undertaken by photography enthusiasts across the country. Back in the UK, I had to devise ways to continue my fieldwork remotely, including maintaining presence and connection with research participants whom I had met in Iran, as well as those with whom I had connected purely online. This brings me to a discussion of the specific manners, modes and affordances through which I principally conducted online qualitative research throughout my doctoral project, and retrieved my ethnographic data online.

Remote ethnography: developing digital and visual methods for research in/on Iran

So far I have accounted for my lack of a certain physical experience of 'being there' in my research for a sustained period of time. Given the classical definition of anthropological research described earlier in this chapter, this predicament presented me, as a student anthropologist conducting digital research online remotely, with an epistemological quandary. In this case, I was faced with what Postill suitably describes as a certain 'epistemological angst' (Postill 2016); an anxiety linked to the process of conducting remote ethnography, stemming from a sense of thwarted purpose and method, given the virtue of physical presence upon which anthropological fieldwork is traditionally based. This requires further reflection here, in order to epistemologically situate the digital-visual research methods I eventually took up in my research. In the first instance, the fact that difficult and limited access to Iran was/is not uncommon for fieldwork-based researchers more generally provided a certain level of acquittal to my epistemological angst at the time, as I began exploring my digital-ethnographic research remotely. Hegland (2009: 53) terms this limited access to Iran for non-native anthropologists a 'professional dilemma', stemming from the broader history of political tensions between western powers and successive post-revolutionary governments, which largely accounts for the dearth of anthropological research in the country since the revolution of 1979. As a result, research trips to Iran (sometimes on tourist visas) have not been uncommon for Iranian and non-Iranian researchers. In these cases, then, as in my own experience, the rationale of doing 'quick ethnography' or 'zip in and zip out fieldwork' (Hegland 2004) in Iran is a pragmatic antidote to travel injunctions, outweighing ideals of 'being there' for sustained periods of time. Moreover, the issue of lack of physical presence is not exclusive to anthropological research on Iran, nor necessarily tied to geopolitical factors. Anthropologists are often faced with restrictions of multiple kinds, affecting how one accesses and how much time is spent in the field, ranging from war and natural disasters to local political turbulence, or more prosaically, lack of funds. All of these have been cited, to varying degrees as factors *contextualising* – but not *excusing* – the conducting of remote digital ethnography today (Postill 2016). Remote ethnography, Postill notes, can prove a useful option for researchers in both planned and unplanned circumstances, and in shifting socio-political circumstances (p. 5). Remote ethnographic research can also take a variety of forms; from the use of remedial technologies (social media; Skype; email, and so forth), or via other layers of non-technological mediation, such as the use of research assistants, translators and other influencing agents, which contribute to and make up the researcher's mediating lens (ibid.: 5). In the case of my research, as I will demonstrate below, remote methodologies proved central to much of my understanding of photo-blogging in/of Iran, and the people who partake in it as producers and viewers of images across the globe.

In the following section, I consider the specific choices I made in pursuing my research remotely online through digital and visual ethnographic methods. The principal research participants taking part in my study were all born and grew up in Iran. They had then either remained living in Iran or migrated abroad, often to pursue higher education. Mobility is therefore a central aspect and conceptual metaphor in photoblogging. It involves: (1) the *physical* movement of photobloggers across the globe; (2) the *digital* circulation of digital images they produce; as well as (3) the *epistemological* mobility many photobloggers themselves seek to initiate by sharing 'normal' photographs of their country online as a way of 'moving' the country's international image beyond dominant visual tropes, as I earlier described. At the time of my research, the photobloggers who became my main participants were based in six countries: Iran, the USA, the UK, Germany, Italy and Australia.[2] Their multimodal activities of producing subjective visual discourses in multitemporal frameworks (including different time zones) begged the question of how to study them online over an extended period of time. An early *digital* step I took in my research was to set up a research photoblog for my visit to Iran. I did this fairly simply through Tumblr. com, a popular blogging platform, which provided a stand-alone digital space for the research project, aside from my own and my participants' more general social media platforms. Through the research photoblog I aimed to provide a personalised account of my own photographs and experiences as a researcher in and travelling across Iran. This fieldwork method, and the images that it contained, subsequently formed a useful basis for discussion with research participants. In recent years, and with the increasing use of digital technologies in anthropological fieldwork, these kinds of digital practices, which actively include research participants in the research process, have been termed 'e-Fieldnotes (Sanjek and Tratner 2016) and have become increasingly widespread.[3] The process of actively including research participants (and/or co-collaborators) in this manner indicates what Horst (2016: 7) describes as a 'knowing beyond the self' of the solo researcher, involving an epistemological framework that is collectivised/socialised and developed through the research process itself. Technology-facilitated collaboration was something that I developed instinctively throughout my research with Iranian photobloggers, given the very subject matter of my research: mobile individuals/groups and their digital-visual practices. As part of this pursuit, I co-constructed a unique methodological apparatus with my research participants, in direct conversation with my thematic focus and sites of research: a digital photography exhibition: www.photoblogsiran.com (Figure 8.3) (Walton 2016).

The exhibition was designed and employed in my doctoral project with the participation and approval of the exhibiting photobloggers. The rationale for developing it directly relates to the broader epistemological framework of my digital-ethnographic research. The exhibition aimed to show a range of self-selected digital photographs from the photographers' pre-existing digital archives on their photoblog sites. These selected images would then form the basis for discussion among participants and myself and be used for research purposes with broader on- and offline publics. In developing the digital exhibition as a method, I effectively made use of what Gubrium and Harper (2013: 173) suggest is the primary goal of placing exhibitions online in the form of online web 2.0 platforms, namely, 'to make materials available to a wider public', while attending fully to the ethical implications of this endeavour.[4] Ethical considerations were intrinsic to the theoretical conception of the exhibition. Participants would maintain copyright of all of their photographs, and these would be featured on the site with their permission. The photographs would be introduced, contextualised and presented as part of a wider research process, as described in the 'about' and background' sections of the site. Apart from LGOIT, who officially maintains public anonymity, each photographer is introduced with their real name. This reflects a conscious ethical policy agreed with all participants in my study that real names would be used, as they exist in other public online platforms, including in their own photoblogs. Here, I

Contemporary Iranian Popular Digital Photography

Pages

About

Background

Photographers
— Amir Sadeghi
— Kiana Farhoudi
— 'Life Goes on in Tehran'
— Ehsan Abbasi
— Saleh Ara
— Vahid Rahmanian
— Omid Akhavan
— Nikzad Shahidian

Cover image for the Facebook fan page of the popular photoblog 'Life Goes on in Tehran'.

Figure 8.3 Digital Research Exhibition.

Sources: www.photoblogsiran.com home page; www.photoblogsiran.com/blog/.

effectively treat photobloggers in the digital research process akin to artists – a common practice in the anthropology of art, for instance, is to refer to the artist and their work, but also to anonymise sections of interview material where desired or deemed appropriate. More broadly, this strategy of using real people's real names in online research reflects Bruckman's (2014) broader conceptualisation of online participants as 'amateur artists', describing the process by which the researcher honours public individuals' desires to be named in order to acquire the recognition of their work and/or views. Overall, the digital exhibition forms what I term a 'site-specific methodology', whereby the form of research method (a digital exhibition of digital photographs/photoblogs) was carved out of the field site (photographers' practices in online environments). Here, participants and I could 'meet', reflect upon and explore the research theme within the safety and confines of a platform we co-created precisely for this purpose. In more general terms, curating a digital research environment such as this can prove beneficial in all kinds of research in/on the digital, in constructing a discursive virtual space made of an ensemble of people from across multiple countries and time zones, and whose multi-sited/multi-temporal ontology cannot exist in the offline, physical world. In this sense, digital-visual methods offered ways of knowing and being in my research than other, physical fieldwork methods could not provide.

In broader fieldwork activities, I carried out online participant observation of Iranian photoblogging for 12 months, during which I became a 'consequential social actor in online space' (Boellstorff et al. 2012). With the permission of the individuals I was conducting research with, I took hand-written notes and recorded video and audio calls on Skype using a relevant software application. I also printed and physically archived emails, chat correspondence and interview transcripts.[5] Many of these research activities involved establishing live digital co-presence with participants across multiple physical locations; an ontological aspect that has been cited as one of the unique features of doing digital ethnography today (Boellstorff et al. 2012; Marcus 2012; Pink et al. 2015). Technologically-facilitated 'being there' together allowed me to be with participants as they were out and about taking photographs in Iran, as well as in their own homes where they attend to the technical maintenance and social lives of their photoblogs. According to Urry (2004: 35), blogs are 'one of those machines, that allow people and networks to be connected to, or to be at home with "sites" across the world – while simultaneously such sites can monitor, observe and trace each inhabited machine'. Conducting this kind of 'home ethnography' (Larsen 2008: 156) in my study of Iranian photoblogs invariably involved being virtually present with participants in their own homes, which, incidentally constituted one of the main *physical* manifestations of my various digital research fields. Invariably, individuals would also move between platforms and mobile devices in their daily digital practices. I needed to be attentive to these online digital migrations, as well as maintaining a clear sense of where they physically were, in Iran or otherwise through our wider communication. Here, photobloggers' uses of locative media and the geotagging of their images (to Google Maps) helped me, as a researcher to locate them, physically. These digital traces also allowed me to experience being both 'in' the live moment of the event, and accessing their logged activities as an archived online record afterwards on their photoblogs and social networks pages through what has been termed 'trace ethnography' (Geiger and Ribes 2011). In such cases, as has been noted by (Gray, in press, cited in Postill 2016) 'being *then*', or the researcher's 'presence' in *past* moments digitally mapped/traced online, becomes as important as being *there*.

At this point, a more general theoretical note on the specificity of the ethnographic method in digital research will help to situate some of the methodological choices described above. Digital anthropology involves the conducting of what was originally termed 'virtual ethnography' (Hine 2000).[6] The methodology follows an epistemological and ontological approach that 'transfers the ethnographic tradition of the researcher as an embodied research instrument to the social spaces of the Internet' (p. 8). Here, the ethnographer studies physically disparate peoples by creating meaningful social relationships that are not necessarily less 'authentic', or *more* mediated than offline face-to-face communication, as Goffman (1959, 1975) earlier argued. In digital anthropological/ethnographic research, then, it is just as important to 'be with' participants, observing them in the routine practices of everyday life, as it is to actively solicit information from them. In fact, this soliciting should be carried out in conjunction with wider processes of proximity building with individuals. In this notion, a certain amount of trust is established due to having been knowingly present in participants' everyday lives and lifeworlds over a period of time. Beyond bouts of actively retrieving data through direct forms of direct contact with individuals in interviews and other digital forms of communication, one can therefore explore and orientate oneself within what may be termed the 'negative spaces' of the research; involving other kinds of latent endeavours taken up and explored during the research. One term coined to describe these kinds of latent online activities is 'lurking' (Hine 2008), a notion that recognises the importance of obtaining unsolicited data in social research on the web. Lurking created a passive form of 'being there' that I found useful in situating myself as a participant observer of Iranian photoblogging. An important aspect of my research was the fact that photoblogs could be viewed and revisited at any time provided they remain public and online. Hence, part of my digital-ethnographic portrait of photobloggers was drawn from unsolicited, pre-existing knowledge sources on the Internet. To illustrate, as public social actors, my research participants had shared information online over a number of years. Some of them had conducted interviews with or provided information about themselves and their practices to other parties, including journalists, photographic organisations and other bloggers, and much of this remains publicly available information online. Revisiting and recording information online in this manner, retrieved and used within the overall ethical framework of the research, proved a useful source of 'para-ethnographic' (Holmes and Marcus 2008) material, akin to obtaining relevant historical documents, (which I also pursued online), that contributed to my budding corpus of online data.

The digital and visual methods used in my research on photoblogging that I have described in the latter part of this chapter contribute broader theoretical insights into why and how researchers might engage in 'remote fieldwork' (Postill 2016). Here, as Postill (p. 8) observes, this type of enquiry is much more than a remedial measure, or a 'second best choice for anthropologists unable to reach their field sites ... it often helps us to observe familiar people and things from a different perspective, thereby creating a richer engagement with the world of our research participants'. In the case of my research, the fact that I was able to maintain presence remotely – in a digital *and* ontological sense – with my participants by sharing in the kinds of digital practices they do (updating their photoblog, commenting on each other's work, and communicating locally and transnationally), all the while being critically self-aware of our physical distance from each other, made for a curious but creativity-inducing epistemological and ontological predicament. The research dialectic, being primarily a digital one, was in one sense rendered even more visible a construct than one based purely on physical proximity. Connection speeds, arranging online availability, and censorship of many websites in Iran all heightened my awareness of the digital ethnographic research process *as* a consciously constructed process. At the same time, this is arguably no substantively different, despite an ontological shift to the virtual space, to problems of access, integration and disruption encountered in offline research pursuits. Furthermore, this heightened awareness of the digital-ethnographic research framework, as I have discussed, also had a qualitative impact on the *type* of information that I was able to retrieve by virtue of being online and virtually connected with people. Having spent months getting to know each other online, my research participants would voluntarily share with me photographs, stories, memories, anecdotes, URL links and people to connect with that they deemed to be relevant to the research, trusting that it would be used in an ethical manner. In this sense, the digital methods I employed stemmed from and operated within the ontological and epistemological parameters of the digital environment, the research and the established rubric of ethics.

In sum, in the case of my research on Iran, the unplanned nature of having limited time in Iran essentially begat my multi-sited and multi-modal methodology. The methodology was incrementally crafted and pieced together along different ontological and epistemological axes, involving off- and online research conducted *in situ* and remotely, via a range of technologies. From a classical anthropological perspective, as I have discussed, a 'professional dilemma' stemmed from the fact that I was left at least 11 months short of conducting *bona fide* anthropological research, traditionally involving physically 'being there' for a sustained period of time. The contemporary remote ethnographer is hereby left in a liminal position, floating between orthodoxy and innovation in their dealings with the digital. In the strict epistemological context of discipline-based knowledge regimes, weighty claims are staked on how such research is authenticated and ultimately validated. It is comforting to learn now what was unbeknown to me at the time as I stepped into the digital unknown, that anthropologists finding themselves in similarly restricted conditions of physical access have equally admitted to doubting the validity of their research based on traditional epistemological and ontological parameters. The stringency of these disciplinary dogmas makes those operating outside of the methodological status quo feel that they are somehow 'cheating' (Postill 2016, p. 8). Addressing this predicament, this chapter has sought to explain how digital and visual methods, rooted in both the ethnographic tradition and in cross-disciplinary engagement, are ushering in a nascent epistemology and ontology for anthropological research and beyond.

Conclusion

In this chapter, I have introduced and critically discussed a range of digital and visual methods employed and developed in my research with Iranian photobloggers, inside and outside of Iran. In presenting these methods, I have discussed how they can be applied to develop specific (social) research questions, or to help raise them in the first place. In the case of my research, I showed how the predicament of having limited access to Iran at a particular period of political and diplomatic capriciousness had a direct influence on some of the choices I made to engage with digital research methods online in the decidedly visual and ethnographic manners in which I did. I showed how a range of these methods allowed me a unique way of collaborating with individuals based in different countries, and with other participants in Iran, without necessarily always being physically present with them – as traditionally characterises the anthropological *modus operandi*. In my partial supplanting of *physical* presence with a *digital* one, I found that relationships with participants in 'the field' could be forged effectively and maintained through long-term digital-visual communications. This effectively allowed me to overcome the so-called 'professional dilemma', or 'epistemological angst' of not physically being in Iran for a sustained period of time. Digital and visual ethnographic methods, I suggest, therefore raise a host of timely epistemological, ontological and ethical questions concerning how qualitative digital researchers can 'be in', mediate and represent an increasingly interconnected world. The broader implications of this prospect, I contend, extend beyond the disciplinary concerns of anthropologists, offering a host of researchers working in/on the digital a range of relevant tools for accessing and understanding nascent epistemologies and research ontologies evolving alongside fields of study with which they are connected.

Notes

1 For a focused discussion on the specific issue of 'truth' in Iranian photoblogs, see Walton (2016).
2 My research sample reflects strongholds of the Iranian diaspora, the largest being in the USA (Los Angeles), with sizeable communities across various parts of the UK, Australia and Germany.
3 For a relevant discussion on producing 'live field notes' using digital applications, see Tricia Wang's (2012) report: http://ethnographymatters.net/blog/2012/08/02/writing-live-fieldnotes-towards-a-more-open-ethnography/
4 For a relevant discussion on the ethics of making digital research material public, see Gubrium and Harper (2013: 45–69).
5 See Horst (2016).
6 (Digital) anthropologists such as Horst and Miller (2012) replace the term 'virtual' with 'digital'. This follows from their emphasis on continuity between on- and offline spheres, as opposed to the implied 'unreality' of *virtual* reality.

References

Balaghi, S. and Gumpert, L. (eds) (2002). *Picturing Iran: Art, Society and Revolution*. New York: I.B. Tauris.

Boellstorff, T., Nardi, B., Pearce, C. and Taylor, T. L. (2012). *Ethnography and Virtual Worlds: A Handbook of Method*. Princeton, NJ: Princeton University Press.

Bruckman, A. (2014). 'Studying the Amateur Artist: A Perspective on Disguising Data Collected in Human Subjects Research on the Internet', *Ethics and Information Technology*, 4(3): 217–231.

Cohen, K. R. (2005). 'What Does the Photoblog Want?' *Media, Culture and Society*, 27(6): 883–901.

Dabashi, H. (2010). *Iran, the Green Movement and the USA: The Fox and the Paradox*. New York: Zed Books.

Geiger, R. S. and Ribes, D. (2011). 'Trace Ethnography: Following Coordination through Documentary Practices', in Proceedings of the 44th Annual Hawaii International Conference on Systems Sciences.

Ginsburg, F. (1994). 'Culture/Media: A (Mild) Polemic', *Anthropology Today*, 10(2): 5–15.

Ginsburg, F. (1991). 'Indigenous Media: Faustian Contract or Global Village?' *Cultural Anthropology*, 6(1): 92–112.

Goffman, E. (1959). *The Presentation of Self in Everyday Life*. New York: Doubleday.

Goffman, E. (1975). *Frame Analysis: An Essay on the Organization of Experience*. Harmondsworth: Penguin.

Gubrium, A. and Harper, K. (2013). *Participatory Visual and Digital Methods*. Walnut Creek, CA: Left Coast Press.

Hegland, M. E. (2004). 'Zip in and Zip out Fieldwork', *Iranian Studies*, 37(4): 575–583.

Hegland, M. E. (2009). 'Iranian Anthropology-Crossing Boundaries: Influences of Modernization, Social Transformation and Globalization', in S. R. Nadjmabadi (ed.) *Conceptualizing Iranian Anthropology: Past and Present Perspectives*. New York: Berghahn Books.

Hine, C. (2000). *Virtual Ethnography*. London: Sage.

Hine, C. (2008). 'Virtual Ethnography: Modes, Varieties, Affordances', in N. Fielding, R. M. Lee, et al. (eds) *Handbook of Online Research Methods*. London: Sage.

Holmes, D. R. and Marcus, G. E. (2008). 'Para-Ethnography', in L. M. Given (ed.) *SAGE Encyclopaedia of Qualitative Research Methods*. London: Sage, pp. 595–597.

Hookway, N. (2008). 'Entering the Blogosphere: Some Strategies for Using Blogs in Social Research', *Qualitative Review*, 8(1): 91–113.

Horst, H. (2016). 'Being in Fieldwork: Collaboration, Digital Media and Ethnographic Practice', in R. Sanjek and S. Tratner (eds) *eFieldnotes: The Makings of Anthropology in a Digital World*. Philadelphia, PA: University of Pennsylvania Press.

Horst, H. and Miller, D. (eds) (2012). *Digital Anthropology*. New York: Berg.

Khatib, L. (2013). 'The Politics of (In)visibility in Iran', in L. Khatib (ed.) *Image Politics in the Middle East*. New York: I. B. Tauris, pp. 72–113.

Khosronejad, P. (ed.) (2013). 'Digital Art, Political Aesthetic and Social Media: Case Study of the Iranian Presidential Election of 2009', *International Journal of Communication*, 7: 1298–1315.

Larsen, J. (2008). 'Practices and Flows of Digital Photography: An Ethnographic Framework', *Mobilities*, 3(1): 141–160.

Malinowski, B. (1922). *Argonauts of the Western Pacific: An Account of Native Enterprises and Adventure in the Archipelagoes of Melanesian New Guinea*. London: Routledge.

Marcus, G. E. (2012). 'Foreword', in T. Boellstorff, B. Nardi, et al. (eds) *Ethnography and Virtual Worlds: A Handbook on Method*. Princeton, NJ: Princeton University Press.

Mead, M. and Bateson, G. (1942). *Balinese Character: A Photographic Analysis*. New York: The New York Academy of Sciences.

Mottahedeh, N. (2015). *#iranelection: Hashtag Solidarity and the Transformation of Online Life*. Stanford, CA: Stanford University Press.

Naficy, H. (2011). *A Social History of Iranian Cinema*. Durham, NC: Duke University Press.

Pink, S. (2006). *The Future of Visual Anthropology: Engaging the Senses*. London: Routledge.

Pink, S., Horst, H., Postill, J., et al. (2015). *Digital Ethnography: Principles and Practice*. London: Sage.

Pinney, C. (2008). *The Coming of Photography in India*. London: The British Library.

Postill, J. (2016). 'Doing Remote Ethnography', in L. Hjorth, H. Horst, et al. (eds) *Routledge Companion to Digital Ethnography*. London: Routledge.

Sanjek, R. and Tratner, S. (eds) (2016). *eFieldnotes: The Makings of Anthropology in a Digital World*. Philadelphia, PA: University of Pennsylvania Press.

Sreberny, A. and Khiabany, G. (2010). *Blogistan: The Internet and Politics in Iran*. New York: I.B. Tauris.

Tapper, R. (ed.) (2002). *The New Iranian Cinema: Politics, Representation and Identity*. London: I.B. Tauris.

Turner, T. (1991). 'The Social Dynamics of Video Making in an Indigenous Society: The Cultural Meaning and the Personal Politics of Video-making in Kayapo Communities', *Visual Anthropology Review*, 7(2): 68–76.

Underberg, N. M. and Zorn, E. (2013). *Digital Ethnography: Anthropology, Narrative and New Media*. Austin, TX: University of Texas Press.

Urry, J. (2004). 'Connections, Environment and Planning', *Society and Space*, 22(1): 27–37.

Walton, S. (2015). 'Re-envisioning Iran Online: Photoblogs and the Ethnographic "Digital-Visual Moment"', *Middle East Journal of Culture and Communication*, Special Issue: Critical Histories of Photography, 8: 398–418.

Walton, S. (2016). 'Photographic Truth in Motion: The Case of Iranian Photoblogs', *Royal Anthropological Institute,* 2(Online Open-Access).

Wang. T. (2012) 'Writing Live Fieldnotes.' Available at: http://ethnographymatters.net/blog/2012/08/02/writing-live-fieldnotes-towards-a-more-open-ethnography/

Part II

Engaging research informants

Digital participatory methods and data stories

9 The visualisation of data in a digital context

David A. Ellis and Hannah L. Merdian

Introduction

Science is often driven by datasets and a curiosity to explore them. While these investigations are typically guided by hypotheses, acting as a lens during exploration, good study design also allows researchers to create a story with their data (McCandless, 2009). The advent of digital research methods has led to the emergence of larger and multifaceted data sets, be it through the appearance of new platforms for established research methods (e.g. online social media) or the generation of mobile and cloud-based systems for data capture (e.g. smartphones); thus, transitioning from raw data to a story that can be shared with others has become increasingly complex, often requiring the simultaneous development of computational models alongside larger and constantly evolving data sets (McGrath and Scanaill, 2013).

In psychology and the social sciences more broadly, two main issues have emerged as a consequence of increased digitalisation; (1) the ethics of social research, with regards to maintaining ethical research practices alongside secure data ownership, and (2) the approach to the collection, management, and analysis of very large data sets. While the former remains a challenging (and complex) topic in itself, we have dedicated this chapter to the exploration of the latter, which can also be termed "scientific storytelling". We have argued previously that the digitalisation of psychological research requires a "digitalisation" of our approach to data analysis and data visualisation, which could provide new benefits for psychological research, including applied domains within clinical and forensic settings (Ellis and Merdian, 2015). This also provided examples of interactive data visualisation as a way to enhance the communication and teaching of basic and complex statistical functions (Lowe, 2003). Therefore, the aim of this chapter is to introduce interactive visual graphics as one response to the digitalisation of psychological research. We will consider current challenges and the development of new visualisations before discussing the future impact on psychology as a whole.

Data visualisation in psychology

While psychological scientists have traditionally designed and conducted research to test predictions, visualise data, and provide statistical output, the introduction of digital data has changed the research environment dramatically. For example, it has now become standard practice to run experiments and surveys online. Psychologists are now able to access pre-existing administrative data sets or access increased samples through the use of mobile technology (Ellis and Jenkins, 2012; Woods, Velasco, Levitan, Wan, and Spence, 2015). Field research also has the capacity to produce very large data sets (e.g. Andrews, Ellis, Shaw, and Piwek, 2015), both in terms of the absolute sample size as well as the amount of information collected about each participant (Keuleers and Balota, 2015). Similar to theoretical paradigm development, research methods evolve gradually with accumulative knowledge and in response to social processes (Kuhn, 2012), and psychological research has indeed made considerable progress when it comes to exploratory, non-linear research designs (Columb and Sagadai, 2006; Huberty and Morris, 1989; Rothman, 1990; Sainani, 2009; Saville, 1990). However, developments concerning other statistical practices, data management, and visualisation have not kept pace with these developments.[1]

Historically, psychological research has seen a number of paradigms with regards to what defined the generation of "new knowledge". In 1987, Gigerenzer and Murray identified the *inference revolution*, the adoption of significance testing, as the essential paradigm for conducting empirical research and an essential component if research was to become published. But a shift in focus from significance testing to the exploration of effect sizes and confidence intervals (Sainani, 2009; Schmidt, 1996; Wilcox, 2006) suggests a move away from the significant vs non-significant dichotomy that has dominated the empirical literature in social sciences. This correlates with a gradual rise in innovative methods for visualising and interpreting data (Friendly, 2008), allowing a more flexible approach to data management. However, despite the importance of visualisation and exploration of data for psychology as a discipline, it has failed to become integrated into standard statistical practice (Gelman, 2012; Zuur and Ieno, 2016). What is often presented within or as a supplement to existing publications does not reflect recent advances in data collection and analysis. The communication of most research continues to rely on numerical or visual representations that are centred around the concept of static, paper-based journals.

In reality, almost all of our standard visual representations of data remain grounded in developments of almost 100 years ago. Friendly (2009) defined the second half of the nineteenth century as *The Golden Age of Statistical Graphics*, due to

> the unrestrained enthusiasm not only of statisticians, but of government and municipal authorities, by the eagerness with which the possibilities and problems of graphic representation were debated and by the graphic displays which became an important adjunct of almost every kind of scientific gathering.
>
> (p. 505)

According to Friendly, this rapid development was due to a combination of the increasing quantification of social data, advances in statistical thinking, and advances in technology that allowed images to be created more quickly. In contrast, in the first half of the twentieth century, Friendly and Denis (2000) argued that visual data representations largely disappeared from many journals, particularly within social and personality psychology, returning to representations in the form of numbers and tables. This move was partly driven by the development of statistical theory, which led to the standardised implementation of correlation and regression (Stanton, 2001). By 1908, Gosset had developed the t-test and between 1918 and 1925 Fisher had extended early ideas underpinning the ANOVA and experimental design further (Lovie, 1981). Through the enhancement of statistical theory in psychology, numbers came to be viewed as more precise than graphs, with visual representations of data used predominantly to support rather than confirm the statistical narrative (Figure 9.1).

These static graphical illustrations may remain perfectly adequate in some instances; however, their static nature can lead to a lack of transparency and information loss. In many cases, they can be fundamentally misleading (Allen, Erhardt, and Callhoun, 2012). For example, Anscombe's Quartet (Figure 9.2)

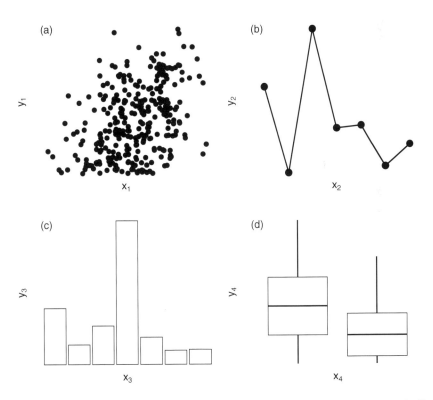

Figure 9.1 Typical static data visualisations used in psychology (a) scatter plot, (b) line graph, (c) bar graph, and (d) the less common box plot.

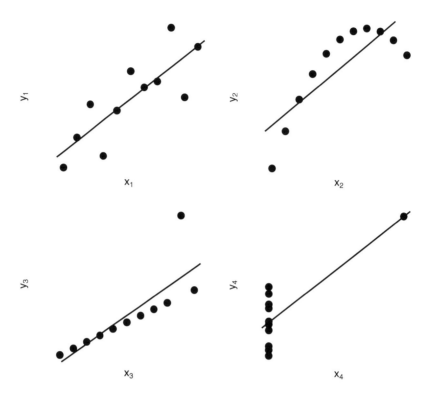

Figure 9.2 Anscombe's Quartet effectively demonstrates how very different distributions of data can return identical summary statistics.

reveals how very different distributions of data can be associated with numerically equal summary statistics; these different distributions would be readily disguised within traditional data portrayals, such as bar graphs. In addition, the benefits of illustrating data and its associated distributions that were previously emphasised in many publications and introductory statistical text-books are frequently ignored within academic publications (Zuur and Ieno, 2016). For example, data visualisations can typically provide insights concerning fundamental assumptions required by traditional statistical tests (e.g. normality). The lack of appropriate data visualisation in psychological journals has resulted in a lack of concrete examples that directly relate to psychological data, leading to new developments being frequently overlooked even within statistics itself (Gelman, Pasarica, and Dodhia, 2002).

We have previously summarised some of the limitations of static data visuali-sation, pointing to the restricted depth of these representations that are not adequate as larger and/or more complex data sets emerge (Ellis and Merdian, 2015; Heer and Kandel, 2012; Weissgerber, Milic, Winham, and Garovic, 2015). Indeed, the use of static graphs, such as bar graphs or box plots, as a standard way of reporting data can still lead to information loss that can be alleviated even by a small addition of interactivity. For example, interactive visualisations allow users to display the raw data points on top of any plot, thus instantly revealing the consistency of any underlying effect; these data points can then be hidden so the data is displayed in a summary format. Similarly, a trend line that is hidden or revealed can allow for the additional exploration of any linear (or non-linear) trend. Moreover, recent research has demonstrated that static data representations such as bar graphs are routinely misinterpreted by students (Newman and Scholl, 2012), with Moreau (2015) suggesting that visual and dynamic visualisations may be more appropriate when teaching complex statistical concepts. To exemplify this, in a previous paper, we presented an interactive regression as a teaching example where the model could be recalculated in real-time according to the research question, for example, to investigate differences between male and female participants separately (Figure 9.3).[2] In addition, these visualisations in isolation raise more questions about the data itself or may encourage an alternative analysis; here, in contrast to static figures, dynamic representations can provide a limitless supply of additional information (Ellis and Merdian, 2015).

In response to the digitalisation of psychological research methods, data figures have and will continue to evolve in order to maximise their expressive power, both with regards to conveying the content and structure of the data as well as informing the analysis process (Campitelli and Macbeth, 2014; Marmolejo-Ramos, 2014). So far, this has included computational developments, such as the expansion of box plots to include information about both

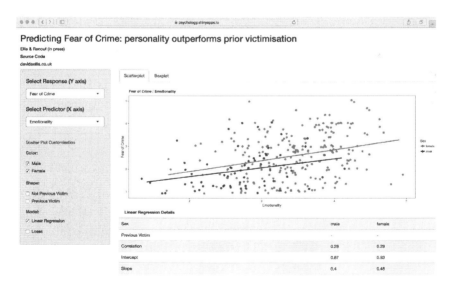

Figure 9.3 An interactive dashboard that provides a range of visualisation and analysis options.

distribution and density of the data (Marmolejo-Ramos and Matsunaga, 2009; Marmolejo-Ramos and Tian, 2010) or explorations of different data visualisations for particularly skewed data sets (Ospina, Larangeiras, and Frery, 2014). Many research groups have also started to develop new ways of visualising moderation analyses (e.g. Tay, Parringon, Huang, and LeBreton, 2016). Of course, while visualisation can provide tools for driving domains of interest, its adoption and adaptation is ultimately determined by the ability to build accurate and relevant models that produce useful answers. Surprisingly, very few papers actually explain how to build accurate data representations, and available resources appear to neglect the possibility of dynamic, software-based visualisations (Fry, 2007).

Developing dynamic data visualisations

To exemplify the ease of application when creating interactive data visualisations from scratch, we have developed both a website and related materials that will help anyone build simple visualisations and statistical applications that can quickly be deployed online.[3] These use *Shiny* (https://shiny.rstudio.com/), a web application framework for *R* (www.r-project.org). *Shiny* allows for the rapid development of data visualisations that enable researchers, practitioners, and members of the public to interact with the data in real-time and generate custom graphs and tables as required. The development of such dynamic visualisations previously required specialist knowledge of HTML, CSS, or JavaScript, which would often turn many researchers away at the outset. However, it is now possible to quickly produce interactive data visualisations that can supplement and support a variety of research findings. Digital researchers are therefore in a prime position to make meaningful contributions when it comes to developing innovative methods for visualising and interpreting findings.

At a universal level, the development of any interactive visualisation can be split into several smaller steps (Ellis and Merdian, 2015). This includes the preparation of data; here, it is crucial to ensure that the narrative the researcher is aiming to convey with the data is easy to understand by the reader, without the need to conduct any additional analysis. At this stage, the researcher may conclude that static visualisation is adequate. However, dynamic visualisations will often add additional value and transparency to the data set, particularly when it comes to enabling reviewers and other interested parties to explore the data in a fashion that is not reported within the original publication (Tay, Parringon, Huang, and LeBreton, 2016).

Following our earlier discussion concerning the limitations of bar graphs, the case study below demonstrates the value of interactive visualisation even within a relatively small data set, and provides a further introduction into the development of interactive graphics.[4]

Quantifying and assessing group differences remains a key part of psychological science and traditionally, if one wanted to test for a significant effect between two independent groups, they would compare the differences between

---

Case study: predicting smartphone operating system from personality and individual differences

This research study aimed to investigate if smartphones could provide clues about the individual behind the screen (Shaw, Ellis, Kendrick, Ziegler, and Wiseman, 2016). Extended Self-Theory suggests that the greater power and control a person has over an object, the more it becomes part of his or her self-identity (Belk, 2013). Aspects of a smartphone, including the type of operating system, can therefore be considered within this context and one can make sensible predictions grounded in the context of brand personality, which is quantifiably different between Android and iPhone smartphones.

This study therefore employed a straightforward between-subjects design where the researchers wanted to compare differences between two groups of smartphone users based on their operating system of choice (*Android* or *iPhone*). These devices account for over 90 per cent of all smartphones sold worldwide (IDC, 2016) and the final sample in this study consisted of 310 iPhone owners and 219 Android users. Participants completed a standard personality assessment, which measured six factors of personality (Ashton and Lee, 2009). They were also required to answer a number of additional questions about themselves and their attitudes towards smartphones.

The data can be reported in several ways, depending on the original research questions; for example, comparing means alongside a series of t-tests will reveal differences between the two groups. However, a more advanced analysis may subsequently aim to develop several regression models that could then predict future smartphone ownership based on the differences observed between the two groups.

---

means using several t-tests. However, these, like ANOVAs, are not always robust to outliers, particularly when only a small sample is available (Wilcox and Keselman, 2003; Wilcox, 2012). Similarly, measures of effect size including Cohen's *d* are also not robust in this respect (Wilcox, 2006). Graphically, even with a seemingly straightforward data set (see case study), static data visualisations (a single table or graph) could lead to information loss and incorrect conclusions. For example, a bar graph displaying the mean difference between two groups or conditions does not inform the reader about variance or outliers. Here, even a small addition of interactivity to the visualisation and statistical analysis can provide considerable insight. Displaying the original data points that make up each result is highly revealing when it comes to any outliers that might be driving significant results. Some argue that displaying raw data points leads to a rather messy and cluttered visual presentation, but dynamic presentation actually provides the best of both worlds in this instance – transparency of analysis alongside some detailed and informative visualisations.

To exemplify, we have built an interactive visualisation plot of the outlined study above using *Shiny* (https://psychology.shinyapps.io/smartphonepersonality/). The controls on the left allow visitors to explore the raw data set. A direct link to the location of the data is visible. Copying the URL into a web browser will allow anyone to download the original data set. The *x*-axis variable will default to *Smartphone*, which in this case is a categorical variable. Changing the *y*-axis will update the data display accordingly and allow a visitor to explore the differences between Android and iPhone users. Individual data points in the scatter plot can also be coloured based on a specific variable.

All graphics on the right will update in real-time based on the selections made on the left. This includes scatter plots and box plots. It is also possible to zoom into specific areas of these graphs by dragging the mouse over a specific area and double-clicking the mouse in the selected zone. Further, one can reset the viewpoint by double-clicking anywhere on the graph. Finally, the table will update with data points that are within the area of interest.

This simple visualisation can be adapted to suit other data sets where two groups or conditions are being compared. Provided the raw-data set is in a similar format, the data will simply transfer through the application with little or no modification to the existing code.

Generating impact with digital dashboards

Static visualisations typically become exponentially more difficult to understand as the complexity of the content they aim to display increases (Teknomo and Estuar, 2014). However, with careful management, dynamic data visualisations can provide a data format that is more accessible for a variety of user groups including other researchers, practitioners, interested members of the public, and students.

Benefits to the research community

Given the sheer number of scientific publications that appear every day, the challenge for researchers not only concerns getting papers published, but ensuring that others notice and engage with their work. This is before any attempt is made to reach out to other interested parties and stakeholders affected by the research findings. Providing access to an interactive storyboard, which can be shared with the public and journalists, is likely to lead to increased numbers of people engaging with the research; in the long-run, this may lead to more citations (Piwowar and Vision, 2013).[5]

Perhaps most importantly, the addition of dynamic data visualisation tools may also encourage active data sharing and transparency within the analysis. It is almost impossible for a reviewer to keep their statistical expertise current given the rate of progress concerning analysis (Siebert, Machesky, and Insall, 2015). Therefore, ensuring that the process of analysis and visualisation is clear will help share these developments, while simultaneously illuminating results. Computer code that sits alongside visualisations further enhances this usability (Gorgolewski and Poldrack, 2016).

An online, interactive dashboard also encourages good data management particularly if the associated data is also available from an online repository or directly from within the visualisation. Open data is almost certainly going to become standard practice for psychology in the next few years, with the 2015 RCUK Concordat on Open Research Data (Grand, Davies, Holliman, and Adams, 2015) stating that good data management is fundamental to all stages of the research process and should be established from the outset; all data must be curated so that it is accessible, discoverable, and useable.

The benefits of data dashboards for psychology are not simply limited to improved understanding and dissemination of research (and the related data), but also feed into issues surrounding transparency and replication. Data sets can now be issued and cited with DOI numbers, and these might be taken into account when it comes to future grant applications or replication research. However, this data will only become valuable if it is visible and easily accessible. This would allow researchers to revisit a paper's analysis and re-analyse the original data with improved methods in the future.

While cloud-based data repositories can improve research practices by ensuring that past research is integrated into current work, they still require a user-friendly interface that allows for rapid re-analysis and visualisation if they are to be successful. Given the fast nature of these developments and the associated ethical implications, it remains imperative that the twenty-first-century digital researcher remains vigilant and pro-active throughout. For example, the ability to compare multiple or pairs of replications side by side is now possible by providing suitable user interfaces. Tsuji, Bergmann, and Cristia (2014), for example, have recently developed the concept of Community-Augmented Meta-Analysis (CAMA), which involves a combination of meta-analysis and an open repository (e.g. PsychFileDrawer, 2016; Spellman, 2012). Developments such as these can improve research practices by ensuring that past research is integrated into current work, contributing to accumulative knowledge in psychology and beyond.

Benefits to society (bridging the practitioner–researcher gap)

We have argued previously, that dynamic data visualisation and cloud-based data sharing has particular benefits for applied psychology, where research sits at the interface between science and practice (Ellis and Merdian, 2015). In forensic and clinical psychology, research is often based on single-case studies (e.g. clinical intervention research) or small and diverse sample sizes (e.g. clinical subtypes, offending populations). Frequently, a large amount of data is collected for each case, resulting in limitations when it comes to the type of analysis that can be conducted as the assumptions for linear testing are not fulfilled, for example, with regards to offender profiling (e.g. Canter and Heritage, 1990; Goodwill, Lehmann, Beauregard, and Andrei, 2014) or offender classification and risk assessment (e.g. Merdian, Moghaddam, Boer, Wilson, Thakker, Curtis, and Dawson, 2016). Dynamic data visualisations are ideally placed to aid in the data display, exploration, outlier identification, and analysis of applied data sets, especially when it comes to more complex visual representation as required for multidimensional scaling. Using dynamic data plots, a researcher could easily display different types of cluster analysis (e.g. using different distance measures) and compare these alongside each other; or, by adapting examples outlined previously, develop an application that plots the progress of individual clients over several years, providing information on treatment change, outliers, and group trends over time. Thus, dynamic data visualisations hold specific appeal for applied psychology, and have the potential to become a shared platform for both scientists and practitioners.

Benefits for teaching

Such data-rich representations are likely to be helpful when teaching statistical concepts as data (and the relationships between variables) can be explored in real-time, and from different angles, allowing the student to match their engagement with the data based on their skills and knowledge. Many undergraduate psychology students are now being taught how to use *R*, *Shiny*, and other related visualisation tools (Barr, 2016). This represents a sensible step forward for the next generation of academics and practitioners. However, little research exists on its effectiveness within an educational context (Valero-Mora and Ledesma, 2014) and until recently, very little was known cognitively about how interacting with dynamic information can facilitate learning (Scaife and Rogers, 1996). Many questions remain unresolved in terms of how visualisation can assist with understanding. Memorability, for example, may be a factor as, interestingly; less memorable visualisations tend to be very traditional in their presentation (e.g. line and bar graphs). People appear to be better at remembering visualisations that are colourful and include a human recognisable object, but that does not confirm that viewers fully understand the content that has been presented (Borkin, Vo, Bylinskii, Isola, Sunkavalli, Oliva, and Pfister, 2013). In addition, while an expert user may believe they have created something practical and aesthetically pleasing, much of the literature surrounding human–computer interaction repeatedly demonstrates how a seemingly straightforward system that an expert considers "easy" to operate often poses significant challenges to new users (Norman, 2013). Future research is required in order to fully understand the effect interactive visualisations could have on, for example, a student's understanding of complex statistical concepts.

Future challenges to dynamic data visualisation

The digitalisation of psychological research has sparked the development of new ways to collect, store, analyse, and visualise data; however, if we are to move into the productive use of digital data management, several challenges remain, most predominantly, how to deal with "big data", how to respond to the lack of adequate software, and yet continue to encourage the psychological profession to adjust their own practice surrounding data management and visualisation within existing disciplinary constraints.

Dealing with "big data"

As technology has transitioned from lab-centred, computer-based systems towards Internet and remote collection, researchers are able to amass larger participant samples and thousands of data points from participants. For example, recent research has effectively demonstrated how we can better understand individuals with millions of data points derived from smartphones alongside a variety of other wearable and Internet-connected devices (Piwek, Ellis, Andrews, and Joinson, 2016). As outlined above, the expansion of these data sets brings with it many benefits but also new methodological concerns. Debates surrounding issues of replication alongside data that is arguably no longer suitable for traditional inferential statistics continue to dominate the research landscape (Keuleers and Balota, 2015).

Classic statistical analysis was based on the great insight that not every member of a population needs to be examined to make inferential statements about the whole population, based on the likelihoods of certain events occurring. Unfortunately, if not managed correctly, the focus on big data, and the need to collect, and process, more and more information, can actually be a step backwards with regards to knowledge generation within psychology. Large numbers of variables can also mean that key effects are missed or misinterpreted. However, we would argue that dynamic visualisation could help overcome these issues. It allows the researcher to focus on key variables based on existing empirical and theoretical knowledge of interest in the first instance and build in complexity as required. Even if the work is purely exploratory in nature, large data sets allow researchers to consider multiple questions simultaneously, or different questions at different times, leading to the development of new hypothesises. Returning to our case study, the dynamic data exploration provided an open-access reference point for other researchers, the popular press, and interested members of the public. This also helped stimulate a number of additional research projects. In summary, this dynamic data visualisation did not replace or repeat any statistical analysis within the original publication, but instead acted as a counterweight to help communicate and develop the research further (Shaw, Ellis, Kendrick, Ziegler, and Wiseman, 2016).

Into the cloud: the development and uptake of responsive visualisation software

In the social sciences, little is publicised concerning new ways to visualise and organise large data sets, with new developments often confided to computer science (Ellis and Merdian, 2015). Software to develop interactive visualisations has existed long before the Internet, but today there remains a lack of commercially available software with a simple graphical user interface that can help psychologists develop interactive, data-driven graphics, which can be easily uploaded online. When it comes to analysing and visualising data, almost every psychologist trained in the UK will be aware of *SPSS*. However, visualisation functions within *SPSS* are limited, as the software is no longer as actively developed with many standard analysis and visualisation functions unavailable (JASP Team, 2016). Similarly, the user interface requires refinement and has become overly complex, which makes statistical errors more difficult to spot (Smith and Mosier, 1986). Excellent free alternatives to mainstream statistical packages include *GNU PSPP* (www.gnu.org/ software/pspp/) and *JASP* (https://jasp-stats.org/) and for interactive visualisations *R* and *Shiny* portray accessible alternatives.

A handful of alternative, cloud-based solutions also now exist online that remove the need for any programme code. For example, *Plotly* (https://plot.ly/ feed/) allows for the development of interactive dashboards without a single line of code. However, going beyond basic functionality will require additional time and funding. The most powerful solution at present involves the use of *D3.js* (https:// d3js.org/), which is a JavaScript library for producing interactive data visualisations. However, this requires extensive knowledge from the user concerning other aspects of JavaScript. Commercial cloud services are easier to use,[6] but lack the ability to customise specific visualisation requirements that are very specific to each research design and data set. *Shiny*, on the other hand, sits somewhere in the middle between usability and flexibility. A basic knowledge of *R* is essential, but many free online courses are available and such training is frequently being built into postgraduate and even some undergraduate psychology courses (Barr, 2016). We would argue that recent technological advances will require social science courses to include basic coding modules as part of their research methods training.

Our examples demonstrate that the tools are relatively easy to access, and we hope this motivates the reader to consider their use in future work. The reality for many researchers is that in the digital domain, a small amount of programming knowledge can go a long way – dynamic visualisations can make a technically proficient user more productive, while also empowering students and those with limited programming abilities (Ellis and Merdian, 2015). At this stage, we would favour the flexibility of producing code to fine-tune each visualisation rather than to rely on commercial or point-and-click interfaces. Making these available as part of any publication is essential, for the peer review process, future replication, and the sharing of methodological developments.

Data visualisation within psychological science

While these developments are exciting and promise many benefits for psychology as a whole, they have yet to become commonplace for a number of reasons. As outlined, psychologists are currently ill-equipped to develop these visualisations and even with those skills, it takes longer to develop interactive visualisations in comparison to static graphs. This is further compounded when there is no agreed software platform that will help psychologists develop these new tools.

However, it is our view that open data and the additional transparency offered by dynamic visualisations is going to become standard practice for a number reasons. First, as the issues surrounding research impact are becoming unavoidable, more psychologists will start to use additional methods, including dynamic visualisation, to make these data sets usable and accessible to a larger audience. Second, large funders in the UK and abroad increasingly require data to be made usable and available to other researchers. Finally, there is a growing consensus that regardless of funder requirements, data analysed as part of any publication should be freely available and useable when required by other researchers. Until this is built into the publication process directly, psychology will continue to deal with the associated fallout (Van der Zee, Anaya, and Brown, 2017).

Psychological journals are playing catch-up at this stage, but it remains likely that the same will apply when journals start to integrate interactive dashboards and visualisations as part of their publication output. While publishers may conclude that space remains an issue, this does not apply in a digital context. Graphics have also repeatedly been shown to actually take up less space than their table-based counterparts (Gelman, Pasarica, and Dodhia, 2004). Researchers themselves will govern the speed of this development and if there is a clear demand, old and new journals may start to support this additional interactivity within their publications (Weissgerber, Milic, Winham, and Garovic, 2015). In doing so, psychology itself will lead the way, ensuring that old and new data sets can, for the first time, become an essential resource in their own right.

Theoretical frameworks to guide future development

Finally, the broader introduction of interactive data dashboards calls for the consideration of a theoretical and structural framework underlying these developments. Significant attention has been paid to the graphics used to present data in a variety of contexts, particularly following influential work by Tufte (2001 [1983]); however, this knowledge has not been integrated into theoretical developments. Often in science the theoretical background for a subject is considerable with little applied literature implementing it, but the literature on data visualisation is at the opposite end of the spectrum and often contradictory. Examples are plentiful in many journals concerned with quantitative analysis; however, few articles within psychology are dedicated to the theory of specific graphical forms. A new generation of statistical graphics as a whole, dynamic, or static, may encourage the development of a theoretical rationale concerning visualisations in the digital domain for both quantitative and qualitative data. New evaluative methodologies could be built into future visualisations, for example, to better understand the links between data visualisation and cognition. Scientists could then efficiently use these new tools to their advantage, particularly when attempting to get the attention of those outside of academia (Chen, 2005; Chen, Härdle, and Unwin, 2007).

Beyond theoretical contributions, dynamic data dashboards, like visualisations of the past will continue to depend on similar advances in technology, data collection, and statistical theory (Friendly, 2008). However, researchers also have to reconsider some ethical aspects of their work, particularly when it comes to issues surrounding data ownership, and the long-term security of participants' data. For example, many digital data collection tools and devices collect identifiable information from participants, such as their IP address, and in some countries, even store the data on the collection platform (e.g. Qualtrics). The establishment of ethical frameworks for digital data management and data sharing remains a pressing issue, but existing ethical guidelines for Internet-mediated research may act as a useful starting point (British Psychological Society, 2013).

Conclusion

The current chapter was written in response to the increased digitalisation of research, especially within psychology and across social science. We argue that digital research methods have the potential to revolutionise data management in our respective disciplines but that it has so far failed to be recognised and/or implemented by the research community. We further argued that dynamic data visualisation provide great mechanisms to promote this change, and have exemplified their development with a case study. We have described the benefits of dynamic data visualisations, and considered some of the challenges resulting from the digitalisation of psychological research as a whole. We hope this chapter will highlight the way towards an improved research toolset for the psychological community and help improve access to future research for both psychological peers and other interested parties.

Of course, we recognise that, at times, interactive visualisations will be unwarranted or less useful than static visualisations or tables, and distinctions need to be made between those that benefit experts and end-users with a more general interest. Perhaps more importantly, any form of data visualisation can only provide answers and insights into well-constructed questions. Dynamic data visualisation will never become a magic wand that can make sense from data chaos; however, careful execution and guidance combined with appropriate research questions will often ensure that simple and complex data sets are correctly interpreted and communicated in the digital domain.

Notes

1 Many developments concerning data visualisation have taken place in other disciplines (e.g. computer science). However, these have never been universally adopted across the social sciences.
2 See https://psychology.shinyapps.io/example3/.
3 See https://sites.google.com/site/psychvisualizations/.
4 Instructions and computer code required to build the example outlined in this chapter can also be found at the above address.
5 Other advocates of dynamic visualisation have suggested that academic papers as a whole need to be re-designed for computer screens that are not space orientated liketraditional physical journals. See http://worrydream.com/-!/ScientificCommunication AsSequentialArt.
6 *Tableau* has been used by online mainstream media outlets for many years but, at the time of writing, lacks any statistical functionality without additional development. See www.tableau.com.

References

Allen, E. A., Erhardt, E. B., and Callhoun, V. D. (2012). Data visualization in the neurosciences: Overcoming the curse of dimensionality. *Neuron, 74*, 603–608.
Andrews, S., Ellis, D. A., Shaw, H., and Piwek, L. (2015). Beyond self-report: Tools to compare estimated and real-world smartphone use. *PLOS ONE, 10*(10), e0139004.
Ashton, M. and Lee, K. (2009). The HEXACO-60: A short measure of the major dimensions of personality. *Journal of Personality Assessment, 91*, 340–345.

Barr, D. J. (2016). No more excuses: R is better than SPSS for psychology undergrads and students agree. Web blog post. Retrieved from https://datahowler.wordpress.com/2016/09/10/no-more-excuses-r-is-better-than-spss-for-psychology-undergrads-and-students-agree/.

Belk, R. W. (2013). Extended self in a digital world. *Journal of Consumer Research, 40*, 477–500.

Borkin, M. A., Vo, A. A., Bylinskii, Z., Isola, P., Sunkavalli, S., Oliva, A., and Pfister, H. (2013). What makes a visualization memorable? *IEEE Transactions on Visualization and Computer Graphics, 19*(12), 2306–2315.

British Psychological Society (2013). Ethics guidelines for internet-mediated research. Retrieved from www.bps.org.uk/system/files/Public%20files/inf206-guidelines-for-internet-mediated-research.pdf.

Campitelli, G. and Macbeth, G. (2014). Hierarchical graphical Bayesian models in psychology. *Rev. Colomb. Estadística, 37*, 319–339.

Canter, D. and Heritage, R. (1990). A multivariate model of sexual offence behaviour: Developments in "offender profiling". *The Journal of Forensic Psychiatry, 1*(2), 185–212.

Chen, C. (2005). Top 10 unsolved information visualization problems. *IEEE Computer Graphics and Applications, 25*(4), 12–16.

Chen, C. H., Härdle, W. K., and Unwin, A. (Eds) (2007). *Handbook of data visualization*. Berlin: Springer.

Columb, M. O. and Sagadai, S. (2006). Multiple comparisons. *Current Anaesthesia & Critical Care, 17*(3), 233–236.

Ellis, D. A. and Jenkins, R. (2012). Weekday affects attendance rate for medical appointments: Large-scale data analysis and implications. *PLOS ONE, 7*(12), e51365.

Ellis, D. A. and Merdian, H. L. (2015). Thinking outside the box: Developing dynamic data visualizations for psychology with shiny. *Frontiers in Psychology, 6*, 1782.

Friendly, M. (2008). A brief history of data visualization. In *Handbook of data visualization* (pp. 15–56). Berlin: Springer.

Friendly, M. (2009). The golden age of statistical graphics. *Statistical Science, 23*(4), 502–535.

Friendly, M. and Denis, D. (2000). Discussion and comments. Approche graphique en analyse des données. The roots and branches of modern statistical graphics. *Journal de la société française de statistique, 141*(4), 51–60.

Fry, B. (2007). *Visualizing Data*. Canada: O'Reilly.

Gelman, A. (2012). Exploratory data analysis for complex models. *Journal of Computational and Graphical Statistics, 14*(4), 755–779.

Gelman, A., Pasarica, C., and Dodhia, R. (2002). Let's practice what we preach: Turning tables into graphs. *The American Statistician, 56*(2), 121–130.

Gigerenzer, G. and Murray, D. J. (2015). *Cognition as intuitive statistics*. London: Psychology Press.

Goodwill, A. M., Lehmann, R. J., Beauregard, E., and Andrei, A. (2014). An action phase approach to offender profiling. *Legal and Criminological Psychology*. doi:10.1111/lcp.12069.

Gorgolewski, K. J. and Poldrack, R. A. (2016). A practical guide for improving transparency and reproducibility in neuroimaging research. *PLOS BIOLOGY, 14*(7), e1002506.

Grand, A., Davies, G., Holliman, R., and Adams, A. (2015). Mapping public engagement with research in a UK university. *PLOS ONE, 10*(4), e0121874.

Heer, J. and Kandel, S. (2012). Interactive analysis of big data. *XRDS: Crossroads, The ACM Magazine for Students, 19*(1), 50–54.

Huberty, C. J. and Morris, J. D. (1989). Multivariate analysis versus multiple univariate analyses. *Psychological Bulletin, 105*(2), 302.

IDC (2016). Smartphone OS market share, Q2. Retrieved from www.idc.com/prodserv/smartphone-os-market-share.jsp.

JASP Team (2016). *JASP (Version 0.7.5.5)*. Computer Software.

Keuleers, E. and Balota, D. A. (2015). Megastudies, crowdsourcing, and large datasets in psycholinguistics: An overview of recent developments. *The Quarterly Journal of Experimental Psychology, 68*(8), 1457–1468.

Kuhn, T. S. (2012). *The structure of scientific revolutions.* Chicago: University of Chicago press.

Lovie, A. D. (1981). On the early history of ANOVA in the analysis of repeated measure designs in psychology. *British Journal of Mathematical and Statistical Psychology, 34*(1), 1–15.

Lowe, R. K. (2003). Animation and learning: Selective processing of information in dynamic graphics. *External and Internal Representations in Multimedia Learning, 13*(2), 157–176.

McCandless, D. (2009). *Information is beautiful.* London: Collins.

McGrath, M. J. and Scanaill, C. N. (2013). *Sensor technologies: healthcare, wellness and environmental applications.* New York, NY: Apress.

Marmolejo-Ramos, F. and Matsunaga, M. (2009). Getting the most from your curves: Exploring and reporting data using informative graphical techniques. *Quant. Methods Psychol, 5,* 40–50.

Marmolejo-Ramos, F. and Tian, T. S. (2010). The shifting boxplot: A boxplot based on essential summary statistics around the mean. *Int. J. Psychol. Res., 3,* 37–45.

Merdian, H. L., Moghaddam, N., Boer, D. P., Wilson, N., Thakker, J., Curtis, C., and Dawson, D. (2016). Fantasy-driven versus contact-driven users of child sexual exploitation material offender classification and implications for their risk assessment. *Sexual Abuse: A Journal of Research and Treatment, 30*(3), 230–253.

Moreau, D. (2015). When seeing is learning: Dynamic and interactive visualizations to teach statistical concepts. *Frontiers in Psychology,* 6, 342.

Newman, G. E. and Scholl, B. J. (2012). Bar graphs depicting averages are perceptually misinterpreted: The within-the-bar bias. *Psychonomic Bulletin & Review, 19*(4), 601–607.

Norman, D. A. (2013). *The design of everyday things, revised and expanded edition.* New York, NY: Basic Books.

Ospina, R., Larangeiras, A. M., and Frery, A. C. (2014). Visualization of skewed data: A tool in R. *Rev. Colomb. Estadística, 37,* 399–417.

Piwek, L., Ellis, D. A., Andrews, S., and Joinson, A. (2016). The rise of consumer health wearables: Promises and barriers. *PLOS MEDICINE, 13*(2), e1001953.

Piwowar, H. A. and Vision, T. J. (2013). Data reuse and the open data citation advantage. *PeerJ, 1,* e175.

PsychFileDrawer (2016). PsychFileDrawer homepage. Retrieved from http://psychfiledrawer.org/.

Rothman, K. J. (1990). No adjustments are needed for multiple comparisons. *Epidemiology, 1*(1), 43–46.

Sainani, K. L. (2009). The problem of multiple testing. *PM&R, 1*(12), 1098–1103.

Saville, D. J. (1990). Multiple comparison procedures: The practical solution. *The American Statistician, 44*(2), 174–180.

Scaife, M. and Rogers, Y. (1996). External cognition: How do graphical representations work? *International Journal of Human–Computer Studies, 45*(2), 185–213.

Schmidt, F. L. (1996). Statistical significance testing and cumulative knowledge in psychology: Implications for training of researchers. *Psychological Methods, 1*(2), 115.

Shaw, H., Ellis, D. A., Kendrick, L. R., Ziegler, F., and Wiseman, R. (2016). Predicting smartphone operating system from personality and individual differences. *Cyberpsychology, Behavior, and Social Networking, 19*(12), 727–732.

Siebert, S., Machesky, L. M., and Insall, R. H. (2015). Overflow in science and its implications for trust. *ELife, 4*, e10825.

Smith, S. L. and Mosier, J. N. (1986). *Guidelines for designing user interface software.* Bedford, MA: Mitre Corporation.

Spellman, B. A. (2012). Introduction to the special section on research practices. *Perspectives in Psychological Science, 7*, 655–656.

Stanton, J. M. (2001). Galton, Pearson, and the peas: A brief history of linear regression for statistics instructors. *Journal of Statistics Education, 9*(3).

Tay, L., Parringon, S., Huang, Q., and LeBreton, J. M. (2016). Graphical descriptives: A way to improve data transparency and methodological rigor in psychology. *Perspectives on Psychological Science, 11*(5), 692–701.

Teknomo, K. and Estuar, M. R. (2014). Visualizing gait patterns of able bodied individuals and transitional amputees with the use of accelerometry in smart phones. *Rev. Colomb. Estadística, 37*, 471–488.

Tsuji, S., Bergmann, C., and Cristia, A. (2014). Community-augmented meta-analyses toward cumulative data assessment. *Perspectives in Psychological Science, 9*, 661–665.

Tufte, E. R. (2001) [1983]. *The visual display of quantitative information* (2nd Edition). Cheshire, CT: Graphics Press.

Valero-Mora, P. and Ledesma, R. (2014). Dynamic-interactive graphics for statistics (26 years later). *Revista Colombiana de Estadística, 37*(2), 247–260.

Van der Zee, T., Anaya, J., and Brown, N. J. (2017). Statistical heartburn: An attempt to digest four pizza publications from the Cornell Food and Brand Lab. *PeerJ Preprints, 5*, e2748v1.

Weissgerber, T. L., Milic, N. M., Winham, S. J., and Garovic, V. D. (2015). Beyond bar and line graphs: Time for a new data presentation paradigm. *PLOS BIOLOGY, 13*, e1002128.

Wilcox, R. R. (2006). Graphical methods for assessing effect size: Some alternatives to Cohen's d. *Journal of Experimental Education, 74*, 353–367.

Wilcox, R. R. (2012). *Introduction to robust estimation and hypothesis testing.* Amsterdam: Academic Press.

Wilcox, R. R. and Keselman, H. J. (2003). Modern robust data analysis methods: Measures of central tendency. *Psychological Methods, 8*, 254–274.

Woods, A. T., Velasco, C., Levitan, C. A., Wan, X., and Spence, C. (2015). Conducting preception research over the internet: A tutorial review. *PeerJ.*, e1058.

Zuur, A. F. and Ieno, E. N. (2016). A protocol for conducting and presenting results of regression-type analyses. *Methods in Ecology and Evolution, 7*(6), 636–645.

10 Designing digital platforms for citizen data and public discourse on climate change

Lily Bui

The proliferation of digital tools has allowed various fields to evolve with regard to how information is collected, for what purpose it is collected, and by whom. Within citizen science, digital tools on the web and mobile applications allow non-scientists to participate in data collection for research conducted by professional scientists (Bonney et al. 2009; Irwin, 1995; Silvertown, 2009). In parallel, public media has a similar goal of representing public discourse and issues of public concern for the general public audience (Clark and Aufderheide, 2009; Price and Raboy, 2003). In recent years, public media stations on TV and radio have adopted similar strategies to citizen science projects to solicit feedback from audiences, whereby individuals are invited to gather and collect information toward the production of a story (ProPublica, 2015; WNYC, 2013). For instance, WNYC's Cicada Tracker involved audience members building low-cost temperature sensors based on an open source hardware and software platform; collecting soil temperature readings over time; submitting this data to a central repository managed by data journalists; and visualizing the data on a map that told a story about the temperatures at which a specific brood of cicada began to emerge in the North-east region of the United States. The motivation behind soliciting feedback from audience members in this way varies, ranging from production of content, audience engagement, and public education. The common thread connecting many citizen science projects and public media projects is this: they are both increasingly mediated heavily by the use of digital tools.

iSeeChange is a digital platform that sits at the crux of both citizen science and public media. It was created by a team of journalists, designers, scientists, and citizens. Inspired by *The Farmers' Almanac*[1] model, the platform allows users to submit observations of climate and weather to a website that would then archive the observations as well as display the posts of other users. The platform adds one additional layer of interaction, which a traditional almanac would not afford: if a user posts an observation with a question about the observed phenomena in their own post, another user can respond to that post and generate discussion around it. Posts can also be sorted by week, season, and year. iSeeChange ran a pilot program in Paonia, Colorado, USA, in 2012 alongside public radio station KVNF. Over a period of two years, community members, comprising mostly rural farmers, submitted photographs, text, audio recordings, and video to the iSeeChange platform. During this two-year pilot run, the site garnered over 700 posts from 137 users. A total of 16 public radio stories were produced and broadcast on KVNF during the pilot phase, with one of them featured on the national radio program, *This American Life*.

The *raison d'être* of iSeeChange is to challenge normative models of environmental reporting that privilege the perspective of experts (scientists) while overlooking, minimizing, or failing to include the perspective of those affected by environmental issues and changes. The platform aims to address a need to prioritize the perspectives of people who would be most affected by environmental change, and to create a digital space in which local knowledge might be exchanged between them. At the same time, the platform's creation came about during a time in which climate scientists were in consensus about environmental change but public discourse was not. It is in this context that the media's role in moderating – and in some ways shaping – climate change discourse becomes important. Although the Intergovernmental Panel on Climate Change (IPCC), convening approximately 2,000 climate scientists, acknowledged that climate change is a threat that can lead to more extreme weather events and natural disasters (IPCC, 2012), public discourse about issues related to climate change, such as global warming, has been divided for some time (Doran and Zimmerman, 2009; Oreskes, 2004). This may have been, in part, due to media practices of covering climate change, which have "depicted conflict rather than coherence regarding scientific explanationals [*sic*] of anthropogenic climate change over time" (Boykoff, 2008, p. 40).

In a sense, communicating climate change effectively to wider audiences can be read as a problem of definition and scale. Schiappa (2003) writes that the beliefs that inform definitions are "human beliefs that are always subject to revision, whether the definition is one advanced by a philosopher, a scientist, an attorney, a legislator, a political activist, or anyone else" (p. xii). While research has revealed that media coverage of climate change has played a significant role in translations between science, policy, and the public (Bell, 1994; McComas and Shanahan, 1999; Smith, 2005), the meaning of climate change itself has shifted over the years, making translation a challenge. For instance, the term "global warming," first used in 1975 in an article by geochemist Wallace Broecker, often is conflated with "climate change," which dates back to 1956 in a study on carbon dioxide and climate science done by Gilbert Plass (Conway/NASA, n.d.). While the former refers to the increase in Earth's average surface temperature due to rising levels of greenhouse gases, the latter refers to a long-term change in the Earth's climate or a region of the Earth. Both terms have been used interchangeably, to the detriment of public understanding, as they refer to different notions. The more holistic term climate change refers not only global changes in temperature (both increases and decreases) but also to change in wind, precipitation, length of seasons, and frequency of extreme weather events.

Callison (2014) writes that a central challenge to communicating about climate change to mass audiences is how to render scientific facts meaningful and worthy of major address. One can argue that this can be read as a question of scale. Goodman et al. (2008) emphasize that understanding how scales are "jumped" or "shifted" is essential to understanding "power dynamics and relations that operate across biophysical and socio-political articulations of local, national, and global political ecologies" (see also Bracken and Oughton, 2006; Glassman, 2006; Massey, 2001; Swyngedouw, 2000). The project of relating the larger global phenomenon of climate change to local impacts on livelihoods and lifestyles involves a politics of scale construction and manipulation. Depending on how media coverage of climate change is framed with respect to scale, the perceived risks and consequences can vary. For example, a weather report about extreme weather in the Pacific during an El Niño year operates on a different scale than if the same story communicated the potential risks of the same storms on transportation, homes, and human safety. Callison writes:

> Engaging the public and politicians, explaining the science, and transforming scientific data into quantitative and/or economic rationales for policy changes with a range of direct and indirect ramifications – these are the difficult tasks that confront those wishing to see climate change addressed in the political and public arenas.
>
> (2014, p. 168)

For Callison, engaging more parties affected by climate change and building an evidence base for decision-making about climate policy is central to addressing the challenges of communicating about climate change. With the emergence of new digital technologies that further enable people to engage with media entities through mobile platforms, commenting on environments, and social media, environmental reporters increasingly have access to their audiences (and vice versa) through digital means. By doing so, actors within the citizen science and public media landscape confer value to local knowledge as an essential part of public discourse (Corburn, 2005; Huntington, 2000; Irwin and Michael, 2003).

Incidentally, design research and design processes play a critical role in how digital tools for research and public engagement manifest. The functionalities of digital tools used within citizen science and public media applications are usually determined, to some degree, by designers during an involved process of engaging stakeholders, assembling user research, and negotiating the costs and benefits of certain design choices. Thus, the design process of digital tools bears much influence on how effective the tools are in the field, whether its application is for data collection or public engagement around an issue such as climate change.

In 2014, the iSeeChange team expanded the platform beyond its pilot location. An additional partnership with NASA's Jet Propulsion Laboratory included technical support to incorporate into user posts open data from the Orbiting Carbon Observatory (OCO-2), the first dedicated satellite mission designed to monitor regional variations in atmospheric carbon dioxide (CO_2). The objective was to combine two different scales and types of data within climate change discourse: OCO-2 data would provide a global view of carbon dioxide levels, a greenhouse gas connected to human activity and increasing global temperatures, while user observations would continue to reveal weather and climate patterns at ground level. The collaboration with NASA-JPL and a new national focus necessitated a redesign of the pilot version of the iSeeChange platform.

This expansion of the pilot presented new design challenges specifically with regard to issues of definition and scale in translating knowledge about climate change across multiple audiences as opposed to only one. This chapter will offer a discussion of the methods involved in re-designing the iSeeChange platform between 2014 and 2015. I focus here on the design process rather than how the platform is used because it offers a novel perspective from which to view the relationship between researchers, media, citizen science, digital tools, and climate change discourse. In particular, this discussion will touch upon the key challenges in bridging quantitative and qualitative data among stakeholders, scaling global data down to local contexts, and making local knowledge relevant to global climate change discourse with the use of digital tools. Finally, the chapter ends with a brief discussion about what social researchers might be able to learn from the best practices within design research.

The design framework

During initial design stages, our team discussed at length the ability to use iSeeChange not only as a storytelling platform but also as a citizen science platform on which participants could explore data relevant to climate science. The principal stakeholders in this design project were the iSeeChange team, iSeeChange pilot participants, current and potential public media partners, and NASA-JPL. Our iSeeChange team consisted of seven individuals with backgrounds in journalism, citizen science, user experience design, software engineering, and public engagement. iSeeChange pilot participants were users from Paonia, Colorado, who had volunteered their feedback on the platform. Public media partners included KVNF radio and a consultant for public media stations. The NASA-JPL team included a software engineer and public engagement director for data applications at the lab.

The two core design challenges were: (1) interpreting quantitative, global-scale climate data from scientists for an audience of non-scientists (comprising media partners and iSeeChange participants); and (2) making qualitative, local-scale observations of environmental change from non-scientists relevant and useful to scientists. In order to begin addressing an approach to these challenges, the iSeeChange team abstracted and prioritized concepts that the platform should aim to connect in future design iterations: local to global, citizen science to public media, qualitative data to quantitative data, and weather and climate events to larger patterns. These relationships served as a baseline for discussions held throughout the design process (Figure 10.1).

By attempting to connect local perspectives of environmental change generated by non-expert publics to global perspectives generated by a government

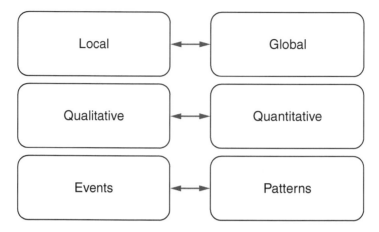

Figure 10.1 Chart outlining categories of information that the new iSeeChange platform
aims to combine.

agency, we hoped to provide a means of revaluing forms of knowledge production from the bottom up. Similarly, but attempting to design and build a platform
that enables connections between qualitative and quantitative data, and likewise
between events and patterns, we hoped to generate new ways for informal knowledge communities to construct meaning across different scales of information.
In a more general sense, this framework also gestures toward the affordances of
participatory approaches in research when working within the digital space. That
is, the wide availability of digital tools and platforms has enabled more experimentation within many fields and areas of interest in order to collect or generate
data for public interests (Johnson and Turner, 2003).

The design research

For our design team, there was a need to understand how existing users were (or
were not) interacting with the pilot version of the platform. Because our team
wanted to learn about the experience of pilot participants in Paonia, Colorado, in
order to inform design decisions for potential new users, we chose a human-
centered design approach (Greenhouse, 2012; Roschuni, Goodman, and
Agogino, 2013), which involves foregrounding the feedback and recommendations from the then-current user base and principal stakeholders to inform
different stages of the design process.

An immediate challenge to a human-centered approach was that while the
core user base was located in Paonia, Colorado, most of our team was dispersed
throughout the rest of the United States and had chosen to convene in New
Orleans, Louisiana, where the iSeeChange leadership was based. Because
the likelihood of meeting with the Paonia pilot community was low, we
adjusted our methods to involve participants using remote and digital methods of

communication. To begin the design research process, the core iSeeChange team developed and distributed a community survey to assess how users interacted with the pilot version of the platform and to get a sense of what features users would be interested in for future iterations of the site. In order to design the survey questions, three members of the iSeeChange team collaboratively drafted survey questions on a mutual Google document in order to share ideas. A finalized version of the survey contained nine questions that were entered into a SurveyMonkey form. To recruit respondents, the iSeeChange team distributed the survey link in a community newsletter to current iSeeChange users. The survey link was also posted on the iSeeChange social media accounts. A total of 27 people responded and completed the survey.

We then followed up with semi-structured interviews with participants who volunteered to speak with us over the phone, Skype, or e-mail. Interview questions interrogated how users typically navigated the site and suggestions for new features or improvement of existing features. With consent, some interviews were recorded and played back to our design team once all the team members had convened in New Orleans. By combining survey responses with interviews, we developed an understanding of general attitudes toward interaction with the pilot version of the platform.

We recognize that respondents to the survey were likely regular users of the site and not necessarily the most representative sample of the entire user base, which is a limitation for the design research; however, these respondents were the most reliable and accessible informants for learning about the attitudes of those who were already engaged with the platform and project mission. Due to the team's limited timeline and budget for design research and development, we chose this sample population and set of methods to gain a preliminary understanding of users' attitudes and behaviors on the site. To be clear, our survey and interview process was oriented toward the design process and was not a rigorous academic study. Our analysis of the results was cursory and did not involve additional statistical modeling. The survey questions were designed to capture very broad attitudes toward the platform, as well as the general behavior of participants who used the platform regularly.

While the survey allowed us a cursory look at user interaction with the platform, the interviews provided insight for more nuanced experiences and user decision-making processes that participants went through while navigating the site. A general summary of our findings from the survey and interviews are as follows:

A: Participants who engage with iSeeChange regularly are vigilant about understanding weather patterns and actively seek out weather information.

Many respondents reported that outside of using the iSeeChange platform, they were also regular checkers of "weather news," "temperatures, storms," "western snow pack reports, regional climate synopses and predictions." Respondents also reported checking factors like "highs and lows, first and last frost." Some respondents gave specific reasons for checking weather data, from a desire to check daily readings to trip planning. One respondent mentioned monitoring drought, snow water, and water vapor.

B: Participants look for weather information from various sites and sources.

Respondents' sources for weather data included NOAA, AccuWeather, Weather. com, "weather sites online," CoCoRAHS, National Weather Service, public radio stations, satellite data, and a service called Intellicast. Some also mentioned that they checked local temperature or weather stations, and one respondent reported monitoring the impacts of livestock grazing on arid public lands through a number of NGOs.

C: Participants are interested in being able to explore specific variables that constitute weather information that is particularly relevant to their personal interests.

Respondents cited wanting the ability to track factors like moisture, warming, temperature, global and polar ice melts, oceanic temperatures, wind speed/ direction, precipitation, annual rain/snow, first/last frost, and annual highs/lows in temperature. Other respondents more familiar with farming reported wanting to track seed germination, planting dates, plant growth, when flowers bloom, and other phenologies. For example, a respondent was interested in "how fast it warms up in the spring and cools down in [*sic*] the fall ... and how they relate to plant growth over time." Another respondent wanted to know if each year is getting increasingly warmer, as she is interested in plotting duck migration arrival times.

D: Reasons that some respondents stop using the platform over time varied, spanning not having access to the internet to not being able to make sense of the observations being posted on the platform.

Some respondents reported not being able to access a computer when the idea occurred or not being able to post from a smartphone or mobile device. One respondent replied, "Most information is way too anecdotal to be useful and I don't want to join that crowd." Another thought that their observations would not have been significant enough to report on the platform.

E: Participants recommended specific changes in the platform's interface design to improve their experience.

Some called for better sharing and comparing features on the site, i.e. being able to share posts and comparing against others' posts. More than one respondent suggested displaying posts by region so that users could compare stories and data from one area to another. Other respondents suggested a way to aggregate posts based on how many people were talking about the same thing. Another suggestion was to include data from local weather stations for the purposes of data accuracy.

From findings A, B, and C, our team learned that the participants who were most engaged with the pilot version of the platform are curious about weather information and seek ways to access it. They also validated for our team that a citizen science approach to the platform would appeal to the types of participants the platform is meant to attract, in that enabling more non-scientists to engage with scientific information through iSeeChange would be among the interests of those already using the platform. Findings D and E gave our team valuable insights on which design changes the participants wanted to see most in the next version of the platform.

These findings related closely with the needs our team identified in our design framework. Our interpretation of findings A, B, and C led us to recognize the need to personalize – and thus localize – weather information that otherwise came from sources that represented data at different scales, so that participants could explore information that was most relevant to them. We also recognized the need to help participants make meaning and draw clearer relationships between the qualitative, "anecdotal," local-scale observations that they were providing on the platform with wider climate trends that might be better explored through quantitative, global-scale data from weather data sources. These findings are what most informed our conversations during the design process and reinforced our belief that design could lead to an improvement of the experience of participants.

The design process

Over the course of three days, the design team met in New Orleans, Louisiana, in order to review design research materials, as well as to develop a "minimum viable product" version of the new iSeeChange platform, based on the survey and interview findings. Most important during this process was to constantly reflect upon the implications of each design decision on each principal stakeholder (i.e. the iSeeChange core team, the iSeeChange pilot participants, the current and potential public media partners, and NASA-JPL). While the core iSeeChange design team met physically in person, individuals representing all other principal stakeholder groups joined in at least once remotely through the phone, Skype, chat, or e-mail.

First, our design team constructed user "personas" in order to conceptualize the different typologies of users who would engage with the iSeeChange platform. Personas are considered "fictitious, specific, concrete representations of target users" of a platform (Pruitt and Adlin, 2006). A persona can represent an aggregate of user typologies that share common behavioral or attitudinal characteristics. As Miaskiewicz and Kozar (2011) write, personas also "limit the design choices available to designers to allow for calculated design decisions." In other words, by limiting for whom the product is designed and what features are vital, personas help prioritize design decisions. Having developed the personas also allowed our team to systematically think through the myriad value systems and incentives that would draw the user to the site throughout the weekend.

To create the personas, our team reviewed survey and interview responses in their entirety over a four-hour period. Each team member took notes on recurring themes and patterns in the user feedback. The design team shared notes by capturing ideas on Post-its, then placing them all on a board visible to everyone (Figure 10.2). Collectively, the team created and curated clusters of user feedback on the board based on characteristics they had in common. For example, if several people had placed notes on the board about users who preferred certain features or had certain attitudes, those notes would end up clustered together. The clusters were then given categorical names. Five categories of users eventually emerged: (1) the curious layperson, which included students and citizen scientists; (2) media makers, which included journalists and storytellers; (3) scientists, which included researchers and others in academia; (4) data providers, which included national government agencies with open data sets like NASA and NOAA; and (5) policymakers. This typology reflected who the design team either observed to be users of the site or envisioned as potential users of the site after the redesign. Each time a design decision had to be made during the workshop, the team would refer back to how the decision might affect each of these personas.

Figure 10.2 Post-its and whiteboard during the wireframing process.

User personas became especially important when the team began to conceptualize how to construct meaning from the combination of different scales of information on the site. For instance, when it came to discussing how NASA's OCO-2 data would be displayed, thinking through the different user roles reminded the design team that there would be varying levels of expert knowledge among users. The language could neither be too technical, which might deter the "curious layperson," nor too abstract, which might receive scrutiny for not being rigorous enough from the scientific and research community. The design team extensively discussed different ways that NASA data could be combined with text and images, but discussion alone had its own limitations. Because the team was faced with designing something that did not yet exist, there were few precedents that the team could point to and use to exemplify abstract design ideas and suggestions.

At this point, the team decided to take on more visual forms of sharing and communicating ideas; we broke into smaller teams of people, tasked with drawing out basic wireframes, or rough sketches that illustrate the functional elements of a web page, for the next version of the platform (Figure 10.3). Our design team divided into smaller groups to draw wireframes for specific tasks and functions. For example, one team was tasked with designing how the user would interact with satellite data while another was tasked with designing how a user would generate a typical post on the platform. We produced our drawings on Post-its, scratch paper, and whiteboards, and then came back together to discuss our results. The team eventually voted on ideas that seemed appropriate and collectively eliminated other ideas that seemed extraneous or less fitting.

After the conclusion of the design workshop, the collaborative sketches, diagrams, and ideas generated by the design team were documented and captured in photographs, shared documents, and audio recordings and further refined over subsequent months. More finalized wireframes, or sketches of each page on the platform, were produced, and a developer on the iSeeChange team built a new front and back end for the iSeeChange platform, which incorporated many of the design tenets discussed during the weekend workshop. During a soft launch period, the iSeeChange team invited representatives from each principal stakeholder group to test an early version of the site and asked for additional feedback, which was taken into account for further refinements to the platform.

The final and most recent version of the iSeeChange platform directly addresses the findings uncovered during the design research and design process phases of this work. To address participant tendencies to explore different types of weather information, the new platform consolidates different types of weather and environmental data. A post on iSeeChange can contain an image and some text that records a user's observation about the environment (Figure 10.4). Below each post is an option called "data," which expands into a map that displays the latest NASA OCO-2 data in various forms. There is a map-based view that displays the post's location in relation to the most recent track of the OCO-2 satellite. Different levels of carbon dioxide in parts per million (ppm), an overall volume of carbon dioxide where the satellite has passed by, appear in different

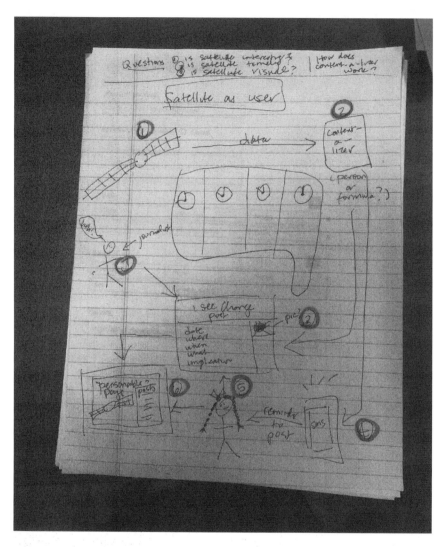

Figure 10.3 Team sketches during the wireframing process.

colors on the map. These colors coordinate with the spectrum directly above the map, which indicates the relative level of ppm (low to high, from left to right) in the atmosphere. It is also possible to zoom in and out of the default view in order to see surrounding areas. This more visual method of communicating OCO-2 data avoids using more complex, technical jargon associated with the data set. The platform also includes additional weather information from a weather data aggregator called Forecast.io. This weather information is location-specific and is tied directly to each user post. For example, if a user were to post an

Figure 10.4 New interface for the iSeeChange platform.

observation from San Diego, California, the user would be able to view and explore NASA carbon dioxide level data and weather information specific to San Diego right alongside their original post.

Additionally, the new version of the platform directly incorporates design changes that originated from the recommendations of engaged participants from the pilot version. There are now ways to share individual posts on social media, more location-specific ways of organizing and viewing the posts, new ways to create "back posts," that allow users who do not have Internet access at the time they capture an observation to upload their observations at a later date and time.

These design choices were directly informed by participants in iSeeChange's pilot platform, but they were supplemented by additional feedback from representatives of each stakeholder group at different points of the design process.

At the time of writing, the new platform has been launched, and users from the previous version of the site have migrated to the new version, submitting regular posts, with new entries each week.

Looking ahead: is design for digital participation enough?

The task of navigating and negotiating the needs of each stakeholder group required that the design team think across disciplines and audiences. This project involved a human-centered design approach to the redesign of the iSeeChange platform in order to design a digital environment that combines two types (quantitative and qualitative) and scales (global and local) of climate data. The design process itself as a unit of analysis for this work reveals meaningful insights not only of how researchers situate digital tools in social research but also of the design process itself within social research. The human-centered design approach bears resemblance to certain aspects of participatory action research approaches; both place emphasis on collaborative data collection and generation with the community being studied (Israel et al., 2003; Nelson and Wright, 1995; Whyte, 1991). Within the realm of design, human-centered design allows users of a product or process to directly influence the outcomes of the design of that product or process. The results are also meant to be transparent to the users who participated in the design process. Within the realm of scholarly research, participatory action research methods directly involve affected communities in developing research agendas and tools; results of the research are also usually shared or distributed among affected communities as well. More participatory approaches in design and social research may potentially lead to more meaningful interactions between designers and researchers, and target audiences and communities being designed for or studied.

iSeeChange's design interventions may also face new challenges in its future in the form of evolving citizen science and media technologies, developments in climate science, and sustainability of partnerships involved in the project in its current state. Another challenge lies in motivating use of the platform over time and developing a more robust understanding of why current users are incentivized to participate. One final challenge is more of an existential one and can be summed up in a single question: *is design for digital participation enough?* Because the iSeeChange platform involves participation in a project with a clear stance on environmental change – that it is, indeed, occurring – it can be viewed as a form of civic participation or digital activism as much as it is an act of citizen science (Joyce, 2010). However, it remains to be seen where the long-term impacts of digital participation may lead.

Future scholarship should investigate whether participation in climate change campaigns within digital spaces also translates into offline participation and advocacy beyond the digital environment as well. The project of making meaning out of climate change science for various publics is one that will continue well into the future, but whether or not online discourse and participation extend to offline action such as attitude changes, behavior changes, and policy changes, deserves further study.

Note

1 *The Farmers' Almanac* is an annual North American periodical that has been in continuous publication since 1818. Published by Geiger of Lewiston, Maine, it is famous for its long-range weather predictions and astronomical data.

References

Arnstein, S. R. (1969). A ladder of citizen participation. *JAIP, 35*(4), 216–224.

BBC. (2015). COP21 climate change summit reaches deal in Paris. BBC Science and Environment. Available at: www.bbc.com/news/science-environment-35084374 (accessed December 17, 2015).

Bell, A. (1994). Climate of opinion: Public and media discourse on the global environment. *Discourse and Society, 5*(1), 33–64.

Ben-Joseph, E. (2011). City design in the age of digital ubiquity. In T. Banerjee and A. Loukaitou-Sideris (Eds.), *Companion to urban design*. London: Routledge.

Bonney, R., Cooper, C. B., Dickinson, J., Kelling, S., Phillips, T., Rosenberg, K. V., and Shirk, J. (2009). Citizen science: A developing tool for expanding science knowledge and scientific literacy. *BioScience, 59*(11), 977–984.

Boykoff, M. T. (2008). Fight semantic drift!? Mass media coverage of anthropogenic climate change. In M. Goodman, M. T. Boykoff, and K. Evered (Eds.), *Contentious geographies: Environmental knowledge, meaning, scale* (pp. 39–57). Farnham: Ashgate.

Bracken, L. J., and Oughton, E. A. (2006). 'What do you mean?' The importance of language in developing interdisciplinary research. *Transactions of the Institute of British Geographers, 31*(3), 371–382.

Broecker, W. (1975). Climatic change: Are we on the brink of a pronounced global warming? *Science, 189*, 460–463.

Callison, C. (2014). *Forms of life: How climate change comes to matter*. Durham, NC: Duke University Press.

Chapman, C. N. and Milham, R. P. (2006). The persona's new clothes: Methodological and practical arguments against a popular method. In *Proceedings of the Human Factors and Ergonomics Society*. HFES, pp. 634–636.

Clark, J. and Aufderheide, P. (2009). *Public media 2.0: Dynamic, engaged publics*. Washington, DC: Center for Social Media, American University.

Conway, E./NASA (n.d.) Available at: www.nasa.gov/topics/earth/features/climate_by_any_other_name.html

Corburn, J. (2005). *Street science: Community knowledge and environmental health justice*. Cambridge, MA: The MIT Press.

Doran, P. T. and Zimmerman, M. K. (2009). Examining the scientific consensus on climate change. *Eos, Transactions of American Geophysical Union, 90*(3), 22–23.

Glassman, J. (2006). Primitive accumulation, accumulation by dispossession, accumulation by 'extra-economic' means. *Progress in Human Geography, 30*(5), 608–625.

Goodchild, M. F. (2007). Citizens as sensors: The world of volunteered geography. *GeoJournal, 69*, 211–221.

Goodman, M., Boykoff, M., and Evered, K. (Eds.). (2008). *Contentious geographies: Environmental knowledge, meaning, scale.* Farnham: Ashgate.

Greenhouse, E. S. (2012). Human-centered design. *Livable New York resource manual.* New York: Nova Iorque.

Huntington, H. P. (2000). Using traditional ecological knowledge in science: Methods and applications. *Ecological Applications, 10*(5), 1270–1274.

Irwin, A. (1995). *Citizen science: A study of people, expertise and sustainable development.* Hove: Psychology Press.

Irwin, A. and Michael, M. (2003). *Science, social theory and public knowledge.* Maidenhead: McGraw-Hill.

IPCC (2012). *Managing the risks of extreme events and disasters to advance Climate change adaptation. A special report of Working Groups I and II of the Intergovernmental Panel on Climate Change.* C. B. Field et al. (Eds.). Cambridge: Cambridge University Press.

Israel, B. A., Schulz, A. J., Parker, E. A., Becker, A. B., Allen, A. J., and Guzman, J. R. (2003). Critical issues in developing and following community-based participatory research principles. *Community-Based Participatory Research for Health, 1*, 53–76.

Johnson, B. and Turner, L. A. (2003). Data collection strategies in mixed methods research. In A. M. Tashakkon and C. B. Teddlie (Eds.), *Handbook of mixed methods in social and behavioral research* (pp. 297–319). London: Sage.

Joyce, M. C. (Ed.). (2010). *Digital activism decoded: The new mechanics of change.* London: IDEA.

Koonin, S. (2014). Climate science is not settled. *Wall Street Journal.* Available at: www.wsj.com/articles/climate-science-is-not-settled-1411143565 (accessed December 17, 2015).

Massey, D. (2001). Geography on the agenda 1. *Progress in Human Geography, 25*(1), 5–17.

McComas, K. and Shanahan, J. (1999). Telling stories about global climate change: Measuring the impact of narratives on issue cycles. *Communication Research, 26*(1): 30–57.

Miaskiewicz, T. and Kozar, K. A. (2011). Personas and user-centered design: How can personas benefit product design processes? *Design Studies, 32*(5), 417–430.

Moore, S. (2015). The myth of 'settled' science. *Washington Times.* Available at: www.washingtontimes.com/news/2015/mar/15/stephen-moore-climate-change-not-settled-science (accessed December 17, 2015).

Nelkin, D. (1987). *Selling science: How the press covers science and technology.* New York: Freeman.

Nelson, N. and Wright, S. (1995). *Power and participatory development: Theory and practice.* ITDG Publishing.

Norman, D. A. (2005). Human-centered design considered harmful. *Interactions, 12*(4), 14–19.

Oreskes, N. (2004). The scientific consensus on climate change. *Science, 306*(5702), 1686–1686.

Price, M. E. and Raboy, M. (2003). *Public service broadcasting in transition: A documentary reader.* Dordrecht: Kluwer Law International.

ProPublica. (2015). ProPublica's 'Get Involved' aims to spur more crowd-powered news. *ProPublica.* Available at: www.propublica.org/article/propublicas-aims-to-spur-more-crowd-powered-news (accessed April 6, 2017).

Pruitt, J. and Adlin, T. (2006). *The persona lifecycle: keeping people in mind throughout product design.* San Francisco: Morgan Kaufmann.

Roschuni, C., Goodman, E., and Agogino, A. M. (2013). Communicating actionable user research for human-centered design. *Artificial Intelligence for Engineering Design, Analysis and Manufacturing, 27*(02), 143–154.

Schiappa, E. (2003). *Defining reality: Definitions and the politics of meaning.* Carbondale, IL: SIU Press.

Silverman, C. (2015). Lies, damn lies, and viral content: How news websites spread (and debunk) online rumors, unverified claims, and misinformation. Tow Center for Digital Journalism.

Silvertown, J. (2009). A new dawn for citizen science. *Trends in Ecology and Evolution, 24*(9), 467–471.

Smith, J. (2005). Dangerous news: media decision making about climate change risk. *Risk Analysis, 25,* 1471.

Swyngedouw, E. (2000). Authoritarian governance, power, and the politics of rescaling. *Environment and Planning D, 18*(1), 63–76.

Whyte, W. F. E. (1991). *Participatory action research.* London: Sage.

Wilson, K. M. (1995). Mass media as sources of global warming knowledge. *Mass Communications Review, 22*(1, 2): 75–89.

WNYC. (2013). Cicada Tracker. WNYC Radio. Available at: https://project.wnyc.org/cicadas (accessed April 6, 2017).

11 In search of lost purpose
The dream life of digital

Erinma Ochu

Phenomena are unstable and impermanent – a dance of particles – an instability we are unable to control. We cannot create permanence.

(Jaya Graves, 2010)

Introduction

Beyond making the findings discoverable and accessible to non-academics, how else might the cultural legacy of digital science projects be broadened when they are finished? How might the before and afterlives of these projects be experienced, by whom, and for what purpose? How might the cultural life of digital research projects fuel people's imaginations, right wrongs, shape identities, and foster social care?

This chapter is an auto-ethnographic exercise to recall, speculate on and consider the unintended consequences of digital citizen science methods and the potential impact they have on people's lives. By situating my ethical failings as a young scientist and curator of digital research methods alongside community stories, I aim to enhance my reflection on the design and evolution of two consecutive participatory digital citizen science projects, Turing's Sunflowers and #Hookedonmusic. My aim is that this approach paves the way to attend to emerging ethical concerns to help us begin to think about living and thriving with the pervasiveness of digital technology.

Essentially, this chapter aims to evolve digital scholarship to embrace diverse socio-political realities. It encourages marginalised scholars to tune into the creative direction of our lived experiences, particularly in navigating the conflicts and tensions that often emerge at the boundaries of public and private space and the differences in reality between our inner and outer worlds (Burton and Kagan, 2003).

I invite digital scholars to consider which values they choose to carry forward into the art and crafting of digital spaces and the extent to which they support cultural democracy. Here I offer a social praxis through which to reflect on how digital scholarship is performed in order to imagine different futures. I ask what shared values, social purposes and stewardship must emerge.

A seat at the table

In writing this chapter, I am inspired by using an open-ended approach that touches on the ways in which academia is performed (Cooper and Condie, 2016), embraces auto-ethnographic, black feminist traditions of intellectual activism (Hill Collins, 2014), embodied intersectionality (Mirza, 2017) and Tim Berners-Lee's vision for the World Wide Web which is 'about anything potentially being connected to anything and this decentralising core principle, freeing us from the hierarchical classification systems to which we have bound ourselves … it brings the workings of society closer to the workings of our minds' (1999, pp. 1–2).

As a queer, politically black academic, I am mindful of becoming a 'professionally defended type of academic who's only half-alive, intellectually and otherwise' (Dollimore, 2016, p. 1034) and find myself with a pent-up desire to offer an oppositional gaze (hooks, 1992).

On re-entering academia, I had an existential crisis in writing my biography: how do I honour and embrace the publication gaps which jump from neuroscience (Ochu, Rothwell and Waters, 1998) to citizen-led digital innovation (Whittle et al., 2012) to citizen science (Swinton and Ochu, 2016)? My academic performance has changed radically, disrupting my scientific identity in the process, as it has other black scientists before me (Carlone and Johnson, 2007; Opara, 2017). While embracing digital methods is part of that, it is far from the full story. I wonder how best to recount my experiences of social injustice that created the political lens that deeply informed my methodological approaches, and under this direction, how my digital methods dream of finding a social purpose. Turning to feminist auto-ethnography, therefore, offers the opportunity to recognise the limits of scientific knowledge and to queer normative paths (Ettorre, 2017).

And, as my fields of digital science communication and, specifically, citizen science begin to embrace narrative methods (Roberts and Constant, 2017) and to communicate scientific concepts by leaving traces of memory to aid future recollection that informs future actions and strategies (Downs, 2014), it is crucial to position these approaches alongside the narrative traditions and actions politicised by black activists, artists, writers, cultural producers, feminist, disabled and queer, scholars and allies (Ochu, 2017). Who might you invite to your methodological table and why? 'You need your favourite feminist books close to hand; … Kick-ass feminist books have a special agency, all of their own. I feel propelled by their kick … their words teach me. Wherever I go, they go' (Ahmed, 2017, p. 240). My aim is to assert the value of imagination, independence, resistance, friendship and lateral thinking, when considering how to approach digital methods. This involves considering how methodological decisions are experienced, by whom and to what ends. Through reflexivity and a focus on affective learning by telling stories, attending to feelings and human values (Hawkins, 2017), I encourage an exploration of designing digital and non-digital interactions in the making of the method to transform scientific identity with social actions (Opara, 2017) and giving back to others (Carlone and Johnson, 2007). 'We cannot escape the legacies of the past, but we can use them to model our future' (Eddo-Lodge, 2017, p. 223).

Favourite things: towards participatory digital research

I grew up in the East End of London with no idea I was poor, black, female and queer until I won an assisted place to attend a private secondary school. Raised by my mum and her diverse network of friends, in between school, church and playing out in the streets, I danced to my sister's records and cut out and collected images of viruses from the newspaper. My mum gave me a red box to store these scientific dreams.

I daydreamed about getting a computer, but it was out of my price range. Instead, I saved £1 a week for 13 weeks from a paper round to buy a miniature Kodak camera. I agonised over owning a machine that, at the click of a button, could capture my version of events, given analogue photography's 'privileged relationship to reality' (Mulvey, 2006, p. 18).

To my utter joy, for Christmas, my mum's partner gave us a black and white TV with a ZX81 Sinclair computer. I taught myself to code from a magazine and wrote games. The creative possibilities that a computer offered did not occur to me as I dodged bullets and shot down pixelated alien ships.

Without warning, aged 11, going to *that* private school, the belief that black children from the most deprived part of London do not amount to anything, burst into my world. A torrent of fear swept up my dreams. A fear that creates shame, guilt and over years, seething anger. James Baldwin articulates this particular fear:

> It was not at all like the fear I heard when one of us was ill or had fallen down the stairs or strayed too far from the house. It was another fear, a fear that the child, in challenging the white world's assumptions, was putting himself in the path of destruction.
>
> (1963, p. 31)

My older sister gave me a copy of Baldwin's *The Fire Next Time* but, today, in a digital age, the urgency of these messages has lost its bite. If it wasn't for the book, I would have imagined that I was going crazy. The injustices and racial abuse that myself and peers faced growing up as teenagers and studying as young adults at British universities persisted. By all accounts, the outcomes for ethnic minorities on health, education and employment are still utterly bruising (Gov UK, 2017; YouGov et al., 2015).

Drawing on marginalised standpoints produces counter-cultural ways of knowing (Mirza, 2017). This knowledge also comes from bearing witness to systemic injustice, which creates a perspective on knowing the world, a praxis that Ferreira da Silva calls 'knowing at the limits of justice' (2013, p. 44). He further elaborates that:

Knowing at the limits of justice is at once a kind of knowing and doing; it is a praxis, one that unsettles what has become but offers no guidance for what has yet to become. Knowing the limits of justice, nonetheless, is an ethical-political praxis; it acknowledges all the effects and implications as well as the presuppositions informing our accounts of existing with/in one another … perhaps, a horizon of radical exteriority, where knowing demands affection, intention, and attention.

(p. 44)

These systemic undercurrents are extended to the politics of the digital realm (Fenton, 2016). My sharpened perceptions of social injustice prepared me to design and consider digital research approaches that build trust, create care, reciprocity and friendship. This kind of engagement often requires a leap of faith, particularly when trying to reach marginalised or ostracised folk, because of the pain that exclusion causes (Burton and Kagan, 2003; Novembre et al., 2014; Mirza, 2017). It is therefore essential to create safe spaces in which to hold the vulnerability and creative potential of marginalised folk.

By focusing across digital projects, I aim to create touchpoints as storyteller, researcher, cultural practitioner and activist. Ideally, you as the reader, can get under the skin of my choices and craft a more equitable digital research practice as a consequence. An ambition in looking back, as digital technology allows research methods to evolve, is, reminiscent of how Mulvey (2006) describes the digital evolution of cinema, allowing time to pass, to shift 'perceptions of relations and aesthetic patterns and these shifts are, in turn, accentuated by the new horizons formed by new technologies' (p. 12). Further,

at a time when new technologies seem to hurry ideas and their representations at full tilt towards the future, to stop and to reflect on cinema and its history also offers the opportunity to think about how time might be understood within wider, contested, patterns of history and mythology

(pp. 22–23)

This is particularly timely as conversations about decolonising the academy resurface (People's Knowledge Editorial Collective, 2016; Mirza, 2017; Tandon et al., 2017). And, bell hooks tugs at my side, reminding us that: 'the ability to manipulate one's gaze in the face of structures of domination that would contain it, opens up the possibility of agency' (1992, p. 116).

Case study 1: Turing's Sunflowers

Turing's Sunflowers was a citizen science project celebrating the centenary of Alan Turing's birth by encouraging community groups and individuals to grow and nurture sunflowers, count the spiral patterns in the sunflower seed heads and submit digital pictures as evidence to an online website to be analysed by computational biologist, Jonathan Swinton. Alan Turing, hoping to better understand how plants grow, had been grappling with the challenge of how Fibonacci number patterns work in sunflowers when he worked at the University of Manchester (Swinton and Ochu, 2016). A visionary mathematician, codebreaker and the father of modern computing, Turing was a gay man at a time when homosexuality was illegal and found himself at the centre of controversy and injustice as he was convicted of gross indecency. He was posthumously pardoned. The centenary celebrations of Turing therefore, marked a transformation in his status (Sumner, 2012). While Turing's Sunflowers offered me the opportunity to openly identify as being a queer scientist, I failed to ensure the social justice angle was stated in the project's goals:

- To raise awareness of Alan Turing's work on Fibonacci numbers by involving 3000 people from Greater Manchester.
- To explore the role of math in nature through a series of public engagement activities.
- To collect sufficient data to carry out the math analysis and present the results at Manchester Science Festival.

Natalie Ireland, the Museum's Science Festival director, who commissioned the project, explained that Jonathan Swinton walked into her office with a sunflower seedhead in a lunchbox, wanting to inspire people about Alan Turing but she knew the power of the story had more potential (N. Ireland, pers. comm., 2017).

There was incredible enthusiasm for the project in the museum, and externally, but time was short. I bought some sunflowers for a short film shoot with the BBC to launch the project. After an afternoon brainstorming, a story emerged – what if a whole city came together to grow sunflowers to finish Turing's work? There was still no mention of Turing's homosexuality and what subsequently happened to him, but we had a science story, with which to launch.

The kindness and generosity continue as I contact potential partners – 'we can donate seeds, pots and gardening canes, we can run an event, we can grow sunflowers, why don't you apply to us for funding for gardening tools?' Armed with a list of fears, potential failures and a limited budget, I draw on the community organising practices that I learned from activists and community organisers who campaigned against racism, fascism and the effects of government cuts on communities in the 1980s and 1990s. Community, cultural partners and individuals can join the project at any time. These approaches encompass communities of practice (Wenger, 1998), mobilising community assets through asset-based community development (Kretzmann and McKnight, 1993) while opening up and diversifying where knowledge comes from and when (Wynne, 2004). These ideas made their way to my craft through activism: together we came up with creative solutions, learned from failure and developed shared assets. Further, we encouraged stories to be spread by word of mouth and social media as people wrote blogs, tweeted, commented on and critiqued the project. An approach that, with more critique of the scientific goals, might connect with scientific citizenship (Irwin, 1995) and scientific agency (Miah, 2017) models of science and digital engagement with research, respectively.

While the objectives were clearly focused on data collection and the public awareness of mathematics and Alan Turing's mathematical contributions to biology, there seemed to be an unspoken, underlying cultural driver to the project, fuelling global interest. Indeed, later, Freitag and Pfeffer (2013) established that the citizen science process is as important as the scientific output and that citizen science offers the opportunity to acknowledge the cultural contexts of science in society. Diverse identities can be obliterated by working from the scientific perspective alone (Wynne, 2004), and in much the same way, there is a need to erase the white gaze of institutional control to enable freedom of expression by black cultural practitioners (Williams, 2014). This perspective is missing in the conception of science capital, a lens which aims to extend the idea of cultural capital to attend to socially diverse participation in science (Archer et al., 2015).

After the project was launched on daytime television by gardener Monty Don planting a sunflower, the phone rang with people wanting to get involved or retired mathematicians keen to talk through the math. Every phone call and every email brings a new opportunity. It slowly dawns on me that I have no way of knowing how people are getting along with growing sunflowers. I turn to Farida Vis, academic and allotment owner, who asks me: 'Why would growers care about keeping their sunflowers?' (pers. comm., 2012). A huge risk is the phase between sunflowers being sown and grown, where slugs, squirrels and the weather might throw sunflower growing off course. The web guy, Stuart, converts this challenge into four project phases: (1) get planting; (2) keep them growing; (3) measure and count; and (4) see the results. With the help of BBC producer, Caroline Ward, we then build digitally mediated storytelling campaigns (McrSciFest, 2013) and encourage community-led events around these phases.

This also means that we can work out the digital requirements of the next project phase as we go along, rather than defining everything at the outset. This flexibility became critical, as, for example, when someone tweeted that they were growing Turing's Sunflowers in Palestine, we could add a map to show where sunflowers were being grown. Collecting and visually representing locational data became a way to acknowledge contributions online both for those sunflowers that made it to the final dataset and those that did not.

One of the approaches I had learned from working as a digital producer in the film industry was lead user innovation (von Hippel, 1986). If we could somehow stay connected to those people who adopted the idea of growing sunflowers for our experiment, we could encounter and solve problems quickly, before most other people faced them. Therefore, I hosted public events where I tested draft, unfinished methods of how to measure and count sunflower spirals. Participants helped to refine these initial methods, which were then updated and used to inform the web capture of any data collected. Through this process, I could see what people might struggle with and notice innovations that could make it simpler. Similarly, to get closer to the data we needed to collect for the experiment, I filmed and re-filmed Jonathan Swinton, the academic lead, talking about his dreams for data collection. Sharing the video with participants gets us closer to which data are vital and which are just nice to have.

Engaging with ethics

A range of ethical issues were considered at the planning stage, ranging from data ownership to photographic consents, as well as recognition of public contributions within academic articles. This also included the differing capacities of community groups and schools to participate and to understand the results. In terms of governance, the Museum of Science and Industry had the final say on all decisions, but a creative workshop involving all partners addressed and provided innovative solutions to challenges, including ethical ones at the outset. We agreed that participants would be credited on the Turing's Sunflowers website and on any academic publications that resulted by linking to a credits page on the website. This is encouraged and encapsulated as a principle of the European Citizen Science Association (ECSA, 2015).

Additional issues emerged at the first creative workshop and online via social media including considerations for environmental sustainability and that sunflower seedheads should be composted. Again, sustainability is considered as part of the ECSA principles of citizen science (ibid.). Additional partners were sought or emerged (often via social media) to advise on several issues, including enabling public access to the results data while maintaining privacy over personal data. While a map indicating where participants were growing sunflowers was used to drive participation and to recognise contributions, it was important to avoid pinpointing individual houses where sunflowers were grown. For those who didn't have gardens, people grew at the museum and community-led planting events.

In terms of recognising non-academic contributions, it was remarkable how small gestures mattered. I would get phone calls from people as they submitted their data and watched their computer screens in anticipation of a sunflower popping up near their location. To avoid ownership issues over content, creative commons licensing was encouraged for people to share their content with the museum and more widely, while retaining authorship. Sourcing user-produced content for use within the Turing's sunflowers website enabled recognition of participants' contributions and saved time creating resources from scratch.

In terms of data ownership, people were given the option to submit their results to the research project. Only one person opted out of this. I felt it was important that people were opting into the experiment. To ensure that people could connect with the results, we commissioned a public show, 'Cracking Nature's Code', which explained the results through stories. We invited a community choir, Open Voice, to sing a Fibonacci song at the initial presentation of the scientific results, to demonstrate how Fibonacci numbers were used in music. This was composed by Carol Donaldson, the choral director.

We also participated in a digital hackathon with Hack Manchester where the sunflower dataset was hacked to make a sunflower game and a digital map. I was invited to share the results and joined in an LGBT debate to defend the idea that homosexuality was genetic. Having been to *that* private school where we had learned to debate anything, whether we believed it or not, I adopted a comical approach to try to win the argument. In the audience that night, unknown to me, was an older gay man, for whom the legalisation of homosexuality had changed his life. I saw the tears in his eyes as our eyes met. His voice cracked as he defended his argument and my attempt to win at all costs became trite. I admitted defeat, we hugged and I later bought him a whisky in the pub as he shared his story. The powerful 'why', of the lost purpose of this particular digital project crystallised for me in that moment.

Turing's Sunflowers, with the community-led events, exhibitions, stories and songs, got me outside and away from my desk, changed my outlook on life and work – but, what cannot be articulated in words is a feeling wedged inside my brain and felt in my heart every time I look at or think about sunflowers. Perhaps, Turing's Sunflowers has created, as part of our conscious experience, the feeling of what happened (Damasio, 2000). Supported by digital technology and the media, science became entangled with society through mutual reciprocity – Fibonacci numbers, Alan Turing and Sunflowers are now an interconnected part of my emotional, social and scientific world, distinct from Van Gogh's sunflowers, yet embedded with sunflower songs and a sense of queer pride and social justice. These moments of symbolic exchange both online and offline tap into the mutual desire to bring people into a shared social world (Pelaprat and Brown, 2012) and emphasise the importance of learning in social settings (Lave and Wenger, 1991). For me, the symbolic culmination of the science and social worlds recognising one another is witnessing the police handing out sunflowers to the public as they watch several Turing's Sunflowers floats pass through the Manchester Pride Parade. One of the floats had a Fibonacci sequence painted on the side 1, 1, 2, 3, 5, 8, 13, 21, 34. This experiment gave me a sense of pride and belonging in ways that academia rarely can (Gabriel, 2017).

Brian Lobel's interactive performance, 'Purge' (Lobel, 2016) interrogates the boundaries of these perspectives further. Lobel gave complete strangers the opportunity to decide whether to keep or delete over 1000 of his Facebook friends. His friends' responses to being purged, and subsequent fall-outs, reconnections and reflections in real life on the appropriateness of such a performance, demonstrate just how closely entangled our social, emotional and online worlds are.

Case study 2: #Hookedonmusic

After the perceived success of Turing's Sunflowers, the museum wanted a second citizen science project. Hosted at the University of Manchester in the school of Life Sciences, I took up a residency at the Museum of Science and Industry. Since the responsibility of the project falls under the direction of a new

Science Festival director and a citizen science project manager, we build in the hunt for the citizen science project into the recruitment process to get potential candidates excited and dreaming about what this new citizen science project could be.

The idea to find a project around music is put forward by the new Science Festival director, Marieke Navin. Her excitement, enthusiasm and contacts lead us to Hooked! a music recognition game that crowdsources responses via a smartphone app and, by reaching a large audience, aims to explore individual differences in musical memory. The game is devised by music cognition researchers to explore what makes music catchy (Burgoyne et al., 2013). I flew out to Amsterdam to visit two of the researchers, Ashley Burgoyne and Henkjan Honning. After lunch, I play the existing game – I don't quite understand it – but I love their enthusiasm and passion for what they do. Playing the game, I experience several barriers to immersing myself in it. The design of the branding is a fish on a hook, the name, Hooked! has associations with drug use and the biggest challenge of all, is that you need a premium account with Spotify to access the music you'll need to listen to. This accessibility challenge is a major barrier to entry and will exclude those who don't have a smartphone and cannot afford a premium account. If we are to reach the tens of thousands of participants the researchers dream of to create a big dataset, this and the other challenges need to be solved.

I am challenged by Jean Franczyk, the Museum Director, who has worked as a journalist, to find out why playing #hookedonmusic matters, why would the public care? I ask the researchers – musical memory has implications for future research into Alzheimer's disease. And music is also important as a social connector for people with Alzheimer's disease and for those who care for people with Alzheimer's (Clair and Ebberts, 1997; McDermott, Orrell and Ridder, 2014), and music-based interventions can help reduce the stigma and social isolation associated with the disease (Harris and Caporella, 2014). Like Turing's Sunflowers, albeit more explicitly, we now have a story.

I worked up several concept documents – one is just images, a practice I learned from my film industry days to imagine and convey the look and feel of the experience and the settings in which people might play the game or experience the concept. A one-page project proposal outlining the aims, objectives and benefits of the project grows to a four-page document, as investigative journalist, Katy Jones, interrogates it and connects us to BBC radio stations. The concept is further shaped by pitching it to people, inside and outside of the museum, and asking or guessing, based on people's age, what a memorable piece of music might be for them. I build playlists for people and share the idea at festivals, meetings and events. I take a Massive Open Online course on music and creativity and another on human computer interactions from Stanford University to help me to better understand the cultural value of music and to ensure that this can be built into the design requirements of the game. Importantly I learn the value of Wizard of Oz prototypes which allow you to test out user experiences and elicit tacit knowledge on unfinished or mock-up versions of an experience.

When the game is not ready and we have to launch the concept to the public, we instead host a silent disco as a visual device to articulate the idea that the game player is the DJ tuning into the memorable music of their past. This later informs a music experiment to investigate the social grouping behaviours of dancers listening to music that they control via a silent disco headset (Mooren, Burgoyne and Honing, 2017).

Doing this 'guerrilla' research shows me that choosing and sharing music with strangers put people in incredibly personal and vulnerable positions. With this in mind, we choose an image of a guy wearing headphones to indicate that that is what people will be expected to do and discard another image of a record playing music. This image, of someone wearing headphones, becomes the project brand and backdrop to the game. The web designers hired to make the game find a solution to the challenges that I experienced when I first played the game. There is a new name, #Hookedonmusic, and a more accessible online science game played via a web browser on a laptop, tablet or desktop. The game is a test of your popular musical memory, sharing snippets of popular songs to see how quickly you recognise them (Korsmit, Burgoyne and Honing, 2017).

Engaging with ethics

During the initial engagement phase of #Hookedonmusic, the museum's core audience for the game is 16–24-year-olds. This excluded the very people who could benefit most from the project – socially isolated older people and younger people who might find a way into learning about science through music.

While visiting my sister and her kids, I decide to see if they can understand this concept of playing a game to recognise a musical hook. The Harlem Shake meme has been sweeping the country so we make a Harlem Shake video to explore what a musical hook is. The Harlem Shake has a repetitive musical hook that suddenly changes. It's at this point of change, that people in Harlem Shake videos break out of routine into crazed antics in an office, a lecture theatre or a kid's bedroom. After several attempts of falling about laughing, re-taking and figuring out how to set up, film and edit a Harlem Shake video on an iPad, unprompted by me, they show their video to their dad and explain what a hook is.

I share the idea behind the video with the festival director who explores what can be done with people under 14. The next time I visit my sister's children, I tell them about how we are going to have a kids' show. They shrug their shoulders and run off into the garden. Later, my niece tells me a story she wants to shoot on her iPad. We brainstorm the story, shoot and edit it. She picks the music, writes the script and stars in it. I cannot be sure that this is influenced by us making the meme together, but the reciprocity of creating and making together, for my project and then hers, is as it should be (Gauntlett, 2011; Pelaprat and Brown, 2012). Later I am horrified to discover that the Harlem Shake meme is an appropriation of a dance that was instigated by Harlem-based African Americans in the 1980s; the project suddenly problematises the ways in which participatory culture and black culture can be misappropriated for digital commodification, rather than the liberation of marginalised groups (Steele, 2013) and digital citizen science must take note.

When we came to develop the public engagement for #Hookedonmusic, a core ethical proposition was how to engage those so-called 'vulnerable' communities, at risk of social isolation who could benefit from engaging with a music project. These attempts to design this commitment into the project just did not catch fire and we must acknowledge and explore these ethical failings together in the future. However, the ethical dots connect through an interim social justice action: I reduce my fellowship contribution to #Hookedonmusic and re-direct resources to an art-science project to reach out via Greater Manchester Community Umbrella organisation, MACC, to small organisations and community groups to partner with researchers and artists to address a social challenge through small seed pilot funds. Following community consultations, the most pressing challenge to address in the current context of local government cuts and the devolution of the health and social care budget is to address social isolation. Following a meeting of researchers, artists and community organisers facilitated by Theatre in Prisons and Probations, we imagine how to make social isolation worse, in order to explore how to make it better. A call for proposals invites partnerships to creatively tackle and engage those at risk of social isolation.

To my joy, one of the projects allocated seed funds is a community choir drawn from Manchester African and Caribbean folk living with Alzheimer's and their carers. The following year, while #Hookedonmusic is still running at the Science Festival, we invite this community choir to open a panel event about living with Alzheimer's. Every audience that this choir sings to is educated in Alzheimer's friendly approaches. I am overjoyed that the project has connected to the social purpose that I had dreamed of.

Decolonising the digital and what remains

At the funeral of Jaya Graves, an activist friend of mine, I am moved to see the many people who recall her all-encompassing, attentive presence. She told people exactly how she saw things, however challenging, and wrote letters describing the injustices of museum displays and community panels that kept communities from the 'Global South' at a distance – a step removed from objects that had been taken – 'no, stolen, Erinma, stolen' – and isolated behind glass walls, away from their context, their language and, their very being. In remembering Jaya, I search for her presence on the internet. Unsuccessful, I remember instead her heartfelt hugs and mischievous laugh.

In the same way, much of the work that I learned from community organisers, activists and artists is uncredited in academic literature, invisible, not dissimilar to the ways that Frantz Fanon and Virginia Woolf previously warned (Woolf, 1929; Fanon, 2008). Therefore, I must write about these influences and my own lived experience in solidarity with black female scholars (Gabriel, 2017).

Just as colonial museum objects, disconnected from their places and cultures of origin, continue to unlock financial capital for institutions in the 'Global North', we have to ask questions and pay attention to whose dreams they bring to life, whose dreams they exclude and why, and in whose presence we might be invited to share our dreams in these institutions. Similarly, as academia's digital methods seek to investigate and learn about people's lives through the digital data they leave behind, how do marginalised communities begin to set the digital agenda around research that might frame our lives, our histories, our futures?

With this story alive to me, I recall a troubling ethical challenge posed by #Hookedonmusic, which, fuelled by global media coverage, enabled the spread of Western popular music to 200 countries around the world. The democratisation of science, on the one hand, and the potential to homogenise local cultural identities, on the other:

> How can general knowledge be nurtured in postcolonial worlds committed to taking difference seriously? Answers to these questions can only be put together in emergent practices; i.e. in vulnerable, on-the-ground work that cobbles together non-harmonious agencies and ways of living that are accountable both to their disparate inherited histories and to their barely possible but absolutely necessary joint futures.
>
> (Haraway, 2003, p. 1)

This social praxis of research is already considered for community-based participatory research (Banks et al., 2013), for citizen science projects facilitated by the internet (Haklay, 2013; Geoghegan et al., 2016) and it accompanied me, in the curation and subsequent evolution of participatory digital science methods. While the scientific legacy of these projects (Swinton and Ochu, 2016; Korsmit et al., 2017) has now been published, the making of and the cultural legacies of these projects are barely acknowledged.

In remembering and understanding what it feels like to be excluded, it is possible to call to mind the values, gestures and ethical implications of digital methods. The use of storytelling builds in practice on critical race theory, feminist theory and queer theory to extend the ethical principles of community-based participatory research (Banks et al., 2013) and the principles of citizen science (ECSA, 2015).

I finally realise what funerals are all about: they are not about the dead, but the living. My friend Jaya's presence lives on in her poems, the stories people tell about her and the way in which people came together to celebrate her life. A wonderful thing is that Open Voice, the community choir that sang the Fibonacci song for the Turing's Sunflowers project, sang to Jaya while she was in hospital and again at her funeral. In typical Jaya fashion, when we gathered around her hospital bedside to sing, she encouraged us to take a step back so that everyone on the ward could hear us sing songs from around the world. An older lady, who, we were later told, didn't speak a word of English, awoke from her sleep and began singing along to one of the songs, a distant memory stirred? This pivotal moment left a deep impression, of Jaya's kindness and generosity to strangers in her presence, even as she faced death. And, I witnessed the true power of musical memory in a patient who suddenly came to life through song. It is in considering these moments that I understand how you move forward in life, what you carry into tomorrow and what you leave behind. Jaya's work lives on in mine.

Invited to give a talk, I went back to *that* private secondary school where racism tried to eat my soul. From what I witnessed, things had changed, I was welcomed and shown around the school by kind people. All that remains are the remembrance of that past in my mind. My experience is erased from history, invisible, as if it never happened. The internal trauma returns, until, I am given access to my school records which includes letters of support from the school warden to prospective universities I have applied to. It seems extraordinary that a letter of support includes details of my having been ill and the economic circumstances of my upbringing. I wonder if all children are spoken about like this to prospective educators. My private life had clearly not been very private. Like dead stars, my past experience, can be used to take measure of the digital universe and to consider a different way forward.

It is important not only to recognise that access to the web and digital technology is not ubiquitous but also that

> Claims for the extension and reinvention of activism through digital media need to be considered in the context of the material social and political world of inequality, injustice, corporate dominance and the financialization of everything. This means taking account of neoliberal formations of the subject, the state, the social and the economic. It is true that a global civil society is developing on the web, it is one that is segmented by interest and structured by inequality.
>
> (Fenton, 2016, p. 19)

And, as companies and the government create and own data about us on the internet, there are growing ethical concerns about the system, how it stores data and for what purpose. But what must also be considered is the system out of which the database was created and why and who else has access to it. When we outsource the creation of various databases into commercial hands, who can assure our privacy?

> A final note on method … in the end it is our own inner tenacity, our passionate intention through which we must judge our path and progress.
>
> (Jaya Graves, 2010)

This chapter draws attention to the engagement that can take place around a participatory digital research project. It highlights the need for nuanced stewardship in these interstitial spaces in which we become entangled and, by association bear witness to and sense the dreams, desires and despairs of diverse communities, including our own (see, for example, Sinfield, 2016). By taking into account lived experiences in the engagement phases of a digital research cycle, might we become better aware of the conditions that facilitate ethically impactful digital research? For community-engaged research projects, Durie et al. (2012) identify an 'engaging' and 'follow-on' period, either side of the 'project delivery' phase. They highlight the 'follow-on' phase as a place for reflection, mutually agreed closure or forward planning.

It is in this 'follow-on' space that a feeling, a sunflower, a piece of music, a dataset, might trigger the imaginations of those who encounter them in new cultural contexts. It is here that stories might transform the design of digital research methods, engaging people in meaningful ways to widen cultural impact by fostering broad and diverse participation. And, it is important for scientists to recognise the role of the arts and humanities (Snow, 1959), alongside science and technology studies and the history of science (Kuhn, 1962) in transforming scholarly practices as they have done for the medical humanities (Fitzgerald and Callard, 2016) and digital humanities (Antonijević, 2015) before them. Further, we must acknowledge that this is unlikely to occur through digital intervention alone (Whittle et al., 2012; Fenton, 2016). The engagement process is essential and generative in that it creates and sustains life through mutual becoming and should be 'vital concerns … for the scientific, social and political institutions that are expected to govern and take care of them' (Braidotti, 2002, p. 2).

In this way, we ask how we might ensure that digital research methods offer

> … a world of opportunities to *create* – where everyone has substantial and sustained choices about what to do, what to make, what to be; with everyone drawing freely on their own powers and possibilities; their (individual and collective) experiences, ideas and visions … this is cultural democracy. This is when people have the substantive social freedom to make versions of culture.
>
> (Martin Green, p. 1, cited in Wilson, Gross and Bull, 2017)

Since the internet is a cultural platform for crafting connectivity, creativity, social exchange and sense-making (Gauntlett, 2011), digital research methods using the internet also have the potential for citizens to be in control of exploring their everyday realities, triggering dreams, reflection and learning (Herodotou, Sharples and Scanlon, 2018). We must take extra care to create boundaries that value privacy yet not exclude people who would benefit from dreaming about and using the digital data that they have had some hand in creating.

Through two case studies, I have considered the cultural legacy in making two databases or digital spaces 'dynamic and subjective' (Manovich, 2001, p. 12). I encourage researchers working with digital methods to recognise their role as datamakers whose digital practices have the potential to evoke the creation of records, artifacts and collective identities (Vis, 2013). We must consider that different parties, ourselves included, may have different interests in making data visible as a means of control or for commercial exploitation (Vis, 2013).

Further, the dream life of digital draws on the ideals of the Afrofuturist movement (Bould, 2007), which seeks to ensure, through the power of imagination, a future for diasporas, by challenging history and mainstream practices that marginalise black people and instead reimagining history, science and science fiction to create different possibilities than those currently imagined for us by the mainstream. Consequently, this chapter seeks to remind us to ask where the missing dreamers are (Southern et al., 2014). Indeed, within academia, we need to consider more equitable pathways to enable all dreamers to take a seat at the table. Given the commodification of higher education and the severe impact that cuts to disabled access support will continue to have on disabled students (Anon, 2017), to keep the dream alive, we must advocate for change (Cullinane and Montacute, 2017).

Consequently, my advice to scholars treading this winding yet impactful path (Banks, Herrington and Carter, 2017) is to stay patient and true. If we choose to persistently nurture the intersection of race, class, gender, disability and sexuality as a social medium to foster diverse identities, digital or otherwise, imagine what futures we can create.

Finally, if marginalised dreams are to be realised, it is worth considering, given the structural inequalities inherent within academia, the value of more equitable governance arrangements that support counter-cultures (McQuillan, 2014), practices of resistance (Kullenberg, 2015), becomings (Braidotti, 2002) and nomadism (Deleuze and Guattari, 1986; Braidotti, 2011) that place resistance to established institutions and nations in order to foster the 'myriad of ways that people place the power of their ideas in service to social justice' (Hill Collins, 2014, p. x). Many academics, myself included, have embarked on this journey through social enterprise (British Council, 2016; Gabriel, 2017).

And, while nurturing the digital commons and the open web is key, we must learn more about our rights and how to protect online privacy. This will be important in protecting cultural and democratic rights in the digital age, including the right to be remembered and the right to be forgotten.

Acknowledgements

I would like to acknowledge the support of a Wellcome Engagement Fellowship under grant number WT099887MA which supported a two-year residency at the Museum of Science and Industry via the University of Manchester. Any opinions expressed are those of the author and do not necessarily reflect the views of Wellcome, the Museum of Science and Industry or the University of Manchester. A list of acknowledgements to non-academic colleagues is given in Ochu (2017).

References

Ahmed, S. (2017). *Living a Feminist Life*. Durham, NC: Duke University Press.
Anon (2017). Disability services transform students' lives – we must protect them. *Guardian*. 7 April. Available at: www.theguardian.com/higher-education-network/2017/

apr/07/disability-services-transform-students-lives-we-must-protect-them (accessed 20 November 2017).

Antonijević, S. (2015). *Amongst Digital Humanists: An Ethnographic Study of Digital Knowledge Production.* Basingstoke: Palgrave Macmillan.

Archer, L., Dawson, E., DeWitt, J., Seakins, A. and Wong, B. (2015). "Science capital": A conceptual, methodological, and empirical argument for extending Bourdieusian notions of capital beyond the arts. *Journal of Research in Science Teaching,* 52: 922–948. http://dx.doi.org/10.1002/tea.21227.

Baldwin, J. (1963). *The Fire Next Time.* New York: Dial Press.

Banks, S., Armstrong, A., Carter, K., et al. (2013). Everyday ethics in community-based participatory research. *Contemporary Social Science,* 8(3): 263–277 http://dx.doi.org/ 10.1080/21582041.2013.769618.

Banks, S., Herrington, T. and Carter, K. (2017). Pathways to co-impact: action research and community organising. *Educational Action Research,* 25(4): 541–559.

Berners-Lee, T. (2000). *Weaving the Web. The Original and Ultimate Destiny of the World Wide Web by Its Inventor Tim Berners-Lee with Mark Fischetti.* New York: HarperCollins.

Bould, M. (2007). The ships landed long ago: Afrofuturism and Black SF. *Science Fiction Studies, Afrofuturism,* 34(2): 177–186.

Braidotti, R. (2002). *Metamorphoses: Towards a Materialist Theory of Becoming.* Cambridge: Polity Press.

Braidotti, R. (2011). *Nomadic Theory: The Portable Rosie Braidotti.* New York: Columbia University Press.

British Council (2016). *Social Enterprise in a Global Context: The Role of Higher Education Institutions.* London: British Council.

Burgoyne, J. A., Bountouridis, D., van Balen, J., and Honing, H. (2013). Hooked: a game for discovering what makes music catchy. In A. de Souza Britto, Jr., F. Gouyon, and S. Dixon (eds), *Proceedings of the 14th International Society for Music Information Retrieval Conference.* Curitiba, Brazil, pp. 245–250.

Burton, M. and Kagan, C. (2003). Marginalization. In I. Prilleltensky and G. Nelson (eds) *Community Psychology: In Pursuit of Wellness and Liberation.* Basingstoke: Palgrave Macmillan.

Carlone, H. B. and Johnson, A. (2007). Understanding the science experiences of successful women of colour: science identity as an analytic lens. *Journal of Research in Science Teaching,* 44(8): 1187–1218.

Clair, A. A., and Ebberts, A. G. (1997). The effects of music therapy on interactions between family caregivers and their care receivers with late stage dementia. *Journal of Music Therapy,* 34(3): 148–164.

Cooper, A. and Condie, J. (2016). Bakhtin, digital scholarship and new publishing practices as carnival. *Journal of Applied Social Theory,* 1(1).

Cullinane, C. and Montacute, R. (2017). *Fairer Fees.* London: The Sutton Trust.

Damasio, A. (2000). *The Feeling of What Happens: Body, Emotion and the Making of Consciousness.* London: Vintage Books.

Deleuze G. and Guattari, F. (1986). *Nomadology: The War Machine.* New York: Semiotext(e).

Dollimore, J. (2016). Alan Sinfield: mentor and lover. *Textual Practice,* 30(6): 1031–1038.

Downs, J.S. (2014). Prescriptive scientific narratives for communicating usable science. *PNAS,* 111(4): 13627–13633.

Durie, R., Lundy, C. and Wyatt, K. (2012). Researching with communities: Towards a leading edge theory and practice for community engagement. *Connected Communities.* University of Wollongong, Australia.

ECSA (2015). Ten principles of Citizen Science. The European Citizen Science Association. Available at: http://ecsa.citizen-science.net/sites/default/files/ecsa_ten_principles_of_citizen_science.pdf (accessed 16 October 2017).

Eddo-Lodge, R. (2017). *Why I'm No Longer Talking to White People about Race.* London: Bloomsbury.

Ettorre, E. (2017). *Autoethnography as Feminist Method.* London: Routledge.

Fanon, F. (2008). *Black Skin, White Mask.* London: Pluto Books.

Fenton, N. (2016). *Digital, Political, Radical.* Cambridge: Polity Press.

Ferreira da Silva, D. (2013). To be announced. Radical praxis or knowing (at) the limits of justice. *Social Text*, 114: 43–62.

Fitzgerald, D. and Callard, F. (2016). Entangling the medical humanities. In A. Whitehead et al. (eds) *The Edinburgh Companion to the Critical Medical Humanities.* Edinburgh: Edinburgh University Press, pp. 35–49.

Freitag, A. and Pfeffer, M. J. (2013). Process, not product: investigating recommendations for improving citizen science "success" *PLoS ONE*, 8(5): e64079. https://doi.org/10.1371/journal.pone.0064079.

Gabriel, D. (2017). Overcoming objectification and dehumanization in academia. In D. Gabriel and A. Tate (eds) *Inside the Ivory Tower.* London: UCL, pp. 25–38.

Gauntlett, G. (2011). *Making Is Connecting: The Social Meaning of Creativity, from DIY and Knitting to YouTube and Web 2.0.* Cambridge: Polity Press.

Geoghegan, H., Dyke, A., Pateman, R., West, S. and Everett, G. (2016). *Understanding Motivations for Citizen Science: Final Report on Behalf of UKEOF.* University of Reading, Stockholm Environment Institute (University of York) and University of the West of England.

Gov UK (2017). Ethnicity facts and figures. Available at: www.ethnicity-facts-figures.service.gov.uk/ (accessed 16 October 2017).

Graves, J. (2010). Buddhism's alternative path. *Guardian*, 28 October. Available at: www.theguardian.com/commentisfree/belief/2010/oct/28/buddhism#comments (accessed 12 October 2017).

Haklay, M. (2013). Citizen science and volunteered geographic information – overview and typology of participation. In D. Z. Sui, S. Elwood and M. F. Goodchild (eds), *Crowdsourcing Geographic Knowledge: Volunteered Geographic Information (VGI) in Theory and Practice.* Berlin: Springer, pp. 105–122.

Haraway, D. (2003). *The Companion Species Manifesto: Dogs, People and Significant Otherness.* Chicago: Prickly Paradigm Press.

Harris, P. B. and Caporella C. A. (2014). An intergenerational choir formed to lessen Alzheimer's disease stigma in college students and decrease the social isolation of people with Alzheimer's disease and their family members: a pilot study. *American Journal of Alzheimer's Disease and Other Dementias*, 29(3): 270–281.

Hawkins, J. A. (2017). *Feelings and Emotion-Based Learning. A New Theory.* Basingstoke: Palgrave Macmillan.

Herodotou, C., Sharples, M. and Scanlon, E. (2018). *Citizen Inquiry. Synthesising Science and Inquiry Learning.* London: Routledge.

Hill Collins, P. (2014). *On Intellectual Activism.* Philadelphia, PA: Temple University Press.

hooks, b. (1992). *Black Looks: Race and Representation.* New York: Routledge.

Irwin, A. (1995). *Citizen Science: A Study of People, Expertise and Sustainable Development.* Hove: Psychology Press.

Korsmit, I. R., Burgoyne, J. A., and Honing, H. (2017). If you wanna be my lover ... a hook discovery game to uncover individual differences in long-term musical memory. In E. Van Dijck (ed.), *Proceedings of the 25th Anniversary Conference of the European Society for the Cognitive Sciences of Music.* Ghent: Ghent University, pp. 106–111.

Kretzmann, J. P. and McKnight, J. L. (1993). *Building Communities from the Inside Out: A Path Toward Finding and Mobilizing a Community's Assets.* Evanston, IL: Institute for Policy Research.

Kuhn, T. (1962). *The Structure of Scientific Revolutions.* Chicago: University of Chicago Press.

Kullenberg, C. (2015). Citizen science as resistance: crossing the boundary between reference and representation. *Journal of Resistance Studies,* 1(1).

Lave J. and Wenger, E (1991). *Situated Learning: Legitimate Peripheral Participation.* Cambridge: Cambridge University Press.

Manovich, L. (2001). *The Language of New Media.* Cambridge, MA: MIT Press.

McDermott, O., Orrell, M., and Ridder, H. M. (2014). The importance of music for people with dementia: The perspectives of people with dementia, family carers, staff and music therapists. *Aging & Mental Health,* 18(6): 706–716.

McQuillan, D. (2014). The countercultural potential of citizen science. *Journal of Media and Culture,* 17(6).

McrSciFest, 2013. *The Turing's Sunflowers Diaries.* [online video] Available at: www.youtube.com/watch?v=QmFxDeFW9gQ (accessed 24 October 2017).

Miah, A. (2017). Nanoethics, science communication, and a fourth model for public engagement. *Nanoethics,* 11: 139. https://doi.org/10.1007/s11569-017-0302-9.

Mirza, S. H. (2017). 'One in a million': A journey of a post-colonial woman of colour in the White academy. In D. Gabriel and A. Tate (eds) *Inside the Ivory Tower.* London: UCL, pp. 39–53.

Mooren, N., Burgoyne, J. A., and Honing, H. (2017). Investigating grouping behaviour of dancers in a silent disco using overhead video capture. In E. Van Dijck (ed.), *Proceedings of the 25th Anniversary Conference of the European Society for the Cognitive Sciences of Music.* Ghent: Ghent University. pp. 142–149.

Mulvey, L. (2006). *Death 24x a Second: Stillness and the Moving Image.* London: Reaktion Books.

Novembre, G., Zanon, Z. and Silani, G. (2014). Empathy for social exclusion involves the sensory-discriminative component of pain: A within-subject fMRI study. *Social Cognitive and Affective Neuroscience.* doi: 10.1093/scan/nsu038.

Ochu, E. E. (2017). A seat at the table ... [Weblog]. 19 November. Available at: https://everyoneandeverything.wordpress.com/2017/11/19/a-seat-at-the-table/

Ochu, E. E., Rothwell, N .J., and Waters, C. M. (1998). Caspases mediate 6-hydroxydopamine-induced apoptosis but not necrosis in PC12 cells. *Journal of Neurochemistry,* 70(6): 2637–2640. doi:10.1046/j.1471-4159.1998.70062637.x.

Opara, E. (2017). The transformation of my science identity. In D. Gabriel and A. Tate (eds) *Inside the Ivory Tower.* London: UCL, pp. 124–135.

Pelaprat E. and Brown, B. (2012). Reciprocity: understanding online social relations. *First Monday,* 17(10). Available at: www.ojphi.org/ojs/index.php/fm/article/view/3324/3330.

People's Knowledge, Collective (2016). *People's Knowledge and Participatory Action Research: Escaping the White-Walled Labyrinth.* Rugby: Practical Action Publishing, pp. 113–134. doi:10.3362/9781780449395.012.

Roberts, E. and Constant, N. (2017). Narratives as a mode of research evaluation in citizen science: Understanding broader science communication impacts. *Journal of Science Communication*, 16(4).

Shirk, J., Ballard, H., Wilderman, C. et al. (2012). Public participation in scientific research: a framework for deliberate design. *Ecology and Society*, 17: 29–48. doi: 10.5751/ES-04705-170229.

Shirky, C. (2011). *Cognitive Surplus: Creativity and Generosity in a Connected Age*. London: Penguin Books.

Sinfield, A. (2016). Humanism and ideology. *Textual Practice*, 30(6): 1121–1133.

Snow, C. P. (1959). *The Two Cultures*. The Rede lecture. Cambridge: Cambridge University Press.

Southern, J., Ellis, R., Ferrario, M. A., McNally, R., Dillon, R., Simm, W. and Whittle, J. (2014). Imaginative labour and relationships of care: co-designing prototypes with vulnerable communities. *Technological Forecasting and Social Change*, 84(05): 131–142.

Steele, C. K. (2013). Shaking off the 'Other': appropriation of marginalized cultures and the 'Harlem Shake'. *Selected Papers of Internet Research*, 14: 1–3.

Sumner, J. (2012). Turing today. *Notes and Records*, 66: 295–300 doi:10.1098/rsnr. 2012.0036.

Swan, A. (2012). *Policy Guidelines for the Development and Promotion f Open Access*. Paris. UNESCO.

Swinton, J., Ochu, E. and the MSI Turing's Sunflowers Consortium (2016). Novel Fibonacci and non-Fibonacci structure in the sunflower: results of a citizen science experiment. *Royal Society Open Science*, 3(5), doi:10.1098/rsos.160091.

Tandon, R., Singh, W., Clover, D. and Hall, B. (2017). Knowledge democracy and excellence in engagement. *IDS Bulletin*, 47(6). Available at: http://bulletin.ids.ac.uk/idsbo/article/view/2828 (accessed 12 October 2017).

Vis, F. (2013). A critical reflection on Big Data: considering APIs, researchers and tools as datamakers. *First Monday*, 18(10).

von Hippel, E. (1986). Lead users: a source of novel product concepts. *Management Science*, 32(7): 791–805.

Wenger, E. (1998). *Communities of Practice: Learning, Meaning, and Identity*. Cambridge: Cambridge University Press.

Whittle, J., Ochu, E., Ferrario, M.A., Southern, J. and McNally, R. (2012). *Beyond Research in the Wild: Citizen-led Research as a Model for Innovation in the Digital Economy*. Proc Digital Futures.

Williams, J. (2014). Black Leadership and the white gaze. In S. Kay and K. Venner with S. Burns and M. Schwarz (eds) *A Cultural Leadership Reader* (pp. 40–46). Cultural leadership programme. Available at: www.co-creatives.co.uk/wp-content/uploads/2014/12/a_cultural_leadership_reader_201007051349381.pdf (accessed 24 October 2017).

Wilson, N., Gross, J. and Bull. A. (2017). *Towards Cultural Democracy: Promoting Cultural Capabilities for Everyone*. London: Kings College, London.

Woolf, V. (1929). *A Room of One's Own*. London: The Hogarth Press Ltd.

Wynne, B. E. (2004). May the sheep graze safely? A reflexive view of the expert-lay knowledge divide. In S. Lash, B. Szerszynski, and B. Wynne (eds) *Risk, Environment and Modernity: Towards a New Ecology*. London: Sage.

YouGov, Gregory, R. and Wyse, G. (2015). Race at work. Business in the Community. Available at: http://race.bitc.org.uk (accessed 16 October 2017).

12 Using digital stories in healthcare research

Ethical and practical dilemmas

Carol Haigh and Pip Hardy

The importance of storytelling as the foundation of communicating human experience cannot be over-estimated. McKibbon et al. (1999) note that the oral traditions were focused upon educating and transmitting knowledge and skills and also evolved into one of the earliest methods of communicating scientific discoveries and developments. According to Greenhalgh (2009), stories are the smallest units by which human beings communicate their experience and knowledge of the world. Although some authors use the word 'narrative' as a synonym for 'story', narrative can be defined as predominantly factual whereas stories are reflective, creative and value-laden, usually revealing something important about the human condition (Haigh and Hardy, 2011). The authors of this chapter would also like to suggest that any good story involves adversity and challenge, offering the protagonist the opportunity to overcome suffering and demonstrate courage, resilience, humour or whatever other human virtue leads to overcoming the challenge (Hardy, 2015; O'Connor, 1969).

This chapter explores the experiences of using digital stories to inform research data collection in the context of healthcare and healthcare education. It will explore issues around veracity and reliability, the concept of power and consent. It will further examine how these ethical issues have an added dimension within the digital storytelling format.

What is digital storytelling?

Digital storytelling, as a specific multimedia form, emerged in California in the early 1990s as a means of enabling 'ordinary' people (i.e. non-media professionals) to create short videos using industry-standard software and hardware in a carefully facilitated workshop environment (Lambert, 2002, 2006, 2012). The resulting 'digital stories' are short, multi-media clips consisting of a series of (mostly) still images and a voiceover recorded by the storyteller. Their power comes from the rich, multi-faceted tapestry that results when the storyteller is able to tell an authentic, personal story by weaving together images, music, story and voice. The focus, content and presentation of the stories are entirely within the storyteller's control and so the stories themselves are a rich source of highly qualitative research data.

In the early days of the digital storytelling movement, the creation of these stories was facilitated by people who had advanced communication and technical skills, together with the ability to help storytellers articulate the experiences they wanted to share and who had been trained in both the medium and the workshop process. A number of small-scale and medium-scale projects were established throughout the USA, led by people who had been trained by the Center for Digital Storytelling (now StoryCenter; www.storycenter.org) in digital storytelling facilitation skills.The BBC's *Capture Wales* project was one of the first large-scale projects which, in turn, spawned a number of other community history projects throughout the UK. In Australia, the Museum of the Moving Image pioneered digital stories in the Antipodes and in 2003 the Patient Voices Programme was founded in the UK. It was the first project to focus specifically on digital storytelling in healthcare

The elements of the Patient Voices programme are:

*   the production and distribution of the Patient Voices digital stories themselves;
*   workshops that enable healthcare professionals, carers and patients to develop their own stories and narratives;
*   consultancy and support on the integration and use of digital stories within healthcare development programmes;
*   research into the uses and applications of digital stories in healthcare quality improvement and as reflective tools in healthcare education;
*   development and identification of resources that support the use of digital storytelling in health and social care.

However, it must also be acknowledged that the word 'digital' has now become ubiquitous and, to some extent, redundant when describing twenty-first-century storytelling techniques. Thanks to the World Wide Web and the proliferation of social media sites such as YouTube, Facebook and Twitter, anyone who wants to, can, potentially, have a global canvas upon which to share their experiences in the form of videos, podcasts, blogs, vlogs, Facebook and Twitter posts – to name but a few possibilities. These artefacts are also often referred to as 'digital stories', as are talking head-type videos – and all of these can also form a rich source of data for researchers via cartoons, music or conventional video. Thus, it can be seen that digital stories come in many forms.

From a research perspective, the formal workshop approach is still the most effective way to collect data on a specific topic; indeed, it is this approach that combines creative writing skills, art and photo therapy in safe, small group processes that has become known in digital storytelling circles as the 'classical' model of digital storytelling. In this chapter, we will be looking specifically at digital stories that are created using this approach and, in particular, stories that have been created as part of the Patient Voices Programme: www.patientvoices. org.uk

How are digital stories created?

It is important to distinguish between digital stories (the product) and digital storytelling (the process). Since the early inception of the digital storytelling movement, approaches to the creation of such stories has developed and evolved partly in response to the needs and demands of particular groups and the requirements of particular projects. Characteristic of the classical approach to digital storytelling is the desire to ensure that the voice of the storyteller is not muted by the process. This places a focus on the development of technical skills and even more on communication and narrative skills. These approaches are usually informed by the framework developed by Joe Lambert and colleagues at Story-Center, initially entitled 'The Seven Elements', which later evolved into 'The Seven Steps of Digital Storytelling' (Lambert, 2010). This framework provides a useful guide for digital story creation (Table 12.1), in that it helps to provide a useful template to manage, what is potentially a complex and emotive process, one that is usually managed over the course of a number of days.

Digital stories in research

The digital world has made the sharing of individual stories easier and more immediate than at any other time in history and the growing acknowledgement of the importance of the voice of the individual in healthcare makes digital stories an ideal tool for researchers. Hitchen and Williamson (2015) have noted that the inclusion of participants as co-researchers provides authenticity to data, empowerment of participants and shared learning between healthcare academics, professionals and service users. This is increasingly important as we strive to understand the experiences of people whose reality is so different from the dominant one – refugees or survivors of violence, for example. Our digital world is already evolving into communities of auto-ethnographers and storytellers. Creating digital stories for research is a new way to explore this.

Using digital stories as data

It was Barney Glaser who famously stated, 'all is data' (Glaser and Strauss, 1967; Glaser, 2007) and the number of free-to-access digital stories on the World Wide Web certainly supports that statement since its content can be described as multi-layered in terms of meaning, for example, the persona display on something as simple as a Twitter feed can be seen as a comment, a provocation or a snapshot of one element of someone's persona; all or any of these elements could be seen as potential research data. These can be of particular use when data collection in the offline world is frustrated by protectionism from external but interested parties. See, for example, Case study 12.1.

Witham et al. (2015) have highlighted, for example, how discursive construction(s) of healthcare professionals, such as a paternalistic approach to service users or a protectionist approach to their own professional reputation can make it difficult to ascertain the views or experiences of certain groups.

Table 12.1 The seven steps of digital storytelling

Step 1	Find your story	This important first step helps storytellers find themselves within their stories. This can be a challenge for some storytellers, especially those who do not see themselves as an integral element of the story they want to tell.
Step 2	Own the emotion	Having encouraged the storyteller to own their story as a personal artefact, the next step is to explore and understand what emotions the proposed story evokes in both the storyteller and the listener.
Step 3	Find the moment	Often storytellers come to digital storytelling workshops with long and complex tales to tell. This step is crucial as it requires the storyteller to strip away the 'packing' and recognise the key moment they want to share. Identifying the issues that come alive in a personal and powerful way connects the audience to the story.
Step 4	See the story	Digital stories are a rich amalgamation of visual and audio content. Storytellers are asked to reflect upon the images their story suggests to them and are encouraged to create a storyboard of images to accompany and augment their words. The complexity and sophistication of these images and the degree of care with which they are chosen can provide another layer of meaning to the story.
Step 5	Hear the story	The essence of the story lies in the authenticity of the narrator. Most digital stories are told by the author. Choice of words and phrases should be driven by the usual speech patterns of the storyteller. Music or ambient sounds, such as bird song, can be used to good effect to emphasise the context and complexity of the story itself.
Step 6	Assembling the story	Once the script is completed to the satisfaction of the storyteller, the images selected and any music chosen, the story can be assembled. Digital stories run on average for around 2.5 minutes; therefore economy of content is important. The key is to provide just enough content to tell the story with careful attention paid to the relationship between the words and the images so that the story is told without overloading the viewer or disrupting the pace and progress of the story.
Step 7	Sharing the story	Most digital stories are created as a way of communicating a personal experience and many are shared, often within specific communities. Generally, the initial screening of a story is a cause for celebration. However, later in this chapter we will explore some ethical situations in which the sharing of stories was compromised.

Source: Based upon Lambert (2010).

Case study 12.1 Talking to 'vulnerable' people about service communication

The study: We wanted to ask vulnerable people accessing cancer services how they thought we could communicate with them more effectively. For the purposes of the study, 'vulnerable' meant people who were perceived as vulnerable prior to their diagnosis of cancer; those with mental health issues or learning disabilities, for example. We anticipated using face-to-face interviews and focus groups to collect our data.

The unanticipated problem: The healthcare provider that had commissioned the work had agreed to recruit patients as part of their partnership agreement within the study. However, they decided every patient who could potentially have been invited to participate was 'too fragile' to even be approached and informed about the study. This left us with no participants.

How digital stories helped: Using the free-to-access stories on the Patient Voices website (www.patientvoices.org.uk/stories.htm), we were able to gather sufficient related data from existing material via a kind of combined data mining and content analysis.

In this instance, we used existing digital stories to provide us with information about cancer-related experiences and vulnerable people. None of the stories we used had been created specifically in relation to this topic. We were able to do this because the Patient Voices project has a robust consent process that allows storytellers to consent to such use. Any research planning on using digital stories as post-hoc data would be well advised to check that such ethical rigour is in operation on the source site. However, such was the complexity of the stories that we found a rich source of material on our topic. Digital stories created as part of the Patient Voices programme are intended to reveal the person behind the patient (or carer) and are less focused on the specifics of a particular disease condition. Thus, universal themes of suffering and despair, as well as courage, hope and resilience are commonly found in the stories. Experiences of poor communication, careless care and gaps in care provision frequently also appear in the stories. This means that a story told by a patient with heart failure, for example, can highlight issues that are equally important for patients with cancer or rheumatoid arthritis, giving the stories' wide applicability and utility (Hardy, 2007).

Haigh and Jones (2007) have noted that good online research will always have an offline component to complement it and that the themes detected in the digital stories correlated well with the themes obtained from face-to-face focus groups. It was interesting to note that the offline components of our study complemented and enhanced the digital story data, allowing us to have confidence in our analysis.

Digital stories as a research method

Compared to other, established methods, digital storytelling as a discipline is still relatively new, having emerged in the early 1990s, therefore, the creation of digital stories is focused more upon the gathering of experiences and is not a commonly used method of data collection. Case study 12.2 outlines how digital stories can be created with the express intention of answering a specific research question.

The inclusion of this particular group was also valued as it provided a voice from a routinely under-acknowledged group, addressing issues of both epistemic injustice (Fricker, 2009) and the need to leave a personal legacy. The stories we collected were created in response to a specific research question: what has it been like for you when accessing services with a life-limiting illness? This meant that the data we collected was far more focused and specific than some of the stories created with a more fluid remit.

The ethical implications of using digital stories

There is often a temptation among researchers to view the ethics of research activity as a kind of 'one-size-fits-all' solution. As research methods and techniques evolve and develop, it is increasingly clear that research ethics in the twenty-first century need to evolve and develop with them.

A plethora of ethical research perspectives is available to the discerning researcher. These include consequentialism, which involves the careful consideration of the risks and the potential benefits provided; virtue ethics, which emphasises the character of the moral agent, rather than rules or consequences, as the key element, and moral relativism, which is the idea that the authority of moral norms is subject to time and place. These norms indicate which actions and behaviours are expected, required, prohibited, permitted, and discouraged.

It can be argued that, despite the many reflexive ethical frameworks available to researchers today, the one that is still the most widely taught in western

---

Case study 12.2 People with alcohol-related cancers

The study: As part of a larger study that explored the experiences of people with a long-term alcohol problem when transitioning across palliative and acute care services and back again. Rather than standard approaches we decided that every experience would be so unique that the creation of a digital story would be the only way to capture the essence of the individual interactions with the different aspects of healthcare.

How digital stories helped: The story creation was useful in a number of ways. It allowed the storytellers the luxury of time to formulate and create their stories, allowing for richer data to be shared. Stories were created around the demands of illness-related fatigue allowing for the inclusion of a participant group who otherwise would be excluded from the information-sharing process.

universities and used by researchers is the principalist approach, formally articulated by Beauchamp and Childress in 1979 but popular since World War II. This approach forms the basis of many professional codes of ethics.

This approach strongly emphasises the 'rights' of individuals which, in practical terms translates into the right of individuals to be consulted about what happens to them. It is argued that such approaches are supported by Beauchamp and Childress' (2001) four key principles:

1 *Self-direction (Autonomy)*: This is seen as a norm that respects the decision-making capabilities of individuals.
2 *Do no harm (Non-maleficence)*: A norm that avoids the causation of harm or damage.
3 *Actively do good (Beneficence)*: A group of norms focused upon the provision of benefit and balancing of risks and benefits.
4 *Fairness (Justice)*: A group of norms that focuses upon distributing benefits, risks and costs fairly.

It has become 'fashionable' to critique Beauchamp and Childress' work, not least because there is no clear foundation theory underpinning their ethical principles. Furthermore, it is not clear how these principles balance each other – are they all of equal importance or are there situations in which the researcher can down-play justice for the benefits of autonomy, for example? While one of the principles (beneficence) is concerned with actually doing good, yet another (non-maleficence) is more concerned with not doing harm. However, the question that has to be asked is, can harm ever be totally avoided? The potential for harm in the testing of an experimental drug is overt and obvious, less so is the potential harm in the creation of a digital story, but it nonetheless exists, as we demonstrate in Case study 12.3.

Despite these criticisms, it can be seen that the principalist approach encompasses many of the foundation characteristics of newer frameworks. For example, the risk/benefit outcomes of consequentialist ethics are reflected in the principalist notion of justice. These indicate which actions and behaviours are required, prohibited, permitted, and discouraged.

One of the weaknesses in virtually all ethical frameworks, but particularly with a principalist approach, as it often presents the principles in the form of a list, is the danger that they are seen as rules rather than principles or guidelines and are interpreted in a strict and linear fashion. This checklist mindset often leads to researchers being content with a 'tick box' approach to the considerations of the ethical implications of their studies. The personal and flexible nature of digital story creation means that the ethical scrutiny must be deeper and more reactive than is often seen in more traditional elements of research. Our experience of applying ethic principles to the digital stories has reinforced the need to take a fresh look at issues such as consent, for example, as digital story methodology requires ethical consideration to be applied beyond the individual participant. To illustrate this point, we present four case studies, contextualised within the four principles of Beauchamp and Childress' framework. Although each case study presented below can be seen in isolation against one of the four principles, where appropriate, we will link the key ethical issues of each study with some or all of the other ethical principles to demonstrate how the interconnected nature of this ethical approach can be operationalised.

Respect for autonomy

Beauchamp and Childress (2001) argue that every individual's unique gifts and abilities must be acknowledged and that this respect for autonomy underpins and informs the right to dignity and humane care. Therefore, every storyteller's ability to make informed decisions should be respected, within the limits of individual capability. A well-constructed consent 'protocol' needs to be deliberately written in an accessible way (Hardy, 2015). For example, the intentions of the Patient Voices programme are carefully and clearly explained, and what will happen at every stage of the process is reiterated throughout the creation of the stories by encouraging the storyteller to return to the documented consent and reflect upon the previous.

Importantly, consent is considered to be a process rather than an event, allowing time for reflection and review of the story that has been created. Editorial control rests with the storytellers and no story is ever released without a signed release approval form. In keeping with the iterative process of consent, the storyteller can change or remove their story at any point in the future.

All of this seems self-evident. Ensuring that storytellers clearly comprehend the storytelling process at every stage, respecting their autonomy in the creation and crafting of their story are defining characteristics of 'classical' digital storytelling and are also at the heart of the Patient Voices programme as they are seen as best practices in the wider digital storytelling community. Even at the end of the process, storytellers have the right to decide not to publish their stories and this decision is always respected.

However, the location of digital stories in the public domain can complicate matters. Case study 12.3 show an example of this complication, when obtaining the consent of the storyteller has to be balanced against the wider well-being of other people who may be, albeit unwittingly, part of the story too. From a principalist position, such as is espoused by Beauchamp and Childress (2001), there is no dilemma here. However, Case Study 12.3 demonstrates that such a position is never black and white.

The key dilemma for the researchers at this point is: to whom do they owe an acknowledgement of autonomy? Is it the storyteller who created the story and autonomously consented to its publication on an open access website? Or is it the subject of the story, whose consent was not sought? It is clear that the relationship between storyteller and subject was strained at best. One could argue that the consent of the subject should have been sought and, indeed, the initial Patient Voices consent form invites storytellers to confirm that they have sought all relevant permissions and consents. However, the emergent nature of digital

---

Case study 12.3 The need for consent from others involved in the story

A storyteller participated in a three-day workshop, preceded by a briefing session. He was delighted with the story he had made, which focused on child and adolescent mental health services. At the end of the workshop, he signed an interim release form and, in due course, he signed a final release form, pleased that his story might be able to raise awareness and help someone else avoid some of the difficulties he had faced in relation to his child.

Some years later, an angry email from the storyteller's former partner arrived, threatening to take legal action if the story was not immediately removed from the website. The child had come across the story by Googling the father's name and had been upset by it.

The storyteller did not want the story to be removed. However, the partner's anger, together with the implication of litigation for the storyteller and the Patient Voices programme, led to the decision to remove the story for the protection of all involved.

---

storytelling is such that often the topic and focus of the product story emerge slowly over the period of the storytelling Indeed, even those participants who come with a story in mind that they wish to tell may find that the story will evolve into something very different from what they had originally planned (Tappen and Brown, 1989).

One can argue that this is likewise an issue for non-digital researchers, for what is an interview if not a story, albeit one whose structure (and sometimes content) are dictated by the researcher? The difference lies in two ways. First, in interview research, the ethical focus is often upon creation and protection of anonymity, with the participant's real name only being attached to their data if they absolutely insist (Tetley, Grant and Davies, 2009). In digital stories, the converse is the case; most storytellers are keen to have their real names attached to their story, as an acknowledgement of their creation, in much the same way that an author wishes to be acknowledged for writing a book, a musician for composing a symphony, an artist for painting a masterpiece. Only rarely do participants choose to publish their stories anonymously (Livingstone, 2008) and these are often for reasons of safety. This may be explained by the intimate nature of story crafting, every word, every picture, every soundtrack is chosen and controlled by the storyteller. Second, the final destination of the stories is usually an open access website, which renders them far more likely to be found than if their anonymised data is buried in the depths of a research report or published paper, providing recognition for the effort the storyteller has invested in their creation.

In this instance, the dilemma that faced us was this: did we put our respect for the autonomy of the storyteller above the need to avoid harm to the subject (and, given the litigious nature of their correspondence, to ourselves)? Reluctantly, we adopted a utilitarian approach to the problem. Utilitarianism contains the concept of 'the greatest good for the greatest number' (Bentham, 1907) and maintains that, in all circumstances, we ought to produce the greatest possible balance of value over disvalue for all persons affected (Mill, 2010). Part of that decision was an attempt to address the tension between respecting the autonomy of the individual against the obligation to avoid harm – harm which would clearly have accrued to the subject of the story as well as his parents and the digital story-telling facilitators.

The implication of this scenario, for a researcher wishing to gather stories that illustrate specific issues, is the potential (harmful) impact of the stories on the subject of those stories, should they discover them by accident. This is an issue that should be discussed at some point in the process, if at all possible.

Beneficence

There are a number of risks inherent in encouraging people to tell a personal story. Not only storytellers, but also people who view the stories, can find the experience of watching a digital story deeply emotional and, in some instances, disturbing. However, these risks can be weighed against the cathartic and eman-cipatory consequences that are often reported by storytellers when describing the experience of creating a story (Banks-Wallace, 1998).

Mindful of Wordsworth's notion of 'emotion recollected in tranquillity' (2003), when developing digital stories for research, we encourage storytellers to participate only after they have had a period of time to reflect on and, to some extent, process their experiences. Telling a story in the middle of a crisis may be just too difficult and too painful, and it is almost impossible to make any kind of sense without the perspective afforded by time. The management of potential stress before, during and after the storytelling experience is crucial. Although this may seem at odds with notions of autonomy, it introduces the concept of beneficence, actively seeking to promote good while respecting the ability of the individual to direct, and be responsible for, their own actions.

One of the criticisms highlighted earlier in this chapter was the temptation to use Beauchamp and Childress' (2001) four ethical principles as a kind of check-list which could lead to a dismissal of ethics as something that, once completed at the start of the research study, need never be referred to again throughout the life of the project. However, our experience with digital stories has shown us that, in some cases, the principles themselves stand upon shifting sands. Case study 12.4 demonstrates this point.

In this instance, the original benefit or 'good' within the story was the close-ness of the family, in addition to the potential common good of the opportunity to illuminate the experience of living with someone who has dementia. By using a happy family event to illustrate how strong the family unit was, and recounting how this strength made caring for her husband a little less onerous, not only did the storyteller feel good about her family but it was also an optimistic story for those who watched it.

Case study 12.4 A change in circumstances

A woman made a story about caring for her husband who had Alzheimer's. She illustrated the closeness and caring nature of the wider family with images of her daughter's wedding. The story offered deep insights into the challenging world of looking after someone with dementia.

A few years later, the daughter was divorced and did not want the reminder of the story. It was suggested that the images could be changed, but the daughter was adamant and the story was removed from the website.

As the case study shows, however, the beneficial effects of this story were affected by time and the ethical obligation to ensure the promotion of 'good' changed from supporting a display of family solidarity to supporting a member of that family (not the storyteller). Once again, the secondary autonomy of a peripheral subject of the story was acknowledged, as well as the promotion of benefit for that individual.

The implications for researchers in this type of scenario are difficult. For offline researchers, there is a standard clause in most participant information sheets that outlines the fate of an individual's data, should they choose to withdraw from the study. In these cases, it is relatively easy to withdraw raw data but to also make a case to retain anonymised data that has already been included in analysis. When using digital stories, the raw data (i.e. the story) often is part of the analysis, in so far as the content (the data) has already been analysed by the storyteller, but of course the story can also be exhibited publicly. Researchers who adopt a digital storytelling approach to gathering data may find themselves in a position where their research report will carry obsolete URLs which linked to a story which has had to be removed. It can be seen as good practice to have a strategy in mind for the management of such situations, should they arise. So, for example, best practice might be, in the case of removal of a story, to replace the story with a message stating simply that the story has been removed at the storyteller's request.

Justice

Digital storytelling is part of a worldwide movement towards social justice, personal empowerment and personal and collective emancipation. According to both storytellers and users of stories, the potential risks of sharing personal stories are far outweighed by the myriad benefits to those who create them and those who view them (see, for example, Corry-Bass, Critchfield, and Pang, 2014; Hardy and Sumner, 2014; Shea, 2010). The personal cost is minuscule in comparison to the benefits that accrue from both the process and the products of digital storytelling workshops.

Participation in digital storytelling activities can also be argued to address issues of injustice, especially epistemic injustice, as articulated by Fricker

(2007). The concept of epistemic injustice encapsulates the notion of testimonial injustice. Fricker argues that this is a special kind of injustice that arises when the experience, views and attitudes of an individual are disregarded, usually because of prejudice towards a particular group (such as patients, women, people with a particular religious or gender bias). The use of digital stories addresses this kind of injustice by offering dispossessed or disenfranchised people a platform upon which to share their lives, 'where they can be heard in any lecture theatre or conference venue anywhere in the world' (Hardy, 2007). Thus, the role that digital stories can play in promoting justice for an individual or a group is not insignificant as it can often be seen to provide a voice for the voiceless in our society. However, researchers can face a challenge when the threat to justice comes, not from the dominant ideological group, but from within the storytellers' own circle.

In Case study 12.5, it is hard to see which of the four ethical principles have not been violated. Clearly the storyteller's autonomy has been eroded by her daughter's actions and the requirements to do no harm and actively promote good have been compromised by the threat of estrangement. However, what causes the most concern is the complete disregard for the principle of justice. The issue here is that the storyteller has worked hard to produce a resource that would be useful to healthcare professionals, carers and service users alike. This is a story that may well have eased the path of a patient (or a carer) travelling the same road, or

---

Case study 12.5 Whose consent, whose approval?

A woman attended a workshop and created a story about her own experience of dementia, how it feels and its impact on her life. She was especially delighted with the story, and even sent a 'thank you' card for helping her to create something that she hoped would provide insight into the lived experience of Alzheimer's, including her despair at receiving the diagnosis, but also her growing ability to cope with her situation.

Although she signed a final release form at the end of the workshop, she was encouraged to show the story to her family before the story was released.

A few weeks after the workshop, she phoned to say that her daughter had watched the story and was horrified by its honesty. The daughter threatened not to speak to her mother if the story was released. She had understood that the video would only be used locally and would not appear on a public website 'for any Tom, Dick and Harry to see'.

In discussion, suggestions were made about how the story could be altered and, if necessary, anonymised, and the release approval could be changed to cover only local use of the story, rather than appearing on a website, but the storyteller felt that she didn't even want to re-open discussions with her daughter for fear of fanning the flames of anger. She was very sorry, as she had enjoyed making the story and wanted to help others understand what it's like to feel your memories disappearing, one by one.

Her story will never be seen or heard now.

sparked increased compassion in a nurse or doctor, but the patient's voice is silenced, through no fault of her own. Testimonial injustice, indeed. This case study also highlights that researchers need to be aware that storytellers exist in a world that is distinct and separate from the safety and comfort of the storytelling environment and may have responsibilities and obligations that impact upon, but are separate to, the needs of the researcher. As indignant as a researcher may be at the perceived abdication of responsibility to the wider patient community, the storyteller's semi-autonomous (informed as it was by her daughter's actions) decision was that her loyalty to her family over-rode her obligations to strangers in a similar situation to her own. In situations like this, there is not much a researcher can do but concede defeat, although a compromise solution that is anonymous and text-based could be an option. The important thing is to ensure that the lines of communication between researcher and storyteller remain viable.

Non-maleficence

Stories are phenomenally powerful (Haigh and Hardy, 2011; Hardy and Sumner, 2014; Lambert, 2012) and, like electricity, they have the capacity to do harm as well as good. Whereas the principle of beneficence is often seen as a deliberate action to promote good, non-maleficence is often perceived as slightly more passive, and centres upon the need to prevent harm, even though this is not always the case.

Case study 12.6 shows how the principle of non-maleficence can take priority in certain situations.

It is clear that, of all the case studies presented thus far, this one most clearly demonstrates how all of the ethical principles outlined by Beauchamp and Childress (2001) inter-relate by:

Case study 12.6 Safeguarding storytellers

Several women who had taken part in a local health promotion programme all made stories that focused on domestic abuse. They understood the aims of the workshop and the intention of the Patient Voices programme and discussions in the workshop considered the use of imagery that would ensure the storytellers' anonymity. It was essential that their identity not be revealed in the stories for fear of further abuse, but they wanted to describe their learning from the programme that they had participated in and to talk about the courage they had gained and the skills they had acquired to look after themselves.

Post-production work concentrated on finding metaphorical images (clouds, skies, plants, trees, etc.) to accompany their voiceovers about the details of the abuse they had suffered. No names were to be used in the stories; these stories would definitely be anonymous.

The draft stories were shown to the storytellers but, in each case, they decided that it was still too risky to release the stories. The stories have never been released.

- emphasising the autonomy of the storytellers in the direction and content of their stories;
- promoting benefit by facilitating the telling of such personal stories within a supportive group environment;
- providing a sense of justice for the storytellers via the sharing of experiences.

In Case study 12.6, however, the overpowering ethical issue is the prevention of harm. The fear that still was felt by these abused women meant that – despite every care being taken to ensure the anonymity of the storytellers and the miniscule chance of their abusers finding the stories and then identifying the storytellers as their victims – the principle of non-maleficence took priority as the key ethical concern. We had expected the storytellers to show some sign of emotional distress when sharing their experiences since there is a body of literature on the subject (see, for example, Campbell and Lewandowski, 1997) and as a result had to re-evaluate our ethical priorities in the light of the significant levels of fear that still affected these women. It also reinforces the need to have a backup; in a case like this the stories could be analysed in the same way that interviews or focus group data could be but further data collection using interview or focus groups methods would be necessary.

Conclusion

The case studies above clearly demonstrate how the digital story researcher needs to be constantly vigilant because the ethical situation is in a constant state of flux. In all cases we were fortunate that a member of our research team was extremely experienced in the operationalisation of practical research ethics and was able to address any unexpected ethical issues that might occur. We would certainly recommend that digital story researchers should adopt a pragmatic approach to the supplementary ethical issues that may arise during the creation of digital stories by being extra-vigilant and prepared to treat ethical review as an on-going activity.

In conclusion, the key ethical issues that arise when working with digital storytellers are informed by the fact that the stories *can* be viewed as units of raw data that await analysis by the research team but also as discrete, auto-ethnographic, auto-analysed data packets contributed by the storytellers. This, along with the longevity of the data, which is stored in an easily accessible format in cyber-space, means that ethical considerations must encompass the online and the offline world. Notions of identity, control over the message, the management of disclosure and the potential for harm mean that an ethical review must be performed for every stage of the storytelling process.

The fluidity and flexible nature of stories mean that, for the digital story researcher, the standard, pre-project ethical review and approval are merely the beginning of continuous ethical review, which must be carried on throughout the process. This approach requires the researcher to be ethically astute, especially with regard to concepts that are often underplayed in a 'traditional' ethical review, such as threats to justice.

References

Banks-Wallace, J. (1998). Emancipatory potential of storytelling in a group. *Journal of Nursing Scholarship, 30*(1), 17.

Beauchamp, T. L. and Childress, J. F. (2001). *Principles of biomedical ethics*. Oxford: Oxford University Press.

Bentham, J. (1907). *An introduction to the principles of morals and legislation*. Retrieved from Library of Economics and Liberty, www.econlib.org/library/Bentham/bnthPML. html (accessed 18 April 2017).

Campbell, J. C., and Lewandowski, L. A. (1997). Mental and physical health effects of intimate partner violence on women and children. *Psychiatric Clinics of North America, 20*(2), 353–374.

Corry-Bass, S., Critchfield, M., and Pang, W. (2014). Reflection – now we get it! In P. Hardy and T. Sumner (Eds.), *Cultivating compassion: How digital storytelling is transforming healthcare*. Chichester: Kingsham Press.

Fricker, M. (2007). *Epistemic injustice: Power and the ethics of knowing*. Oxford: Oxford University Press.

Glaser, B. (2007). All is data. *Grounded Theory Review, 6*(2). Available at: http://grounded theoryreview.com/wp-content/uploads/2012/06/GT-Review-vol.6-no2.pdf (accessed July 2015).

Glaser, B. G. and Strauss, A. L. (1967). *The discovery of grounded theory: Strategies for qualitative research*. Chicago: Aldine.

Greenhalgh, T. (2009). The illness narrative. Presentation given at Newham University Hospital, 8 November 2009.

Haigh, C., and Hardy, P. (2011). Tell me a story: A conceptual exploration of storytelling in healthcare education. *Nurse Education Today, 31*(4), 408–411.

Haigh, C. and Jones, N. (2007). Techno-research and cyber ethics: Research using the Internet. In T. Long and M. Johnson (Eds.), *Research ethics in the real world*. Edinburgh: Churchill Livingstone.

Hardy, P. (2007). An investigation into the application of the Patient Voices digital stories in healthcare education: quality of learning, policy impact and practice-based value. Available at: www.pilgrimprojects.co.uk/papers/phardymsc.pdf (accessed 18 April 2017).

Hardy, P. (2015). First do no harm: Developing an ethical process of consent and release for digital storytelling in healthcare. *Seminar.net, 11*(3). Available at: www.seminar. net/104-frontpage/256-first-do-no-harm-developing-an-ethical-process-of-consent-and-release-for-digital-storytelling-in-healthcare (accessed 12 January 2015).

Hardy, P. and Sumner, T. (2014). *Cultivating compassion: How digital storytelling is transforming healthcare*. Chichester: Kingsham Press.

Hitchen, S. A. and Williamson, G. R. (2015). A stronger voice: Action research in mental health services using carers and people with experience as co-researchers. *International Journal of Health Care Quality Assurance, 28*(2), 211–222.

Lambert, J. (2002). *Digital storytelling: Capturing lives, creating community*, 1st edn. Berkeley, CA: Digital Diner Press.

Lambert, J. (2006). *Digital storytelling: Capturing lives, creating community*, 2nd edn. Berkeley, CA: Digital Diner Press.

Lambert, J. (2010). *Digital storytelling cookbook*. Available at: http://static1.squarespace. com/static/55368c08e4b0d419e1c011f7/t/561d6222e4b039470e9780c6/1444766242054/ cookbook_full.pdf (accessed 14 December 2015).

Lambert, J. (2012). *Digital storytelling: Capturing lives, creating community*, 3rd ed. New York: Routledge.

Livingstone, S. (2008). Taking risky opportunities in youthful content creation: Teen-agers' use of social networking sites for intimacy, privacy and self-expression. *New Media & Society, 10*(3), 393–411.

McKibbon, A., Eady, A., and Marks, S. (1999). *PDQ: Evidence-based principles and practice*. Ontario: B.C. Deker.

Mill, J. S. (2010). *Utilitarianism*. Calgary: Broadview Press.

Shea, M. (2010). An exploration of personal experiences of taking part in a digital story-telling project. MSc dissertation, Sheffield Hallam University, Sheffield. Available at: www.patientvoices.org.uk/pdf/papers/MarkSheaMScThesis.pdf.

Tappan, M. and Brown, L. M. (1989). Stories told and lessons learned: Toward a narrative approach to moral development and moral education. *Harvard Educational Review, 59*(2), 182–206.

Tetley, J., Grant, G., and Davies, S. (2009). Using narratives to understand older people's decision-making processes. *Qualitative Health Research, 19*, 1273.

Witham, G., Beddow, A., and Haigh, C. (2015). Reflections on access: Too vulnerable to research? *Journal of Research in Nursing, 20*(1), 28–37.

Wordsworth, W. (2003). Preface to the lyrical ballads. *Arts Education Policy Review, 105*(2), 33–36.

13 Conclusion

(Re-)exploring the practical and ethical contexts of digital research

Jenna Condie and Cristina Costa

In this final chapter, we reflect on the decisions, approaches, and innovations that researchers have presented in this collection of digital research. In doing so, we aim to deconstruct some of the emerging discourses presented in the different chapters featured in the book, with a view to reflecting on key research practices as well as the ontological, epistemological and ethical questions that underpin such methodological decisions and developments.

Making a case for digital research and digital methods

The emergence of the web as a space of social congregation and interaction has meant that researchers from a wide range of disciplines have developed and are developing a plethora of methodological approaches. Digital research methods for the exploration of phenomena have grown incrementally in the past few decades with new innovative practices starting to emerge, as the different chapters featured in this collection demonstrate. Nonetheless, given the predominance of digital technologies as part of everyday activities and forms of communication, the appropriation of the 'digital' for research purposes has, more often than not, been as an instrument of data collection rather than a space for the practice of research itself where research participants can be engaged and where their participation can be transformed into meaningful research narratives. This should not come as a surprise, given that research practices in different disciplines enjoy long-standing traditions that substantiate the credibility of the research approaches developed within a given field of inquiry. The aim of this book was not to question such traditions, but rather to open up new discussions regarding the role and potential of digital technologies not only as a research instrument, but also as a research environment. Both approaches are exemplified in this book, thus providing examples of how research in and on the 'digital' is being deployed across fields of inquiry.

What digital research shows us is that there are no static nor prescribed formulas to researching with the web and researching digital phenomena. The research practices that are enabled and/or pervade the digital world are both an indicator and a suggestion that ways of doing research require revision to accommodate the principles and values associated with a growing digital culture in which participation becomes a core source of information. A deep understanding of the 'digital' and the practices therein developed is a key prerequisite to ensuring ethical methodological decisions and empirical practices are taken towards the research (and people) in question. It is crucial to bear in mind how contemporary technological solutions shape social practices and in turn how research projects recognise the interplay between technology and research, not only theoretically but also methodologically.

The chapters in this collection show how a reconceptualisation of taken-for-granted approaches to conventional research practices is realised, required, implemented and can be shared among research communities. Methodological choices should evidence a deep understanding between the research objectives and the strategies employed to achieve them, including the positioning of the researcher and research participants, as well as the conditions under which research participation is included and represented across the entire research journey. Making a case for digital research and digital methods means reconsidering research practices within the contexts of an ever-evolving digital participatory culture. When it comes to digital research, what is most important is not to take for granted the research practices that work or that have often been acclaimed in non-digital environments. This requires a commitment to understanding digital spaces as worthy sites of research, as well as the dynamic, complex, powerful web of relations between technology and people.

The role of the researcher: ontological and epistemological positions

When researching not only about but also within the digital – a social space still relatively new to research and one where social interactions, practices and personal and collective (re)presentations manifest themselves often in unpredictable ways – it is important that researchers interrogate their research practices and the assumptions that underpin their approaches to conducting research. How is your understanding of the phenomenon under study reflected in the research instruments and approaches employed? This implies a reflective knowledge of the different (power) dynamics that can be developed in digital spaces – as a space for conducting research and being researched – as well as thoughtful considerations of the role of the researcher, both as a person and as a researcher generating knowledge through digital means. Relatedly, there are important ontological, epistemological and ethical questions that researchers need to ask themselves when examining the intricacies of the 'digital', both as a tool and – even more importantly – as an environment conducive of a wide variety of research phenomena.

More specifically, the researcher – as in any other type of research – needs to acquire a moral and ethical stance regarding the development of his/her research approach; one that matches his/her epistemological and ontological positions and which in turn justifies his/her methodological choices. In this regard, Guba and Lincoln (1994) are helpful in their reflections even though they were not explicitly making links with digital research practices. They assert that the nature and essence of research paradigms are human constructions that 'represent simply the most informed and sophisticated view that its proponents have been able to devise, given the way they have chosen to respond through the three defining questions' (1994, p. 4) of research practice, i.e.:

- *the ontological question*: the essence of reality under study (how the researcher regards the world in which he/she attempts to develop new knowledge, both in its form and nature);
- *the epistemological question*: the essence of knowledge (how and where knowledge takes place, and what is the relationship between the knower and knowledge);
- *the methodological question*: the source and tool of new knowledge (the means through which new knowledge can be attained taking into consideration the world in which knowledge is developed and apprehended).

To consider the 'digital'– more concretely, the web and the interactive spaces that it enables – not only as a tool but also as a social environment ripe for investigation from different disciplinary perspectives means understanding it from a given ontological and epistemological standpoint. The approach taken, and the disciplinary influences within it, are key to illuminating and justifying methodological decisions applied to and/or through the phenomenon being studied. As the chapters in this collection demonstrate, these involve the considerations and deliberations that researchers take in understanding the topic and focus of their research inquiries and the implications of the digital within the contexts of their research. We are not necessarily proposing that the study of the 'digital' and/or use of digital tools to conduct research has to break away from established research paradigms, but we are suggesting that research in and on the 'digital' requires the revisiting of these research paradigms from a digital perspective. In this vein, the researcher has a commitment to acknowledging the digital in its different facets, as, for example, a communication channel, a repository of information and increasingly as a 'stage' of individual and collective participation and performativity. Such understanding leads to the positioning – and, in some cases, repositioning – of the researcher within the research field. It also implies considering the role of the researcher in relation to the research project, their interactions and participation with the digital environment, and other people implicated in the research process. The blurred boundaries of the digital world mean that different spaces of interaction and social action are often intertwined, making it harder for the researcher to identify and define what are deemed spaces of research and those that are not. A clear and well-defined position of the researcher within the field of digital inquiry is therefore crucial to allow the researcher to account for their subjectivities and pre-empt the issues that may derive from being in a digital field.

[handwritten margin note: Think this should be in any field / type of study]

The field of digital research is still an emergent one, yet literature on research practices involving the digital remains, in its majority – with the exception of some innovative examples, some of which are featured in this book – rather loyal to established research practices and methodological justifications that do not always resonate with the digital world, but which still prevail in digital research because of its recognised value and tradition. The application of less-established research methods, such as those developed with the support of digital tools, and especially those that are digitally enacted, is a practice that is still under-discussed and which more often than not is unrecognised by academic ethics committees, given the lack of debate and awareness of digital research practices within mainstream research protocols. Add to this, the perception of risk that the digital world is often associated with – given the unpredictability, uncertainty and multiplicity of digital practices that pervade the online world – and it is easier to understand the reticence of researchers, as well as funders, of harnessing the potential of the web without attempting to predict the implications of more innovative practices. This often leads to less experienced researchers opting for more traditional methodological solutions, which although they may still yield relevant answers to the questions posed by their research, do not reflect the innovations of an emergent digital culture nor the set of practices that are developed therein.

With this book, we aimed to put together practices and reflections from researchers from different fields not only regarding their research findings but to foreground the ways in which they explored and are exploring their research practices, from the conceptualisation of research to the development and application of research instruments that are entangled with their ontological, epistemological and ethical positionings as digital researchers. The result is a compilation of different studies featuring varied research approaches, from regarding the digital as a tool for research to a social environment ripe for being researched.

Kaye, Monk and Hamlin's Chapter 2 takes us through their journey of conceptualising an 'app-based methodology to explore contextual effects on real-time cognitions, affect and behaviours'. As important the development of an innovative research tool as App is for their study, what is crucial in their account is their deep understanding of the potential mobile applications for their research but also the implications they can generate for their research population. A clear ethical commitment to their research practice is explicit in this chapter, though their reflective accounts, which although not very different to ethical considerations in research developed in traditional settings, equally raise questions that acquire a different dimension when addressed in the context of the digital, where participant-created information is often available to the common user but is not necessarily created and available for research purposes.

Barnes' research in Chapter 3 faces similar questions of accountability of the researcher towards her research participants, when conducting research in an online environment that is not necessarily associated with research practices as is the case for Facebook. Barnes identifies digital research as a moveable space that requires constant examination. Her reflections on how much more we have to think about to do justice to what research participants' social media data means and shows, highlight how far we still have to go with doing digital research. Barnes demonstrates what a duty of care to research participants looks like in terms of not pushing them into an 'empirical dead end' and not finalising people and their experiences based on their digital participation and practices alone.

Another example of a researcher's positioning can be found in Chapter 11 where Ochu encourages researchers to think about who their research is for and reminds us of overlooked and unheard people or 'missing dreamers'. By centring personal histories, Ochu's autobiographical narrative of two digitally mediated citizen science projects, highlights how who we are plays an important role in the research produced and its outcomes. Digital methods are only part of Ochu's academic performance as her commitment to socially just research projects are enabled by the democratic, open, networked, digital, and reciprocal practices she advocates. Who Ochu brings to the table in terms of scholars, from bell hooks to Sara Ahmed, acts as useful signposting to those who want to make a difference and challenge the status quo. For marginalised scholars, Ochu offers encouragement to stick with their research goals and embrace the time it might take to build the kinds of trusting relationships and partnerships required to leave your mark on the world. She dreams of a digital commons and legacy for her digital research projects, and the methodological approaches that she employs enable the flexibility required for change, action, and unforeseen ethical issues that arise during the research journey. Her auto-biographical analysis provides us with insights into how digitally mediated citizen science projects emerge and their unexpected endings.

Research ethics for the digital

New ethical guidelines for digital research practices are needed, given the increased tendency to make use of digital technologies in research. Guidelines suitable for digital research are, however, often provided as an addition to established research codes of practice and ethics, rather than embedded into existing research protocols or as a guide in its own right. Although one can argue that research ethics – independently of contexts – should adhere to a certain type of conduct, the 'digital' and its emergent participatory features demand a specialised understanding of the complex social world as well as the technical terrain it provides for research.

Through regulatory bodies such as research ethics committees, the development of research governance practices in the past few decades has led researchers to devise a strong set of research principles and procedures regarding the moral and appropriate exercise of research. Practices safeguarding research participants' interests and rights to be informed about the intent of the research, as well as their right to anonymity and wish to withdraw from the research, need to be guaranteed. As Davies (2017) reminds us, such approaches derive from the assumption that researchers are able to control and protect their research data. Online, however, that is not always possible. The emergence of the web – with its participatory features – comes to problematise such ethical requirements in that the participants' 'data are already in the public realm, owned and managed by commercial organizations', thus making it impossible to anonymise the data. Several chapters featured in this collection experienced exactly the lack of control derived from accessing participants' accounts in the environments in which they were produced, i.e. in its naturally occurring setting. Take, for example, Kaye, Monk and Hamlin's research (Chapter 2). They had to work within the space of anonymity while also needing to trace participants' activity across time on externally hosted mobile platforms.

Digital research practices in this regard also need to consider the autonomy and responsivity not only of the researcher but also of the researched, and how researchers ensure informed consent is translated into practical solutions that enable the researcher and protect those who participate in the research. Dugdale et al. dwell on this issue in Chapter 4 and suggest that digital research needs to be considered more broadly but also more inclusively as part of research ethics discussions. There is clearly a need to revisit ethical practices within the context of contemporary digital technologies, the environments, practices and the expectations encouraged.

Condie, Lean and James (Chapter 7) go further to reconceptualise and challenge the online/offline, digital/material, real/virtual binaries that often frame understandings of the digital world, using new materialist ideas that draw attention to the boundary-making practices of language. If the online/offline distinction is a false binary, and everything is entangled and interwoven, as people and researchers take technology with them wherever they go, there are many implications for ethical practice.

Another emergent issue brought out by digital research practices relates to questions of authenticity and reliability of the research as highlighted in Chapter 3 by Barnes. Barnes postulates that the online world often inspires more suspicion of the credibility of research practices than other socially constructed spaces accessed offline. Such an assumption seems to derive from traditional views of research that regard the online space as one that is detached from 'real' practices and experiences; an obstacle to research practices that may often be encountered when requesting ethical approval to conduct research in which the instruments of data collection are the digital social environments themselves, as is the case of social networks sites popular with higher education students, for example, Facebook. Barnes overcomes this barrier of perspective by employing phenomenography as a methodology that deals with the issue of authenticity by accepting participants' accounts of their experience as veritable narratives. In this regard, the researcher approaches the online world as just another social space subject to the interpretation of the researcher. Condie, Lean and James (Chapter 7) echo this notion, as from their perspective, online spaces are just as materially real as offline spaces, given that both are entwined and always intra-acting with one another to produce phenomena.

Curiously enough, Ure's research (Chapter 5) does not struggle with issues of authenticity, even though her research is also focused on the study of a given group of people bound by a common interest. The group and online space in which interactions are established are regarded seriously. Ure's research on the accounts of cancer experiences reveals a reality with increased popularity among different audiences regarding patient voice. As spaces of shared practice, blogs recounting the experiences of patients are perhaps more easily justified as a space of 'truthful accounts', because of the topical nature of its contents as well as the veracity of its creators. This, however, does not mean that ethical issues are not raised regarding how participants' voices are accessed, captured and represented when participants' accounts are not elicited but rather encountered as part of a research project. Ure rightly reflects on the dilemma of using the web – and participants' blogs – as sites of access to participant information rather than spaces of engagement between the researcher and the researched. This raises questions not regarding the genuineness of participants' accounts, but rather of the potential intrusiveness of the researcher's practice in accessing information that was not produced with a research project in mind.

Several chapters in this book point out that there is a lack of reflection and debate regarding both the potential and implications that arise from such digital research practices. Nonetheless, the duty of care that the researcher must have towards the participants in their research is of great importance, thus, it is important to make clear the responsibilities of the researcher to obtain informed permission from the author to use their online contributions, or even work, as research evidence, wherever possible. In some cases, where the research dataset is too big and involves too many people, informed consent may not be practical. Anonymity is arguably easier to provide in such cases, particularly if data is analysed and presented quantitatively to research audiences.

The dilemmas of reconstructing informal accounts of experiences as research data, the kinds of accounts often readily available in blog platforms and specialised communities, can be overcome by research strategies that view the web as a space of engagement with and between research participants, rather than the use of the web as an instrument of data collection. Such approach implies an ontological and epistemological shift as to how the digital world is regarded by a research project. Haigh and Hardy (Chapter 12) exemplify this perspective well by employing digital storytelling in their research. They place a stronger emphasis on the autonomy and authorship of research participants in that they make conscious decisions regarding what and how their experiences are narrated. Moreover, such an approach often results in a desire for disclosure of authorship, a release from the anonymity status that has become a standard in research involving human beings. This is equally a form of empowerment by and for research participants from the researcher. Indeed, the blogger in Ure's research on discourses on cancer survivorship (Chapter 5) wanted named acknowledgement for her blog's contribution to the research. These research examples show the transformation that the participatory web is having on research practices. It also reflects that the private and public realms of human experience are indistinguishable. Ultimately, it also reveals that when people choose to provide their story, they often expect their contribution to be acknowledged. Haigh and Hardy call this form of participant legacy a practice of justice, as participants' voices become associated with their name. This is an important aspect to consider, but one which is often disregarded when researchers adhere to standard ethical procedures that reinforce long-standing power relations between researchers and their research populations. The relationship between the researcher and people who participate in research should take into account their online interactions and practices and the way participants envisage their contributions should be taken on board by research. To guarantee anonymity can no longer be regarded as a given of a principled and ethical research practice. To acknowledge participants' contributions according to the terms in which they are understood to be provided is equally important. Research participants can be research partners. As the participatory web shapes social practices so should research practices take note of those changes and reflect on how they affect the dynamics of the researcher-participant relationship.

Significant emphasis has been placed on explicating some of the key challenges faced by researchers who are engaged in research on and in the digital world. The opportunities that digital research presents have also been discussed, such as the uncovering of new insights into social life, the carrying out of research with participants previously unreachable, as well as reflections on methodological innovations that are only possible as well as necessary when digital research practices are embraced and standard ethical practices and protocols are challenged. We hope this edited collection will offer readers – especially researchers – much food for thought when they come to considering their research, not only in relation to the digital, but also in close connection with their research participants and the practices, attitudes and expectations that characterise their experience. This requires a constant reconsideration of the ontological, epistemological and ethical positions we take up in light of the emergent digitally-mediated advances to human practices and experiences.

On a final note, it is important to highlight that a number of the researchers in this collection would be classified as early career, ourselves included. Innovations and advances in social research are often found in the early works of postgraduate and early career researchers, as they try to make their mark on the world. We hope this collection inspires and encourages new researchers, as well as more established ones, to be inventive, critical, reflective and creative, and also to push the boundaries of digital research practices across fields of inquiry.

References

Davies, H. (2017). Ethics of digital research. Retrieved from www.britsoc.co.uk/about/latest-news/2017/april/ethics-of-digital-research/

Guba, E. G., and Lincoln, Y. S. (1994). Competing paradigms in qualitative research. In N. K. Denzin and Y. S. Lincoln (Eds.), *Handbook of qualitative research* (pp. 105–117). London: Sage.

Index